G000088056

lock, stock

Guy Ritchie

Chris Baker & Andrew Day

Bernard Dempsey & Kevin McNally

faber and faber

First published in 2000
by Faber and Faber Limited
3 Queen Square London WC1N 3AU

Printed in Finland

All rights reserved

Copyright © SKA Ginger Productions Ltd., 2000

Guy Ritchie, Chris Baker and Andrew Day, Bernard Dempsey and
Kevin McNally are hereby identified as authors of this work in accordance
with Section 77 of the Copyright, Designs and Patents Act 1988

This book is sold subject to the condition that it shall not, by way of trade or otherwise, be lent,
resold, hired out or otherwise circulated without the publisher's prior consent in any form of
binding or cover other than that in which it is published and without a similar condition including
this condition being imposed on the subsequent purchaser

A CIP record for this book
is available from the British Library

ISBN 0-571-20683-2

10 9 8 7 6 5 4 3 2 1

Contents

EPISODE 1

LOCK, STOCK... & FOUR STOLEN HOOVES

by Guy Ritchie, Chris Baker & Andrew Day

ACT ONE

EXT. UNDERNEATH A FLYOVER -- DAY

Early morning. A luxury camper van stops under a bridge, nose to nose with a van attached to a horse-box. Traffic roars overhead. Engine keeps running. MR. DIGBY, (a middle-class horse-breeder in his fifties, in a wheelchair with his leg in plaster, a neck-brace, wellies, cords, Barbour) turns away in agony as:

A thoroughbred horse is led across our line of view, from the horse-box to the camper van, by MR PIE and MR MASH (two large henchmen).

A case is placed on Mr. Digby's lap. Lid of case flips up. Then we hear the voice of Three Feet. His tone is soft – but the menace is unmistakable.

> THREE FEET'S VOICE
> Pleasure to do business with you, Mr Digby.

We stay on Digby as Three Feet exits and the camper van is driven off. Digby looks into the case – wads of cash. Looks up again – tears stream down his cheeks.

OPENING TITLES

EXT. THE LOCK PUB -- NIGHT

C.U. – PUB SIGN: THE LOCK

Camera tracks back to show the pub and the street that it is in.

> BACON (V.O.)
> Tha's our pub. Now this ain't your ordinary run-of-the-mill
> drinking establishment, anything goes as long as we have an
> angle on it.

CUT TO:

INT. THE LOCK BACK ROOM -- NIGHT

Bacon stands at the front of a ring of spectators, holding them back, with a notebook in one hand, wads of cash in the other, and a pencil behind his ear.

Camera whips round to the spectacle itself:

All the tables have been pushed together to make a line. Five rats are kept at the end of five tunnels, with lumps of cheese up the other end. Each rat has a dot on

2

its back – red, green, blue, yellow and orange.

> BACON
> One, two...

> BACON (V.O.)
> I'm Bacon.

> BACON
> ...three, go!

> BACON (V.O.)
> I'm your man who makes sure everything runs smoothly.

As the rats are released, the room reaches fever pitch. The tunnels are shaken by crazed punters pushing forward and thumping the tables.

One rat doesn't go, the other four scurry along the corridor. One stops, starts again. One slows down and another speeds up. Roared on by the crowd.

> BACON
> Come on...

> CROWD
> Come on...

> MOON
> Move those little legs, come on...

Crowd erupts cheering.

> BACON (V.O.)
> Of course things don't always go according to pian.

INT. PUB KITCHEN -- NIGHT

> BACON (V.O.)
> As for Moon he plays by his own set of rules, he sorts out the nosh. Thing is his brain's more fried than his egg...

Moon cooks. Bacon bangs plate down in front of him, returned.

> BACON (CONT'D)
> Bloke asked for fish and chips.

> MOON
> Fish... Chips.

He points to each. Bacon nods behind him at some bloke in the bar, visible through a window in the kitchen door.

                              BACON
            Reckons this is poncy. Wants to know if the chef's a poof.

Moon marches out of the kitchen.

FREEZE FRAME on Moon.

                                                              CUT TO:

INT. THE LOCK -- NIGHT

Jamie sits round a table in a darkened room, playing with three blokes in ties who don't look very happy.

                          BACON (V.O.)
            Now Jamie. Jamie could talk a nun into having 666 tatooed
            onto her arse if he wanted to. He's a jammy bastard – course
                          he'll tell you it's talent...

Shot of the blokes shaking their heads and folding. Jamie smiles as he cleans up.

INT. THE LOCK BACK ROOM -- DAY

Lee is watching something intently, with an air of authority. Whatever he is watching is moving around.

                          BACON (V.O.)
            Lee's passion is for the ladies, shame it's not a two way deal.
                Still, every now and again he comes up smiling...

                              LEE
            That was great. I liked the way you used the chair. Can we
                        take er, can we take that again ?

                                                              CUT TO:

INT. THE LOCK BAR/BACK ROOM -- DAY

Jamie walks into the lounge to see about twenty girls, most of them pretty tasty – if a bit tarty. They hardly look up. Jamie looks around him, mouths: what the fuck... ?

Walks through to main bar. On the door is a sign in black pen on orange card: 'Audition' with an arrow.

Jamie pushes it open to see Bacon leaning on a video camera, staring at a girl stripping. Lee stands in front of him. Moon is doing the music. Jamie walks straight over to Lee and mutters in his ear.

> JAMIE
> What's goin' on ?

> LEE
> We're auditionin' ero'ic dancers.

> JAMIE
> We ain't gunner 'ave strippers in 'ere!

> LEE
> I know that, but they don't.

Jamie and Lee turn to look back at Bacon who stands in front of the camera jigging up and down to the music. Bacon gives them a wink.

> CUT TO:

INT. THE LOCK BACK ROOM -- DAY

Four lads sit down with beers and peanuts, watching the video show on the big screen. Sense of anticipation.

> MOON
> Go on.

First picture on the screen is the empty bar that they are sitting in. Bacon walks into shot to check the tape is running, winks at camera. Bacon takes two steps back and plants the back of his head right under the camera. The screen shows big close-up of Bacon's bald patch.

The girl's head bobs up and down as she dances. Bacon's head bobs up and down in time to the music, in front of the camera, totally obscuring the girl's body. Items of lingerie are flung out of shot, but still no action for the lads.

> LEE (O.S.)
> Fast forward it.

Someone hits fast-forward. Bacon's head bobs up and down faster. But that's all. End of girl's routine. Bacon glances over his shoulder at the camera with a sly grin, and gives the camera a thumbs-up.

> JAMIE
> You muppet.

5

FREEZE FRAME on Bacon

                                                    CUT TO:

EXT. THE LOCK -- NIGHT

SLOW MOTION SHOT of the four of them, Moon still in his chef's gear, dragging out two blokes who are dripping with beer and blood.

> BACON (V.O.)
> At the end of the day we don't mind getting our hands dirty, we just don't want them cut off. I mean, we know our limits...

                                                    CUT TO:

EXT/INT. ROAD SOMEWHERE IN THE SOUTH OF ENGLAND -- DAY

> BACON (V.O.)
> ...it's a pity our associates don't know theirs...

JOHANN and JORDI cruise along in their van. The back is jammed full of Polish vodka and Tunisian cigarettes. Johann has spiky hair and a tiny little goatee. Jordi has dreadlocks and a moustache. They are listening to German Techno, getting really into it. They pass a spliff between them.

> BACON (V.O.) (CONT'D)
> Since Europe is now an open market, we need to keep up with the times. It's where these two clog heads come in...

EXT. BURGER VAN LAY-BY -- DAY

> BACON (V.O.)
> ... And when it comes to business, they always drive on the wrong side of the road.

JOHANN and JORDI have parked behind Glassjaw's van and are getting out. Johann has a packed lunch and Jordi a suspicious-looking roll-up.

The Flying Dutchmen check out Glassjaw's van, looking laid back, but clearly casing it. They exchange glances.

Glassjaw walks back from caravan eating a packet of crisps.

> JORDI
> Inklish?

> GLASSJAW
> Yeah.

6

JORDI
Cool... We luff Inkland. We are comink here already fife
years. You makink deliffery in London ?

GLASSJAW
Yeah.

JORDI
Well hi, we also. Me ent Johann, we are bringink za cigarettes
ent za booze from za Hook of Holland and comink beck. Ent
go again and again.

GLASSJAW
Alright yeah?

JORDI
Hey... Broderhood of fen driver.

Jordi and Johann clench their fists in solidarity. Glassjaw drops the empty crisp
packet on the ground and dusts his fingers.

GLASSJAW
Lads... I don't think I can get my van out from there, can you
move yours ?

JORDI
You are goink already? Just with only peckid of creesbs? You
are fen driver, you sharink our picnic.

JOHANN
This sentvich is typical foot of Hook of Hollant.

GLASSJAW
Me guts feel a bit funny today.

JORDI
Take some of zis.

Jordi passes him a spliff.

GLASSJAW
Don't usually do puff. Don't really agree with me.

JORDI
No, this is to makink you feel so much better for drifink fen.

JOHANN

Nordern Lights an' Superskunk combo.

> JORDI
> Wicked.

Plants spliff in Glassjaw's gob.

> JOHANN
> Zis is blowink your socks off.

Glassjaw draws good and hard. Doesn't cough, but his eyes almost disappear inside his head.

EXT. BURGER CAFE CAR PARK -- DAY

Glassjaw's van stands by itself, empty, with the doors hanging open.

Glassjaw sits up with a start and emerges from the long grass in a karate pose.

> GLASSJAW
> C'mon then. Let's have some.

Sees empty van with doors open and his arms drop to his sides.

> GLASSJAW (CONT'D)
> Shit!

EXT. SET GARAGES, LONDON -- NIGHT

Johann and Jordi look into the back of their van.

> JOHANN
> Hey Jordi – check it ou-out... triple X porn.

Jordi takes a look.

> JORDI
> Hey – *Beauty and the Farmyard Beasts*, man, cool!

> JOHANN
> Hey – *Monkey Business...*

> JORDI
> Hey – *Old Macdonald Shags His Farm* – you seen that, crazy...

> JOHANN
> That's nothing. Check this out.

8

JOHANN & JORDI
Wow.

Huge gold, jewel-encrusted, mother of a watch. Its hour-hand – an erect penis, the minute-hand and second hand are two spinning balls.

EXT. MIAMI'S PORN CINEMA -- DAY

THREE FEET walks into Porn Cinema.

INT. MIAMI VICE'S OFFICE, WAITING ROOM -- DAY

THREE FEET walks through to BARBIE, Miami Vice's secretary, who clacks away on her keyboard. She is about forty and has a beehive hairdo.

THREE FEET
Morning Barbie.

BARBIE
Morning.

THROUGH TO:

INT. MIAMI VICE'S OFFICE -- DAY

It's a gloomy office, more like an old-fashioned study. Various sporting trophies are mounted above plaques.

Three Feet enters the office.

MIAMI VICE'S VOICE
Three Feet?

THREE FEET
Nefarius says they're 'ere.

MIAMI VICE
Good. Well, bring the Roller round, I think I'll pick 'em up in person.

INT./EXT. MIAMI VICE'S ROLLER -- DAY

JAMIE (V.O.)
Miami Vice. Number one face in this manor. Word is he's
responsible for half the country's porn imports and half of the
stiffs dragged out of the Thames.

Miami Vice and Three Feet are in the back of the car, driven by CHAUFFEUR.

9

MIAMI VICE
'Ow's my 'orse?

THREE FEET
Miami, 'e's a beauty.

MIAMI VICE
Listen... I don't want too much competition on Saturday.
Don't want the 'orse under pressure in its first race.

THREE FEET
The lads are sortin' tha' out. 'E won't 'ave any others breavin'
down 'is neck.

MIAMI VICE
Right. No point takin' a gamble.

THREE FEET
Tha's what I thought.

CUT TO:

EXT. TROJAN TURF ACCOUNTANT -- DAY

The Roller slows to a halt.

JAMIE (V.O.)
This is Nefarius's gaff. A man of many interests. Not just a
bookie, not just the king of kebabs. He's got a podgy finger in
every pie.

INT. TROJAN TURF ACCOUNTANT -- DAY

They walk through the shop and out of the back door into:

INT. ABATTOIR/CORRIDOR -- DAY

JAMIE (V.O.)
And anything you want to buy, whether it's for sale or not,
he'll get hold of it for you. He thinks he's the Onassis of
knock-off road.

The corridor full of goods and on into the abattoir. They thread their way
through the hanging carcasses. Through another door.

CUT TO:

INT. NEFARIUS'S WAREHOUSE -- DAY

C.U. of a set of golf clubs on a stand.

NEFARIUS (O.S.)
Wha' ya thinkin' Mr Vice?

Miami Vice shakes his head, still gazing at the clubs.

MIAMI VICE
No words.

Behind a huge walnut desk sits NEFARIUS, owner of the Trojan Turf Accountant
and several related concerns.

NEFARIUS
'E's gonna miss 'em.

Miami Vice completely ignores this remark.

NEFARIUS (CONT'D)
'Magine it – Nick Faldo ge'in up in na mornin', 'e say, I'll jus'
nip ou' for a quick round before me eggs an' bacon – an'
where's me effin' clubs? Inni?

MIAMI VICE
I don't wanna touch 'em yet. I don't think I'm ready. Put 'em
in the wagon, Three Feet. On the blanket.

Three Feet lays out wads on the table, Nefarius's head nods, counting along.

MIAMI VICE (CONT'D)
I'm so pleased with you Nefarius, I'm thinking of giving you a little something
extra. You discreet?

Nefarius's jowls wobble as he nods vigorously. Miami Vice leans across the desk,
lowers his voice.

MIAMI VICE (CONT'D)
Don't take any bets on Sherbet in the 3.30 at Fontwell
tomorrow. Lower the odds on all the others. You'll clean up.

NEFARIUS
Sherbet. He's gonna win, right?

MIAMI VICE
'E's my 'orse. Here, put a wedge on 'im y'self. You'll clean up
again.

                              NEFARIUS
                Miami Vice, you're a cut above. You know that?

                              MIAMI VICE
                              Yeah. Yeah I do.

INT. THE LOCK BAR -- DAY

The Flying Dutchmen enter with crates of 'Bacradi' rum from the back room. The
four lads surround them and Lee and Moon lower a crate onto the carpet. It is
half-full of unopened bottles of 'Bacradi'.

                              BACON
                         You are taking the piss.

                              MOON
                         Not after last time.

                                                              CUT TO:

INT. THE LOCK BAR -- NIGHT (FLASHBACK)

The Lock is done out for a hen-night. Girls in cocktail dresses, done up to
the nines.

Lee and Bacon emerge from the kitchen with trays of hot dogs. Jamie mixes up
jugs of Bacradi and coke. Party seems to be going well. Inflated condom drifts
across picture. Silly string sprayed through the air. Shrieks of laughter. The
strip-o-gram gyrates vigorously.

                                                              CUT TO:

Atmosphere is less raucous. All the girls are sitting down and chatting. The
strip-o-gram gyrates but to less effect.

                                                              CUT TO:

Girls looks sleepy and sink into the chairs. The stripper begins to look
disappointed.

                                                              CUT TO:

All the women are motionless. Several of them have their eyes open.

                                                              CUT TO:

Five minutes later. The strip-o-gram sits sipping tea.

                                 12

MOON
This stuff must be stronger than it says.

Lee and Bacon go round trying to wake them up, shaking them, slapping their cheeks. Jamie looks straight at one of them.

JAMIE
Shit...

BACON
What?

JAMIE
She's dead. We've killed the fuckin' bride...

LEE
We've fuckin' killed 'em all.

CUT TO:

INT. THE LOCK BAR -- DAY

JOHANN
Eighteen dead botties? No!

JAMIE
Well no, they woke up in the end.

BACON
Wonderin' what happened to the last twenty-four hours.

The Dutchmen laugh with relief.

JORDI
Sank funkink God.

JOHANN
Cheesus Crust!

Jordi wipes his eyes, slips into Dutch. We get subtitles.

JORDI
They were lucky. How many died in Utrecht?

JOHANN
Twenty-four.

JAMIE

So in other words, you can take your Bacradi an' Sod off.

                    JOHANN
                  Hey, guys...

                    JORDI
      Guys... we didn't know. We are fillink so sorry.

                    JAMIE
          We're tryin' to build up a name.

                    JORDI
    Effrybotty, we are puttink it right – right now.

                    JOHANN
                  Right now.

                    JORDI
   First we are takink away za so disgustink booze.

                    JOHANN
    Yah, ent we tell to supplier not to giffink us zis shit
                  stuff, right?

                    JORDI
      Ent zen come look in za back of za fen.

Jordi and Johann pick up the crate and carry it to the door.

EXT. THE LOCK YARD -- DAY

The van doors are open. The lads gaze in on the cabinet with the watch.

                    JORDI
    We take za booze back ent we giff you za porno mooffies.
        If you sell you giffink to us fifty per cent.

                    LEE
            What about the watch?

                    JORDI
        Hey man, you take for free, yah?

Johann looks at his partner aghast. In Dutch, sub-titled:

                    JOHANN
      Not the watch Jordi, the watch is mine...

Jordi ignores his partner.

>   MOON
>   What kind of porno movies?

>   JORDI
>   Wicket. New from Nederlands, Germany, Scentinefya.

>   BACON
>   It's not gay or anyfink is it?

Jordi puts on a serious face.

>   JORDI
>   Hey! No way guys. We are knowink za rules.

INT./EXT. TROJAN KEBAB SHOP -- DAY

KOUROS is behind the counter, he's got his shirt off, displaying his pumped muscles, and a bandana round his head. He works out - doing dips between the fryer and the fridge, chin-ups off the door-frame, power-lifts with the barrels of vegetable oil...

Meanwhile kid is pumping coins into an ancient fruit machine by the door. He kicks and thumps it in frustration.

>   KID
>   Piece of shit...

>   KOUROS
>   Ey!

Kouros comes around the counter and heads for the kid.

>   KID
>   What?... It's bent, I swear!

Kouros grabs him by the collar and cuffs him round the head, then starts to drag him out of the shop. This unnecessary violence looks out of place in the sleepy shop. We move outside with him.

>   KID (CONT'D)
>   Get ya fuckin' 'ands off...

EXT. TROJAN KEBAB SHOP -- DAY

Kouros throws him out onto the pavement. Delivers his line from the doorway, like Dirty Harry.

KOUROS
Get back in da gutter... punk.

Kid gets up muttering. Jamie, Lee and Bacon pull up in Lee's Stag. Lee stays in the car.

BACON
Alright, Kouros. Nefarius in the back?

KOUROS
Ain't been out all day. Got 'iself a noo desk, inni?

INT. ABATTOIR/CORRIDOR -- DAY

Bacon and Jamie enter. Walk through to the back... Rows of skinned cows sway to and fro. They enter...

INT. NEFARIUS'S WAREHOUSE -- DAY

In the middle at the back is a huge walnut desk, with a fitted lamp with a green shade. Looming large on the other side is Nefarius.

NEFARIUS
'Allo lads. Wha's the score?

BACON
Alright. We've... nice desk... no, we've got a bit of business
you might be interested in.

NEFARIUS
Always interested in a little business.

JAMIE
We've got the ultimate in adult entertainment, right here.

Jamie drops five cassettes onto the desk.

BACON
We thought of you first. Bein' the top man in this area...

JAMIE
We're gonna cut you one of the best deals you've had.

BACON
This stuff is the business.

JAMIE
I mean, it's even banned in Bangkok.

16

Nefarius looks with disbelief.

> BACON
> Straight up... I mean this director won six golden dicks at that
> festival...er... what's it called...?

> NEFARIUS
> (Slightly impressed)
> The Little Bo Peep Awards?

> JAMIE
> Yeah – This is the moondust of the porn world and I kid
> you not.

> NEFARIUS
> It's no' gay, issi'?

> BACON
> Do we look like a pair of rear-gunners?

> NEFARIUS
> Nah, it's jus' I got all this fuckin' gay porn, 'n' I can't sell i' to
> any o' my contac'. I mean this is a totally diff'ra market innit?

Nefarius points to a stack of tapes behind him.

> BACON
> This is healthy stuff.

Nefarius steps out from behind his desk and down about a foot. He's now
revealed to be about five foot two.

> NEFARIUS
> Le's 'ave a look then.

Bacon plucks one off the top of the pile, and hands it to Nefarius, who slots it
into a video machine under a widescreen TV. Picks up remote and hits fast-
forward. We cannot see the screen, only their reactions to what appears on it.

> JAMIE
> Bloody 'ell.

> BACON
> Bloody 'ell. That's not faked, is it?

> NEFARIUS
> Jesus tha's a donkey innit?

                    BACON
              Nah, it's an 'orse.

                    JAMIE
        Nice 'orse, though. It's a thoroughbred.

Nefarius stops the tape.

                JAMIE (CONT'D)
        So what's your offer then? 300 tapes.

                  NEFARIUS
    Yeah well, I don't know, might be bi' 'ard t' shift.

                    JAMIE
    Everything's up somebody's street. People who want this kind
        of stuff'll pay through the nose for it too.

                  NEFARIUS
        I tell you what – I'll take 'alf. £350.

                    BACON
        350. 'Alf? Show us some respect.

                  NEFARIUS
            All right. 375 but no more.

                    JAMIE
              Don't waste our time.

                  NEFARIUS
    Is all I can do. It's been a bad week. The hoovers haven't
            shifted as well as I hoped.

Jamie and Bacon look at each other doubtfully.

                    JAMIE
        Bacon, what's that on your forehead?

                    BACON
        Don't tell me it's M. U. fuckin' G.

                    JAMIE
                  Come on.

They go to leave.

NEFARIUS
Alright, alright. I'll give £400 – I can take 'em down to the
blokes at the Rotary Club in Enfield...

BACON
400 for 'alf...

NEFARIUS
For 'alf. But I tell you what else. Runnin' at Fontwell, 3.30 on
Saturday. A dead cert. Fancy it?

JAMIE
I take it you're talking about a horse who ain't being asked to
rely on his natural abilities.

NEFARIUS
I jus' know 'e's gonna win, I 'eard it from the top.

Bacon and Jamie look at each other.

JAMIE
Alright.

Nefarius leans closer and lowers his voice.

NEFARIUS
Sherbet. But don't go shoutin' it about alrigh'?

BACON
Alright, but if your stallion don't come in at the donkey
derby... we'll be back here.

NEFARIUS
Lads, lads, when 'ave I ever done you ou' of anyfink? Get
Kouros to 'elp you bring in the tapes. And tell 'im to put the
pigeon nets up, we're running low on chicken.

Bacon and Jamie walk back through the building.

INT. ABATTOIR/CORRIDOR -- DAY

BACON
That was an eye-opener.

JAMIE
Takes all sorts. What we gonna do with the rest of 'em?

> BACON
> Dunno. Lee's uncle?

> JAMIE
> Firebug?

Jamie looks doubtful.

CUT TO:

INT. WAREHOUSE -- NIGHT

C.U. FIREBUG DOUG, an unlit cigarette in mouth, leans forward... Pulls someone's flaming hand in shot. Lights his fag. Muffled yelps in background.

CUT BACK TO:

INT. ABATTOIR/CORRIDOR -- DAY

Jamie and Bacon continue walking.

> JAMIE
> I ain't goin' near him. The man's a nutter.

EXT. DRIVING RANGE (KINGS CROSS) -- NIGHT

Miami Vice is at the driving range. So it's closed off to the public. Henchmen dotted around. Miami Vice whacks ball. Smiles.

At the other end, some guy in casual wear is trussed up to the flag. The ball pings off his shoulder.

> MIAMI VICE
> Off 'is shoulder?

> THREE FEET
> Gettin' closer every time, Guv.

> MIAMI VICE
> Yeah, I think you're right.

Glassjaw approaches. He doesn't look very happy. Miami Vice about to take a swing.

> THREE FEET
> Guv'ner.

Miami Vice turns to Glassjaw.

MIAMI VICE
Glassjaw... Couldn't wait t'give me my pressy eh?

GLASSJAW
There's been a slight accident...
Er...

Immediately Three Feet is at his shoulder.

MIAMI VICE
Where's my watch?

GLASSJAW
I was poisoned an'...

THREE FEET
You come 'ere with bad news. On the Guv'ner's night off
an' all.

MIAMI VICE
(Calmly)
Where's my fuckin' watch?

GLASSJAW
Well... er...it was like this... There was these two dodgy
Dutchmen... they drugged me an' nicked me van.

MIAMI VICE
D'you know how long it's taken me t' track down that watch?
... Eh? 10 years. That watch was custom made for the
legendary seventies porn maestro Dennis Van Horne... I was
breast-fed on that man's films. 'E was the father I never 'ad.
That watch is an item of...

Very uneasy pause. Miami Vice whacks the ball. Slices it.

MIAMI VICE (CONT'D)
... immense... sentimental value and I haven't even talked
about the cost... An' I'm even more sentimental about
money...

GLASSJAW
I swear I'll... I'll get it back.

THREE FEET
You know what I think Guv'?

                         MIAMI VICE
                   What's that Three Feet?

                         THREE FEET
        I don't think Glassjaw gets it. I don't think he understands
                 what you mean about... sen'imen'al value.

Glassjaw begins to sweat.

                         MIAMI VICE
                Three Feet, I think you're right.

Miami Vice takes another shot. Connects with the ball perfectly. Three Feet
applauds the shot, Glassjaw tries to join in. A henchman's strong arms lock
around his throat and drag him away.

EXT. HENLEY ARMS -- DAY

Cars outside, people unloading gear from vehicles.

INT. HENLEY ARMS -- DAY

An assortment of villains sit around playing cards. Through one door comes an
assortment of goods: fresh meat, cuddly toys, washing machines, sofas, TVs,
booze... What is not waved away is bought for cash or exchanged for other
goods, and then carted out the other door to be loaded into vans, taxis or cars.

                        JAMIE (V.O.)
            Lee's Uncle Doug runs this spill. Small outfit, but highly
              profitable, since most of his punters end up as charcoal.

FIREBUG DOUG and his sidekick HAPPY JACK are in the middle. Next to them is
ROY, five foot seven and sixteen stone. Firebug lights a cigarette with a custom
lighter that gives out a 12-inch flame.

Young geezer approaches with a crate of paints.

                         FIREBUG
           Oi. Put that in the silver BMW yeah? I've just had it re-
          upholstered, so you spill any an' I'll set your balls on fire.
                          Alright?

Lee, Bacon, Jamie and Moon enter and walk cautiously up to Firebug.

                     FIREBUG (CONT'D)
                       It's little Lee...

LEE
Alright, Uncle Doug...

FIREBUG
Alright son... lads... sit yourselves down then.

They do. Silence. Firebug looks at them. No-one wants to speak.

FIREBUG (CONT'D)
Well, get it off your chest.

BACON
We got some dirty vids. If you're... interested... in buying .. to
sell on... y'know.

FIREBUG
How dirty?

JAMIE
Worst I've ever seen.... Good... but ...

LEE
Filth.

MOON
Animals an' stuff.

BACON
Well, not too many animals. Some.

JAMIE
Yeah, most are... y'know...

Awkward laughter.

FIREBUG
No.

JAMIE
Er...

LEE
Kinky stuff.

BACON
We've got about 150.

FIREBUG
150, eh?

ALL THE LADS
Yeah...

FIREBUG
Give yer 250 quid.

BACON
Done.

Jamie, Bacon, Lee and Moon exit, nervously, to get the tapes.

FIREBUG
Lee?

Lee turns around. Jamie, Bacon and Moon exit. Lee sits back down.

FIREBUG (CONT'D)
You seen Dorothy lately? How's she doing?

LEE
Not too bad. Healin' up.

FIREBUG
I told 'er enough times. Why do people try an' push their luck?

Lee shrugs sympathetically. Firebug beckons him closer.

FIREBUG (CONT'D)
You got anyfin' else?

Pause. Firebug then snaps the lighter open inches from Lee's nose. Lee gulps.

LEE
(Blurting it out)
Er... Sherbet.

FIREBUG
What?

LEE
... 3.30 tomorrrow, Fontwell.

Firebug puts a cigarette between his lips.

24

FIREBUG
Dead cert?

LEE
Oh yeah. Well y'know, hush-hush an' all that.

FIREBUG
Put 500 on it then, will ya.

He pulls out a roll of notes and counts out the money in fifties. As he hands it to Lee, he notices Lee's watch.

FIREBUG (CONT'D)
Nice watch, son. Very, very, nice watch.

Flicks lighter. Ten-inch flame leaps up.

EXT. HENLEY ARMS -- DAY

Miami's Roller passes frame as Jamie, Bacon and Moon are unloading the tapes from the boot of their car.

BACON
Do you think we looked scared?

MOON
Nah .. 'e 'ad respect for us.

JAMIE
Yeah, we 'andled ourselves well.

Lee exits Henley Arms checks his watch and walks towards Jamie, Moon and Bacon. Miami Vice, Three Feet and henchmen enter behind him.

LEE
I... let 'im into the tip. 'E gave me some cash to put on it.

INT. HENLEY ARMS -- DAY

Three Feet enters followed by Miami Vice's henchmen. They space themselves out and stand still. Nobody moves. Footsteps.

Miami Vice enters, walks through his crowd of henchmen. Stops in front of Firebug. Tension and suspicion.

MIAMI VICE
Hello Firebug.

FIREBUG
Never thought I'd see the day when you would walk in 'ere,
Miami. Must be somethin' very serious.

MIAMI VICE
Serious alright.

Pause. Miami walks slowly towards Firebug and removes his sunglasses.

MIAMI VICE (CONT'D)
I need to put the word out on a couple of Dutchmen selling
porn videos... and a very special watch. That porn – an' more
importantly, that watch – belongs to me. So if anythin' like
that comes through 'ere do let me know.

FIREBUG
What sort of porn?

MIAMI VICE
Kind that lawyers and bankers go for. Animal classics, shit
like that.

Happy Jack glances at Firebug, but Firebug gives nothing away.

FIREBUG
What sort of watch?

MIAMI VICE
(Great seriousness)
Custom-made erotic timepiece. You'll know it if you see it.

Miami Vice turns towards the door.

FIREBUG
'Ey... Miami....

Miami Vice turns around.

FIREBUG (CONT'D)
'Ere's somethin' to cheer you up, mate. Dead cert – 3.30,
Fontwell tomorrow.

MIAMI VICE
Yeah?

FIREBUG
... Sherbet.

MIAMI VICE
(Sarcastically)
Thanks. You want me to keep that quiet?

Firebug shrugs. Miami Vice walks out. His footmen follow, wary to the last.

HAPPY JACK
You ain't gonna tell 'im then?

FIREBUG
Fuck'im. I ain't got any time for 'im. Flash bastard. 'E's full of
shit... I tell you what, it's good news Lee's got 'is watch? Cos
sooner or later I'm gonna get hold of that watch an' shove it
in Miami Vice's ugly muppet face.

INT. CAB -- NIGHT

All four lads in Taxi.

JAMIE
Now this time, I do not wanna 'ave to leave early – Moon.

MOON
What? She was well into it. And anyway she dropped the
charges – eventually.

EXT. LAPLAND -- NIGHT

Bouncers frame the entrance with the doorman. He is an officious dwarf with
a clipboard. Over the door, the name of the club is in neon, capped with white
snow.

The cab arrives with Jamie, Bacon, Lee and Moon, join a short queue. They look
ready for a good time.

INT. LAPLAND -- NIGHT

Four lads checking in their coats and kissing the girl behind the counter hello.
There is a neon sign reading 'Every Day is Xmas Day in Lapland'.

CUT TO:

INT. LAPLAND -- NIGHT

Meeting the Maitre d' and paying. Walking into semi-glitzy, slightly seventies.
Pole-dancing and lap-dancing. Round tables in cosy alcoves. A few dwarves
serve drinks on trays. Lots of wintry and Xmas touches: fur-trimming, antlers,
fake snow in the corners of the mirrors.

CUT TO:

INT. LAPLAND -- NIGHT

Taking their places around a table in an alcove, waving to the barmaid. A tray of drinks arriving – they know the waitress too.

CUT TO:

INT. LAPLAND -- NIGHT

Lap-dancer wearing antlers and furry boots does her stuff for the boys.

CUT TO:

INT. LAPLAND -- NIGHT

Shot of flaming zamboucas and other disgusting-looking cocktails.

CUT TO:

INT. LAPLAND -- NIGHT

The lads take seats near the pole. Suddenly they look up from one pair of legs to the face and nudge each other, recognising the dancer.

TANYA is sliding down the pole.

> LEE
> Alright Tanya?

> TANYA
> Piss off.

> LEE
> Come on, Tanya. Don't be like that.

> TANYA
> I was 'opin' you wouldn't talk to me.

> JAMIE
> I promise we'll keep Moon on a lead.

> TANYA
> You said that last time.

> JAMIE
> We got a nice little earner for ya. Easy money.

                          TANYA
     If you want me to look after the pub you can fuck off.

                          JAMIE
                        Oh come on.

                          TANYA
              I'm a dancer not a barmaid.

                           LEE
                   You'll be the manager.

                          TANYA
                You mean I'll be on me own?

                           LEE
        You were great last time. Pay you double time.

                          TANYA
      I'll do it if you let me sister 'ave her 21st in the upstairs
                          room...

She twirls round and peers out at him from between her legs.

                      TANYA (CONT'D)
                        For free.

Applause.

                           LEE
                        Alright.

                          TANYA
                       Free booze.

                           LEE
                       Come on...

                          TANYA
                 I'm doin' you a favour.

INT. LAPLAND CORRIDOR/CHANGING ROOM -- NIGHT

She goes through into changing rooms. They follow. Behind the scenes, naked
female flesh everywhere.

                            29

> **TANYA**
> Honestly what's the matter with those doormen. I can't
> believe they let that pervert Moon in.

Turns around startled.

> **TANYA (CONT'D)**
> Keep 'im out of 'ere.

She indicates Moon. Bacon pushes Moon back.

> **MOON**
> What? Me? Oh c'mon Tanya. Don't be like that, I was only
> playing around.

> **TANYA**
> Playing around? Is that what you told the police?

> **BACON**
> Moon, shut it. Look Tanya, are you going to help us out
> or what?

> **TANYA**
> I'll do it if the booze for the party's free.

> **JAMIE**
> Y'know we can't do that.

> **LEE**
> How about we throw in a crate of rum?

Pause. Tanya weighs it up.

> **TANYA**
> Done. Now piss off.

> **LEE**
> See ya tomorrow.

They turn away. Straight into Three Feet, who is supervising the removal of the
bound and gagged Glassjaw with Mr Pie and Mr Mash.

> **THREE FEET**
> What the fuck are you doin' in 'ere?

No answer. Miami's voice booms from next room.

MIAMI VICE'S VOICE
Send them four in will yer Three Feet?

Three Feet nods at the door: 'In you go'. Lads gulp, shrug. Three Feet exits
followed by Mr Pie and Mr Mash, carrying Glassjaw.

INT. LAPLAND, CORRIDOR -- NIGHT CONTINUOUS

Three Feet stops and looks back at Pie and Mash.

MR PIE
Do we 'ave to carry 'im? He's a fat git.

THREE FEET
(Sighing)
Just, put 'im in the Range Rover.

INT. LAPLAND, THE CONTROL ROOM -- NIGHT

The room is very dark. It is lit by a a narrow horizontal strip of window which
overlooks the main room and eight monitors feeding pictures of what's going on
in every corner of the place to a middle-aged bloke in a swivel chair. A bouncer
stands next to him with a walkie-talkie.

Miami Vice has his back to them, looking at the bank of monitors.

MIAMI VICE
(To Moon)
Shut the door behind you, son.

Moon gulps and shuts the door. The lads look at each other, very perturbed.

MIAMI VICE (CONT'D)
First thing. Never approach any of my girls while
they're workin'.

LEE
Course, yeah, stupid of us. It's just that we all went to school
with Tanya.

Miami Vice turns back from the bank of monitors and looks at them all.

MIAMI VICE
I know. That's why you're standing in here and not outside
with ya bollocks kicked in.

EXT. THE JUNCTION -- NIGHT

The Range Rover turns down an alley and comes to a halt. Three Feet steps out and greets two heavies: MR SKIN and MR BONE.

THREE FEET
Alright lads. Sorry about the short notice.

MR BONE
Everything's ready.

THREE FEET
'E's in the back.

MR BONE
Struggler?

Three Feet shakes his head.

THREE FEET
'E won't give you no trouble.

Mr Pie and Mr Mash open the boot. Mr Skin and Mr Bone lift the trussed-up wreck of Glassjaw onto the ground. Gravel crunches underfoot.

INT. LAPLAND, CONTROL ROOM -- NIGHT

MIAMI VICE
Now your pub. What we 'ear is that a lot of business is goin'
through there. Lotta gear, that right?

BACON
We sell a bit of stuff on if it comes our way. Nuffink that 'ot.

MIAMI VICE
Want you to look out for a watch. Custom-made. Gold.
Work of art. Tells the time by a hand-crafted cock and balls.

Strange expression creeps over Lee's face.

LEE
Anyfink like that. Even a bit sim'lar, we'll let yer know.

ALL THE LADS
Yeah.

MIAMI VICE
Yeah.

INT. THE JUNCTION -- NIGHT

32

Inside the carriage. Glassjaw is gagged, but he makes no attempt to struggle or protest. He knows his fate is sealed.

A muffled sniff from Glassjaw. Three Feet steps in.

                    THREE FEET
    What's it to be then? The Gravedigger, or The Postman?

Glassjaw mumbles pathetically into his gag.

                THREE FEET (CONT'D)
            What's that Glassjaw?

Glassjaw mumbles again.

                THREE FEET (CONT'D)
    The Postman, was it? A sensible choice. Less dignity, but
                    more speed.

Three Feet nods to the heavies. They lay down plastic sheeting while Three Feet puts on an apron and rubber gloves. One heavy opens up his suitcase to reveal an assortment of knives and cleavers. The other unpacks wrapping paper and address labels.

                    MR BONE
            Mincemeat or chops, guv?

                    THREE FEET
            Chops, it's quicker.

INT. THE JUNCTION -- NIGHT

The last of about ten parcels has an address label slapped on it. The heavies stand at the door with a bin-liner.

                    THREE FEET
    Thanks lads. Really good service you run, it's a shame more
            people don't know about you.

                    MR BONE
                Cheers.

INT. LAPLAND, THE CONTROL ROOM -- NIGHT

Miami is finishing up telling some horrible anecdote as if it's a really funny joke.

33

MIAMI VICE
So off he goes, his bones showing through 'is elbows, an' 'is
nose in 'is pocket, goin' 'I don't even support Chelsea!'

Miami roars with laughter, his surveillance man and bouncer join in. The lads try
to join in too, but it sounds really forced.

EXT. LAPLAND -- NIGHT

The lads walk down the street.

MOON
Fuckin' 'ell, we got 'is watch!

JAMIE
It's Miami Vice's watch!

LEE
We'll give it back...

BACON
We should give it back NOW!

LEE
We can't give it back straight away – I didn't own up straight away...

JAMIE
'E's got a point.

LEE
Anyway, I quite like it.

BACON
You what?

LEE
You gotta admit...

The other three turn on him.

BACON
You are not fuckin' wearin' that watch around - you fuckin'
take it off when we get 'ome.

LEE
Alright. I'm not stupid.

ACT TWO

INT. BATHROOM -- MORNING

Lee flicks open an old-fashioned cut-throat razor. Lifts it to his soaped-up face. Leans towards the mirror.

INT. BEDROOM -- MORNING

Jamie doing up his shirt in front of the mirror, adding cuff-links.

INT. BATHROOM -- MORNING

Moon furiously greasing back his hair in front of the mirror.

INT. BEDROOM -- MORNING

Bacon tying his tie, in the mirror.

INT. BEDROOM -- MORNING

Jamie puts his jacket on, ties his laces.

EXT. THE LOCK, THE YARD -- MORNING

Moon, Jamie, and Bacon are all suited up. They stand in the yard impatiently.

                              BACON
                         Oi! Come on Lee!

INT. BEDROOM -- MORNING

Lee sweeps cash into his pocket. Last-minute decision: he pulls Miami Vice's watch out from a drawer full of shirts. Straps it on.

EXT. THE LOCK, THE YARD -- MORNING

All four lads in Lee's car, which eventually starts.

EXT. FONTWELL -- DAY

A series of tableaux of the boys having fun.

EXT. FONTWELL -- DAY

Jamie and Lee stroll through the crowd, looking wide, soaking up the atmosphere.

                              LEE
         We should do this more often. We never get birds like that in
                            our boozer.

Lee is staring at a couple of Sloanie girls with hats.

                             JAMIE
                   Time we got these bets in?

Lee looks at his – Miami Vice's – watch. Jamie sees it.

                         JAMIE (CONT'D)
             Lee! That thing's s'posed to be in hidin'

                              LEE
         We ain't exactly gunner run into Miami Vice 'ere...

Whip pan.

                                                        CUT TO:

INT. VIP ENCLOSURE -- DAY

Miami Vice is in a blazer with gold buttons. On one side there are a bunch
of Arab businessmen, on the other a couple of the girls from Lapland in hats
and dresses.

Three Feet looks uncomfortable in his three-piece suit, holding a paper plate
of canapés quite uneasily.

Miami Vice looks at the food with disguised disgust. And watches a posh-looking
woman pop a quail's egg in her mouth.

                          MIAMI VICE
                   See that? That's breedin'.

                          THREE FEET
                     There's no pork pies.

                          MIAMI VICE
     Course not. I might not of been born with a silver spoon up me arse, but I've
         always 'ad an understandin' of the finer fings in life... Sheikh!

THE SHEIKH is now at Miami's side.

                            SHEIKH
           Congratulations on your purchase. I had no idea that you
                         were a horse lover.

MIAMI VICE
Every Englishman's got horses in his blood.

SHEIKH
And I never imagined that Mr Digby would part from Sherbet.

Miami and the Sheikh look over to Mr Digby who is alone in his wheelchair with his drink, looking very morose.

MIAMI VICE
Well, I did 'ave to send in a team of, er, negotiators.
'Ammered out a deal. An' y'know... there's an 'orse of yours I
got my eye on...

EXT. PUBLIC ENTRANCE/PADDOCK -- DAY

Lee, Moon, Jamie and Bacon stand munching hot dogs. A uniform-hat lands at Bacon's feet. He looks over to where it came from.

BACON
'Ello, bit of action...

CUT TO:

UNCLE DEREK, a huge man in his forties, holds a TICKET MAN's lapels in his fists. UNCLE BRIAN backs him up.

UNCLE DEREK
I told you he's six years old - he goes in for fuckin' FREE!

He points to MICHAEL, a boy of about ten. Michael is stealing coins off the counter. Other ATTENDANTS detach their colleague and pull him away. The SENIOR ATTENDANT is a large man, someone to be reckoned with.

SENIOR ATTENDANT
With respect sir, he's at least ten.

AMBER, a small girl of no more than seven years old, grabs the SENIOR ATTENDANT's arm.

AMBER
Listen mate, e's my little brother.

SENIOR ATTENDANT
Rubbish.

UNCLE DEREK
Easy sonny.

AUNT GERALDINE, a woman in her forties with straw-blonde hair and tattoos up both arms decks the Senior Attendant with one punch.

                    AUNT GERALDINE
            Don't you fuckin' insult my nephew.

                                        CUT BACK TO:

                         BACON
            Moon... What're your cousins doin' 'ere?

                          MOON
            They like a bet. I thought I'd tip 'em off.

                         BACON
        When you gonna understand? Your family ain't fit to mix in
                        normal society.

                         JAMIE
            Le's get out the way before they come over 'ere.

                          LEE
        Le's try tha' VIP bit, tha's where all the decent birds are.

                          MOON
                VIP bit? Nah, leave it.

                         JAMIE
            Twenty quid says they'll let us in.

                          MOON
                They won't let us in.

                         JAMIE
                Just let me do the talkin'.

                          MOON
                Alright, twenty quid.

They shake.

EXT. VIP ENCLOSURE -- DAY

Jamie puts twenty quid into Moon's palm as they are ejected from the VIP area.

                     LAURA'S VOICE
                        'Ello Jamie.

                           38

Jamie turns round to see LAURA standing right behind him.

Double-takes and looks her up and down. She's a bit of alright.

                    JAMIE
              Fuck me, Laura?!

All lads look on in disbelief.

                    LAURA
           I was hopin' I'd run into you.

Jamie walks over to her.

                    JAMIE
             You've er, grown up a bit.

She looks at him coyly, sticking her tits out.

                    LAURA
                Meanin' what?

                    JAMIE
    You're not exactly Moon's sweet and innocent little cousin
                  any more.

                    LAURA
          I've learned a lot since then.

                    JAMIE
                  I bet.

EXT. WOOD -- DAY (FLASHBACK)

C.U. - NAMES CARVED IN TREE: 'LAURA 'N' JAMIE'

Trees are blowing in the wind.

                 JAMIE'S VOICE
                  Come on...

                 LAURA'S VOICE
                    No...

                 JAMIE'S VOICE
     All the girls in London do it. If they love yer.

Camera pulls back to show: Jamie and Laura sitting under the tree, holding hands.

                    LAURA
        Look I loves you Jamie, but I ain't like that.

                    JAMIE
            Just stick yer 'and down there...

                    LAURA
                    Noooo....

                                                CUT TO:

Moon, Bacon, and Lee hide behind another tree spying on Laura and Jamie with a pair of plastic binoculars.

                    BACON
        'E ain't even gunner get 'er top off.

                    LEE
                  Tight cow.

                    MOON
        He'll say he shagged 'er though, won't 'e?

                    LEE
                Course 'e will.

P.O.V. – Through the binoculars, Jamie gives them a V-sign in mid-snog.

                                            CUT BACK TO:

EXT. VIP ENCLOSURE -- DAY

                    LAURA
            You think about me, then?

                    JAMIE
            Now and again, y'know.

She laughs.

                    LAURA
            Liar. You're just the same.

Jamie watches Laura saunter off and follows her.

                                                CUT TO:

EXT. RACECOURSE -- DAY

Uncle Derek, patriarch of the Crusty clan, strides towards the bookies, pushing anyone aside if they get in his way. Beefy Uncle Brian follows. They reach the bookie...

                    UNCLE DEREK
            Three hundrid an' fifty quid on...
                     (To Brian)
                 What's 'e's name?

                    UNCLE BRIAN
                     Sher-bet.

                      BOOKIE
                   Too late pal.

They curse and turn away, glaring around them.

EXT. RACECOURSE -- DAY

The horses are off.

EXT. VIP ENCLOSURE -- DAY

Miami Vice rubs his hands as he takes his place again. At least if the horse wins it'll be a good day...

EXT. RACECOURSE -- DAY

The horses begin to space out.

INT. TOILET CUBICLE -- DAY

Jamie and Laura hard at it against the cubicle door.

EXT. VIP ENCLOSURE -- DAY

Look of satisfaction on Miami Vice's face as Sherbet pulls into a huge lead and the three front-runners fall off the pace.

EXT. RACECOURSE -- DAY

Crusty kids weave through the crowd picking pockets.

INT. TOILET CUBICLE -- DAY

The cubicle is in danger of collapsing as Laura coaxes ever increasing vigour from her mount.

EXT. RACECOURSE -- DAY

The other horses lollop along contendedly in a lethargic pack.

EXT. RACECOURSE -- DAY

The lads roar Sherbet on as he thunders past, alone. Lee has doubts:

> LEE
> Bit obvious innit?

> BACON
> Wait a minute...

EXT. RACECOURSE -- DAY

A chestnut mare starts to make ground on Sherbet.

EXT. VIP ENCLOSURE -- DAY

Miami Vice's grin is fading. He shoots Three Feet a sharp glance.

> THREE FEET
> We nobbled 'em all.

> MIAMI VICE
> Seems like this one's got guts of steel.

> THREE FEET
> Relax, guv. We got a plan 'B'.

EXT. RACECOURSE -- DAY

Gasps as the jockey slides out of the saddle. The riderless horse prances alongside meaninglessly as Sherbet charges home to an emphatic victory.

EXT. RACECOURSE -- DAY

Lee, Bacon and Moon cheer.

INT. TOILET CUBICLE -- DAY

Laura and Jamie climax.

EXT. VIP ENCLOSURE -- DAY

Miami Vice's shoulders droop in exhausted satisfaction. Everyone is patting him on the back. The Sheikh walks past with one of the bimbos.

MIAMI VICE
Sheikh! Alright mate. You sure you don't wanna sell any of
them 'orses?

SHEIKH
I'm afraid I'm not a dealer, I'm a breeder.

The Sheikh walks on. Miami turns to Three Feet.

MIAMI VICE
Wanker more like. I wan' im on a drip by the end of the week.
So I can make 'im an offer before Doncaster on Saturday.

INT. RACECOURSE BAR -- DAY

Bacon fishes out the winnings.

BACON
Drinks all round mate.

UNCLE DEREK
Cheers lads. That's very good of you. I'll have a pint of cider.

Bacon looks round and sees the whole Crusty clan piling into the bar. The
barman puts the winnings behind the bar. Aunty Geraldine gives Moon a
tight hug.

MOON
Alright Aunty Geraldine.

UNCLE BRIAN
Pint of cider Derek.

Jamie and Laura enter, flushed.

LAURA
Alright Dad. You remember Jamie.

UNCLE BRIAN
'Ello mate.

JAMIE
How are ya?

Brian stares straight into Jamie's eyes.

UNCLE BRIAN
Got a bit lucky, did ya?

Jamie glances at Laura guiltily.

> JAMIE
> Whassat?

> UNCLE BRIAN
> That horse come in for you?

> JAMIE
> Oh the horse? Yeah, came in.

Uncle Brian puts his arm round Jamie in avuncular fashion. Lee is drinking with Aunt Geraldine. Uncle Derek hands Moon another pint.

> UNCLE DEREK
> You alright Moon? Have another cider. Still looking like
> you've come out of a cow's arse.

Jamie and Uncle Brian finish their pints.

> UNCLE BRIAN
> Another one?

INT. RACECOURSE BAR -- DAY

Bar almost empty. Chairs and tables disarranged. Lads collapsed all round the place. BAR STEWARD wakes Bacon up.

> BAR STEWARD
> I'm afraid we're closing up now, lads.

> BACON
> Right...

Bacon shoves Lee. Lee shambles up to the bar. Points to the envelope with the winnings in it.

> LEE
> Can we 'ave the rest of our winnings back?

> BAR STEWARD
> It's all gone.

> LEE
> There was ten grand in there, pal.

> BAR STEWARD
> Listen, I added it up on the machine.

                         LEE
            Well you added it up wrong, didn't yer.

                      BAR STEWARD
              It's all there. You can check it.

Steward pushes over a long strip of paper.

                         LEE
         We haven't had any crates of Champagne – twenty kegs of
                 cider?! What are you on about?

                      BAR STEWARD
            We helped carry it out to your van.

                         LEE
                      What van?!

INT. LEE'S CAR -- DAY

All four lads in the car looking mournful. Jamie has his head in his hands, Moon
takes deep breaths. It's painful.

                        JAMIE
                 Your fuckin' family.

                        MOON
         It's not their fault. It's the way they were brought up.

                       BACON
                    Oh yeah...

                        MOON
          Yeah. They see something and take it. What's wrong with
                         that?

                       BACON
         What's wrong with taking our fuckin' money? You twat.

Engine starts to splutter, grinds to a sickly halt. Silence.

INT. MIAMI VICE'S ROLLER -- DAY

Miami Vice relaxes in the back with Three Feet. Chauffeur drives them home.
Silence in the car. Three Feet's stomach gurgles. Then Miami's makes the same
gurgling noise.

MIAMI VICE
Right, pull over at that pub... poncy pastry don't fill you up.
Ploughman's oughta do the trick.

They pull into the car park of The Hungry Horse. Behind them a luxury camper
van follows them in.

CUT TO:

EXT. COUNTRY LANE -- DAY

The lads push the car. They are all still very pissed off.

LEE
Christ's sake Moon. If you hadn't have brought your
poxy family...

MOON
What about your stupid car? We'd've been alright if –

LEE
You what? I've lost me winnings! Because of your cousins
and this stupid –

Lee turns on Bacon.

BACON
You can shut up. It was your stupid idea to tell yer Uncle
about the bet, wannit?

LEE
Well I didn't think you'd be stupid enough to give all 'is money
to Moon's cousins did I...

JAMIE
Maybe we should try an' be a bit more positive an' think of
some way to sort this out.

BACON
You can definitely shut up. You got a shag out of it.

ALL THE LADS
Yeah.

BACON
Right, next car we see – we nick.

EXT. CAR PARK, HUNGRY HORSE -- NIGHT

The four lads stand in the car park outside the Hungry Horse, casing the motors.

> JAMIE
> Might as well make it something that'll fetch a price. So we
> can pay Firebug back his money...

They glare at Bacon, who looks sheepish.

They look at the Roller. The chauffeur is still asleep in his seat. They all look at the camper van.

> MOON
> No argument there really.

INT. CAMPER VAN -- NIGHT

The engine revs, he finds a gear, and the van lurches across the car park.

EXT. THE LOCK YARD -- DAY

Lee and Moon stumble out into the yard, still fucked from the day before. Lee opens up the trap door into the cellar. Jamie and Bacon appear down below and pass up an empty barrel. They are looking pretty rough too. Sound of a horse neighing. Lee and Moon freeze, each one thinking the sound was in his head.

> MOON
> I tell you what. I got 'orses on the brain... I jus' 'eard a –

> LEE
> You 'eard an 'orse?

They look at each other. Then the sound of neighing again. Moon walks towards the camper, puts his ear to the back door. The door shudders from an enormous kick.

Bacon and Jamie have climbed up from the cellar to see what is going on.

Moon takes a deep breath and steps forward again. He opens the back door of the camper van, he dives out of the way as Sherbet charges out into the yard. Chaos. The lads run in every direction at once, swearing and shouting.
The horse bucks and rears, gallops to the far wall, kicks over dustbins, and spills their contents.

> BACON
> All we need's a fuckin' 'orse.

INT. THE LOCK BACK ROOM -- DAY

The lads sit round eating breakfast, working out what to do. They all have fry-ups apart from Moon who has prunes and natural yogurt. Outside, the horse is going bonkers: neighing, charging, sending the dustbins rolling round the yard.

> JAMIE
> It's eating the whole yard.

> BACON
> I say we just kill it. See what we can get for its carcass.

> LEE
> You can't kill 'im. What's 'e done to you?

> BACON
> Alright, alright just an idea.

> MOON
> You don't recognise 'im, do yer?

The others look at him strangely. Then there is a huge rumble and crash from outside as something collapses. They look to the window then back to Moon.

> MOON (CONT'D)
> That's Sherbet. The 'orse that won yesterday.

> LEE
> Shit...

Pause.

> JAMIE
> Perfect. Fuckin' perfect. We flog 'im.

> LEE
> Who to?

> JAMIE
> Moon's family. They love 'orses.

> MOON
> (Agreeing)
> They do like an 'orse.

> JAMIE
> Course, we'll 'ave to disguise 'im.

> BACON
> Disguise 'im? As what? A lanky cow?

JAMIE
We go down to Nefarius's tomorrow and spray 'im another
colour, then flog 'im to Moon's nasty family. Pay Firebug back
'is money... an' breathe easy.

LEE
Nice one.

Another crash from outside.

INT. NEFARIUS' WAREHOUSE -- DAY

Sherbet munching on a party-size bag of crisps tied around his neck like a
nose-bag.

Everyone gathered round for the spraying of Sherbet. They've gone for black
with white spots. Moon supervises, Jamie aims the paint.

NEFARIUS
Is unnatural boys, is unnatural.

LEE
'E eats splinters and nails, 'e won't mind a little bit of paint.

BACON
Talkin' of unnatural – how you gettin' on sellin' them vids?

NEFARIUS
'S funny, they goin' li' ho' cakes. I'm runnin' out.

MOON
Give 'im a sock on his leg. For balance.

JAMIE
Eh? Don't get technical.

MOON
Just leave a bit of white down there. Yeah tha's it.

EXT. THE LOCK, THE YARD -- DAY

Firebug wanders up to the horse. Happy Jack goes to stroke Sherbet – sticky.
Looks at his hand – paint. Turns towards the back entrance of the pub.

INT. THE LOCK BAR -- DAY

Moon rushes into the bar looking worried.

                              MOON
              Shit. It's Firebug. He's outside.

                              JAMIE
           Right he's your uncle, you tell 'im.

                               LEE
          Fuck that. It was 'is idea to go an' see im.

                             BACON
              So? You told 'im about the 'orse.

                               LEE
             Alright, why don't we just hide?

                             JAMIE
       What? We can 'ide until we sell the 'orse. Then pay 'im.

Bacon looks towards the doorway.

                             BACON
                       Too late for that.

They all turn. Firebug and Happy Jack stand in front of them. Both beaming.

                        BACON (CONT'D)
              Alright Firebug, I mean Doug...las.

                            FIREBUG
        La-ads. Looks like your tip came off. Well done, boys.

                     LEE'S VOICE WAVERS:

                               LEE
            Uncle Doug, how's Rita? And the k-kids?

Firebug's demeanour changes drastically.

                            FIREBUG
                       Where's my cash?

                             JAMIE
              We had a problem. It's alright though.

Firebug relaxes.

                               50

FIREBUG
Right, so not the sort of problem that means me not getting
my money then.

JAMIE
No, it's just that we've...

LEE
Invested it.

FIREBUG
You've invested my money...

He pulls out a blowtorch.

MOON
In a horse, a very good one.

FIREBUG
You've invested my money in that nag out there, drippin' with
paint and chewin' on a cardboard box?

BACON
You're gonna make money on it. When we sell 'im on.
100 per cent or something?

Looks to the others for assurance.

MOON
We're gonna sell 'im at a profit.

Firebug is now a foot away from the lads.

JAMIE
A big one.

Firebug lights his blowtorch.

FIREBUG
Tell you what Lee, 'ow about you givin' me that fancy watch
of yours instead?

Lee freezes...

LEE
Er... I can't.

.

                        FIREBUG
                An' why's that, nephew?

Sherbet neighs outside...

                          LEE
    You ain'... You're not gonna believe this... but the 'orse has
                        eaten it.

Lads look at Lee in disgust.

                        FIREBUG
                        Eaten it?

                          LEE
    Yeah, we're trying t'figure out 'ow to get it back.

                        FIREBUG
            You're not pissing with me are ya?

                          LEE
                    Course not Uncle.

Firebug and Happy Jack look sceptical.

                        FIREBUG
    Since you're me nephew an' all... I'll give you 24 hours to
    either produce the watch from the 'orses arse or my cash...
            plus 100 per cent... if you're one minute late ...

Pause for dramatic effect...

                    FIREBUG (CONT'D)
        ... I'll just have to roast the lot of yer... alright?

                          LEE
                        Fine...

                        BACON
                Yeah... great... cheers.

                          LEE
                Thanks a lot Uncle Doug.

As a parting gesture, Firebug sets light to the coats on the coat stand with a
casual sweep of his blowtorch.

The lads seize the fire extinguishers and manage to put out the fire before it spreads any further. They open the side door onto the yard to let the smoke out and to get some fresh air.

EXT. THE LOCK, BACK YARD -- CONTINUOUS

All four lads stand by the door breathing in the fresh air.

MOON
Why didn't you just give 'im the watch?

LEE
Cos sooner or later he'd find out it was Miami Vice's, an' then just to piss old Miami off he'd tell everyone he had it, an' where he got it.

BACON
'The 'orse 'as eaten it' – that is the most pathetic thing I've ever heard.

Johann and Jordi enter the yard. They are both loved-up and very touchy, touchy.

JOHANN
Hee-y...

JORDI
Are you ready for rave party?

JOHANN
Who is wanting to neck some E and head for the Ministry off Sound ? Eh?

JAMIE
Not tonight lads.

JOHANN
But you know we tinkink maybe dose dudes are sellink already da porno mooffies ent we can collectink our fifty per cent...

JAMIE
By the way. Where d'you get those vids from?

Pause. Dutchmen suddenly notice the horse.

JORDI
Yikes! Johann, check out za horse!

> JAMIE
> Lee? I think the 'orse is 'ungry again.

> LEE
> 'E's always 'ungry.

> JAMIE
> He's munching on your motor.

Lee dashes over.

> LEE
> 'Kin' stupid animal...

The horse is chewing on the hood of the roof. Lee tries to pull the horse off his car. Fetches a bucket of slop to entice the horse away. That doesn't work either.

No-one helps him. They all stand round laughing.

> LEE (CONT'D)
> Eh, come 'ere, come 'ere, come on...

Plunges his arm into the bucket realising that he needs to take his watch off. He takes the watch off places it on the car and then puts his hands into the bucket bringing out a hand dripping with slop.

> LEE (CONT'D)
> Oi 'orse. Come on there's a good boy, over 'ere.

Lee struggles with horse.

> JOHANN
> Eh Lee, you wantink to relaxink yeah. Take one of these,
> everysink will be cool...

Johann holds out some dubious pills in the palm of his hand. Lee is distracted away from the horse and the car for a moment.

> LEE
> No.

Johann looks furtive, eager to get going.

> JOHANN
> Let's roll, Jordi.

The lads watch the two sad Dutchmen disappear. The horse sinks his mouth into the bucket. Lee pats his nose.

LEE
Hang on, where's me watch?

Lee looks around.

LEE (CONT'D)
No... no... no way.

The horse looks back at Lee with smug innocence.

LEE (CONT'D)
'E's only ate it...

BACON
You what?

LEE
The 'orse's ate me watch...

JAMIE
No, no, Lee tha's the half-arsed story you told Firebug...

LEE
Well now it's 'appened look, you can see by the look on
'is face.

BACON
'E can't've swallowed a watch... can 'e?

EXT. THE LOCK, THE YARD -- NIGHT

Lee, in an apron, stands in front of Sherbet, holding out a prune, and talking
into his ear.

LEE
Just one, please come on, it'll help you go.

Sherbet is not interested.

LEE (CONT'D)
Alright, alright, but shit out the watch, eh?

From the window above, Jamie shouts down.

JAMIE
He ain't gonna shit with you watching him all the time...
you're making 'im nervous.

MOON
Oi Lee, he shits out the other end, mate!

Lee ignores them and keeps talking to Sherbet.

EXT. DUTCHMEN'S VAN, CITY STREET -- NIGHT.

Jordi and Johann get out of their van.

JORDI
I don't like it, man.

JOHANN
Chill out, it's cool.

JORDI
Not our friends, our business partners man! It's bad karma...
Didn't you listen to anything the bagwhan said?

JOHANN
I was stoned. I was just staring at his beard.

JORDI
It's bad yin and yang man. You've cursed us.

JOHANN
Hey... don't get hung up on a materialistic bag. It's... just...
a watch...

ACT THREE

EXT. THE LOCK, THE YARD -- DAY

Lee is still there in his apron. He has taken a break from his vigil and is enjoying
an early morning cigarette.

Moon joins him to read the paper.

MOON
Good news... he's 'ad a shit.

> LEE
> Yeah, right...

Moon points to a pile of manure under Sherbet's tail.

> LEE (CONT'D)
> Excellent.

He pulls on a pair of rubber gloves and dives enthusiastically into the steaming heap. The others look at each other with renewed concern. But Lee is having no luck.

> LEE (CONT'D)
> Bloody hell.

> BACON
> Come on, let's get him in the van.

> LEE
> I better get in the back in case he shits again.

> JAMIE
> It's not gonna come out workin'.

> LEE
> I just wanna see. Here, I made him a nappy.

> BACON
> You fuckin' what?

> LEE
> In case he shits on the journey.

> CUT TO:

EXT. FAIRGROUND -- DAY

The fair is being set up.

At the Treasure Stand, Uncle Derek and Michael are setting up the prizes. Derek hands the kid two sets of hoops.

> UNCLE DEREK
> Yeah, you use these. No bigger or they'll be able to do it. I'll
> come round every 'alf hour and demonstrate with the others,
> with the little dot on. Are you listening boy?

Michael nods.

                    UNCLE DEREK (CONT'D)
    I don't want to be giving out no more of those prizes. Except
                    for them bloody goldfish...

He peers at the goldfish in their plastic bags. None of them are moving.

                    UNCLE DEREK (CONT'D)
                Here, you been feeding them?

Michael sees a swipe coming and legs it. Uncle Derek turns with arm raised.

                    UNCLE DEREK (CONT'D)
              You didn't bloody feed them did...

The three lads make their way towards the stall.

                    UNCLE DEREK (CONT'D)
                    ... Alright boys.

                         MOON
                  Alright Uncle Derek.

                    UNCLE DEREK
                What're you doing here?

Uncle Derek eyes them warily. Pushes a crate of Fontwell Champagne under the
frame of the stall with one foot.

                         MOON
        Thought you might be interested in buying a thoroughbred.

Bacon looks at the goldfish.

                        BACON
                    They dead?

                    UNCLE DEREK
    Having a kip aren't they. Horse, eh?   Always interested in horses.

EXT. FIELD WITH URBAN VIEWS

Dust-track blocked off by two Mercedes. Four pony-and-traps tear down track,
flanked by screaming Crusties and other dubious punters, all exchanging money
and betting slips. Sherbet tears ahead, clearly outclassing the other contenders.
The lads, Uncle Derek and Michael stand in the crowd.

                    UNCLE DEREK
            Bloody fuck! Would you look at him go?

                         58

As Sherbet flies past him, Derek whacks Michael round the head in glee. Michael rubs his head, clearly pissed off. Derek rubs his hands together.

                    UNCLE DEREK (CONT'D)
                    We'll take him, I reckon.

                                                            CUT TO:

INT. HENLEY ARMS -- DAY

Firebug and Happy Jack are playing pool. Happy Jack misses a sitter. Roy - sits watching, and wolfing a burger.

                    FIREBUG
          Eh, Roy? You reckon he's lettin' me win again?

Roy shakes his head.

                    ROY
        'E's doin' 'is best. You rattled 'im with yer safety shots.

                    FIREBUG
            Thought that might be it.

Firebug cleans up. Roy shifts enough food into one cheek that he can get a few words out:

                    ROY
              Got company.

Lee and Bacon approach. Firebug looks up briefly, then goes back to his game.

                    LEE
            We... um, got your money.

Happy Jack looks at his watch.

                    HAPPY JACK
              Tut... tut... tut.

Lee and Bacon look at each other.

                    LEE
          Yeah, er... sorry we're one minute late.

                    BACON
        We got you the 'undred per cent. It's all there.

Bacon puts the wad of notes on the table.

> HAPPY JACK
> What's that?

> BACON
> Eh?

> HAPPY JACK
> Doug said 24 hours. One minute late is one day late. Is one
> day's interest you owe your uncle.

Happy Jack looks at Firebug who nods in confirmation.

> HAPPY JACK (CONT'D)
> Which is another 'undred per cent, I believe.

> FIREBUG
> What I really want is that watch.

> LEE
> It's in the 'orse.

> FIREBUG
> One of you'll 'ave to climb up 'is arse. Come back tomorrow
> with the watch, on top of that...

He pushes the pile of cash back to Lee.

> FIREBUG (CONT'D)
> Or it's a fake tan for the lot of yer. Now fuck off.

> ROY
> Like your vids, by the way. Classy.

Takes another huge mouthful of burger.

INT. THE LOCK BACK ROOM -- NIGHT

The lads discuss the situation. TV on in the background. Lee hands out the beers.

> LEE
> Firebug ain't pissin' about. Now we gotta get that watch
> back. Or I'm emigratin'.

> JAMIE
> So we nick the 'orse back. Tomorrow.

                        BACON
              Off that bunch of psychos?

                        JAMIE
    What choice we got? And anyway we owe 'em a shaftin'.
                 After what they done at the races.

They look at Moon for his reaction.

                        MOON
                 They got it comin'.

Relief all round.

                        LEE
              Fuckin' right. Bastards.

                        BACON
    Yeah we nick that stupid 'orse back off 'em an' we get even.

                        JAMIE
       Then we give the watch to Firebug and flog the 'orse to some
              other geezer an' we're up on the whole deal.

                        LEE
                       Sweet.
                      (Toast)
                      Sherbet.

Everyone grins and drinks up. In the background, the TV is showing a picture of
Sherbet, cutting to Three Feet outside Miami's cinema.

                     THREE FEET
                      (On TV)
       Mr Vice is too gut... distressed to speak to anyone right now...

EXT. OUTSIDE MIAMI VICE'S CINEMA -- DAY

The press crowd around Three Feet. Three Feet speaks haltingly.

                     THREE FEET
       ... a terrible crime... has been done... stealin' a horse an' that.

                                                              CUT TO:

INT. HOTEL ROOM -- NIGHT

The Flying Dutchmen lie on their two single beds in their twin hotel room, watching TV, spliffed out. Three Feet's voice can be heard over this scene.

                    THREE FEET
                    (On TV)
    ... an' obviously we will be offering a reward for...

                    JOHANN
    These English. Still mad for horses... man. Living on an island,
                cut off from reality. I love them. Eh?...

                    JORDI
    I'm not talking to you until you give the watch back. Asshole.

                                                        CUT TO:

INT. HENLEY ARMS -- NIGHT

Firebug and his cohorts watch TV.

                    THREE FEET
                    (On TV)
    Course... that's 'alf a million qui... pounds worth of
    'orse, which we 'ave to consider. Not tha' money is the
                    priority, 'ere...

INT. MIAMI VICE'S OFFICE -- NIGHT

Miami Vice and Three Feet watch themselves on TV.

                    THREE FEET
                    (On TV)
    ... it's the... 'ealth of Sherbet that concerns us.

                    MIAMI VICE
    They know they're in shit now.

                                                        CUT TO:

INT. THE LOCK, BACK ROOM -- NIGHT

Lads watch the TV, open-mouthed with horror.

                    THREE FEET
                    (On TV)
    ... So if anybody can help us out, tell us where he is... we'll
    more than make it worth their while. Thank you very much
                    for your time.

                          BACON
                       We're in shit.

                                                    CUT TO:

INT. HOTEL ROOM -- MORNING

Jordi is talking to the bathroom door.

                          JORDI
        Come on, man. Face the fact. The watch has to go back.
                     They are our buddies.

                    JOHANN'S VOICE
             No way man, the watch is too cool.

                          JORDI
        Hey man, you're gonna have to come out of the toilet, you
              know why? Cos all the gear is out here.

Lights a spliff.

                    JOHANN'S VOICE
        Don't talk to me any more. I'm beginning to meditate.

Chanting comes from inside bathroom.

                          JORDI
             Wow... this spliff is good shit man.

Blows smoke through keyhole. Door flung open.

                         JOHANN
                         OK, OK...

Johann tries to take the spliff. Jordi pulls it away. Johann gives in and takes the
watch off.

                    JOHANN (CONT'D)
        OK, we giving the watch back. For the sake of karma. But I'm
              wanting the 50 per cent on the videos.

                          JORDI
                       Of course.

INT. THE LOCK -- DAY

                            63

Tanya is standing in for the lads. The bar is empty. Except for Firebug and Happy Jack who lean on the bar.

> FIREBUG
> Lee not here? I'm 'is Uncle.

> TANYA
> They've gone to Maidstone.

> FIREBUG
> 'Oliday is it?

> TANYA
> To see Moon's family, they run a fairground or something.

> FIREBUG
> About a horse was it, by any chance?

> TANYA
> (Shrugging)
> 'E's your nephew, 'e ain't even my mate.

The Dutchmen enter.

> FIREBUG
> Where've I seen you before?

> TANYA
> You might've seen me dancin'. At Lapland.

> FIREBUG
> That's right. Yeah, you're good.

> TANYA
> I mean, the other girls ain't got the poise or the stamina. I
> ain't being big-headed or nuffin'. But you can always tell a
> professional. It's the way they carry themselves.

> FIREBUG
> Oh yeah... Excellent.

During Tanya's speech Firebug clocks the Dutchmen with the watch. He leans forward to interrupt.

> FIREBUG (CONT'D)
> Wha's your name?

TANYA
Tanya.

FIREBUG
Listen Tanya. Why don't you take the rest of the day off?

TANYA
I don't think I can do that.

FIREBUG
Jus' do as I say, sweetheart.

Shoves a couple of twenties down her top.

TANYA
Hang on... you can't... treat me like this.

FIREBUG
Or I'll burn your fuckin' face off.

Tanya gets the message. She picks up her bag and gets out of the bar.

Meanwhile, Johann is taking a last lingering look at the watch. Firebug and Happy Jack appear next to Jordi.

FIREBUG (CONT'D)
You been stickin' your hand up horses' arses then?

JOHANN
Eh?

FIREBUG
Where d'you get that watch?

JOHANN
This is a so special watch, y'know. Only one of in all Hollant. I
am luffink, but we giffink to friend.

FIREBUG
Well you're 'giffink' it to me.

JORDI
You jokink wit' us, yeah?

HAPPY JACK
We don't joking with no-one.

65

JORDI
Well we neider, buddy!

They both turn round to face Firebug, breaking beer bottles over the bar and brandishing them.

JOHANN
You are sinkink we are stupid, uh?

JORDI
We are knowink za English rules.

Their faces fall. Firebug is holding a gun.

FIREBUG
(Checks with Jack)
Gun beats bottle, don't it?

HAPPY JACK
I believe so.

EXT. THE LOCK, THE YARD -- DAY

Dutchmen's clothes in a small heap, burning. Johann stands in his Japanese 'rising sun' briefs, shivering. Jordi shivers next to him in his metallic blue posing pouch.

FIREBUG
Oi Adolf, say goodbye to your mate, cos once this gets going –
you're in.

HAPPY JACK
Off with your panties boys...

Happy Jack grins back at him. Jordi and Johann look at each other in consternation. As they take their pants off and chuck them on the fire...

JORDI
We are not knowink zis watch is yours... lads in pub are sellink,
we say very expansive but OK we buy, zey are stealink from
you I sink, yes!

JOHANN
(Subtitled)
What are you saying? What about all that Karma and Yin and
Yang shit?

Jordi ignores him.

                              JORDI
                        (Starting to sob)
        Me ent Johann, we are bringink just za booze ent za feg from
                          za Hook of Hollant...

The fire is shrinking, and almost all their clothes have burned. Happy Jack looks
at Firebug but Firebug is patient. Jordi's upper lip tembles. Both Dutchmen are
holding their balls. All this next section is subtitled:

                             JOHANN
                   There's a drainpipe over there...

                              JORDI
                Look before he burns us I just wanna say...

                             JOHANN
                  We can climb up over the wall...

                              JORDI
        ... That is to say... I love you... Not in a gay way... it's more...

                             JOHANN
                     Can we just leg it, please?

They sprint across the yard. Happy Jack runs after them.

They leap onto the bin and shin up the drainpipe. Happy Jack starts to pull the
pipe away from the wall. Johann jumps onto the top of the wall and helps his
pal to join him, just as the brackets are torn out of the brickwork and the pipe
crashes into the yard, almost landing on Firebug, who is arriving with his blowtorch in one hand and gun in the other. When he looks up again, the Dutchies
have gone.

EXT. ROAD -- DAY

The two naked Dutchmen run down an empty road.

EXT. THE LOCK, THE YARD -- DAY

                             FIREBUG
              Shit. That was gonna be a good one an all.

                           HAPPY JACK
                    'Kin' nice watch though.

Looking at the watch, Firebug has to agree.

FIREBUG
Yeah. Course, this means I'll 'ave to torch me nephew – for
bein' a lying bastard.

HAPPY JACK
We gonna wait 'ere for 'em?

FIREBUG
Nah, let's get the 'orse first. We can make a fuckin' mint on
that bastard, and piss Miami Vice off while we're at it.

He stubs his cigarette out on his hand and sniffs it approvingly.

EXT. KENT COUNTRYSIDE -- DAY

Lads sit in the camper. In the distance the fairground is being set up.

INT. CAMPER VAN -- DAY

Moon is fiddling with copper wire and jump leads.

JAMIE
So I'm goin' on me own, then. Moon?

Moon holds up the electrical gear.

MOON
I've got work to do.

Jamie pulls on a baseball cap and shades.

LEE
So that your disguise, is it?

BACON
'E's only got to find out where the 'orse is and come back. It's
not the fuckin' KGB.

Jamie gets out of the camper and walks off down the road.

EXT. FAIRGROUND -- DAY

Jamie stands behind a bush peeking through at the fair.

ANARCHIST
Alright Jamie?

Jamie turns round to see ANARCHIST: 30's, crew-cut with red mohican, silly tattoos and piercings, combat gear.

ANARCHIST (CONT'D)
'Ow's you?

JAMIE
Er, alright. It's, er, Antichrist innit?

ANARCHIST
Anarchist. Ain't seen you for years. 'Eard you was knocking about wi' me cousin Laura again. Bet she'n a right fuckin' dirty bitch that' one, i'n 'er, eh? Cor! Wha's you doin' 'ere?

JAMIE
Er... came to see Laura.

ANARCHIST
Aah. C'mon then.

Anarchist beckons Jamie to follow.

EXT. FAIRGROUND -- DAY

Anarchist pushes Jamie forward towards a decrepit caravan about ready for the scrap metal yard. He knocks. Anarchist stands in the distance, leering like a goon, gives Jamie the thumbs up. Laura answers - dressed in her fairground gear: tassled suede jacket, bootlace tie, and boots.

LAURA
Jamie?

JAMIE
Hi Laura. I... just 'ad to see yer.

LAURA
Come in.

She steps back to let him through the door.

EXT. KENT COUNTRYSIDE -- DAY

Lee, Moon and Bacon sit in the camper, bored to fuck, listening to the radio.

MOON
How long does it take to find an 'orse, for Christ's sake?

                              LEE
                Reckon they've rumbled 'im?

                             MOON
                  'E can blag 'is way out.

                              LEE
                Told 'im that disguise was sh-

Lee is horrorstruck as Firebug's BMW drives by.

                         LEE (CONT'D)
                Shit... that's Firebug's motor.

They all duck under the dashboard.

                        BACON & MOON
                             Shit.

                            BACON
                  What's he doin' 'ere?

EXT. FAIRGROUND -- AFTERNOON

C.U. – FIREBUG'S BUSINESS CARD

Card reads: PHOENIX IMPORT AND EXPORT ENTERPRISES LTD.

Standing around are: Firebug, Derek, Happy Jack and Michael. Derek and Michael
are in the middle of fixing a car.

                           FIREBUG
          Kosher business, as you can see. What we're after is an 'orse...
                 for our Sport and Leisure wing.

                         UNCLE DEREK
                  You're after an horse, eh?

                           FIREBUG
          Yeah, racehorse. Black and white, bit... sticky. Know the kind
                      of 'orse I mean?

Firebug winks.

                       FIREBUG (CONT'D)
          We can offer you a thousand pounds in cash.

                        UNCLE DEREK
        One thousand? See we haven't got any horses like that
                          round here.

                          FIREBUG
        Alright, course, that's just the cash part of the deal. We also
        got twelve electric toasters, seven juicers... and sixteen non-
                          stick woks.

Firebug opens up the boot of his BMW and shows them the goods. Derek notices
Firebug's gun.

                        UNCLE DEREK
        Come to think of it... we have got a horse just like what you
              just said. Got the cash on you, have you?

Firebug pulls out a wad and plonks it on the box of woks.

                    UNCLE DEREK (CONT'D)
        Proper job. Michael, go and get that horse for these here
        gentlemen. And you know what, I'll chuck in the horse box
                          as well.

Happy Jack and Firebug watch Michael walk off behind a caravan.

Amber, the little girl, bounces up and down in front of Happy Jack.

                          AMBER
                    Lift me up, Mister!

He picks her up with one hand by the collar, her legs dangling.

EXT. KENT COUNTRYSIDE -- DAY

Bacon is pacing up and down while Moon and Lee smoke cigarettes.

                          MOON
                Will you calm down, please.

                          BACON
              Well, where the fuck is 'e?

Looking at his watch.

                          LEE
        'E'll be alright. Works best when 'e's up against it...

                                              CUT TO:

EXT. BUSH BY CANAL -- DAY

BUSH BY ROAD. SUBTITLES:

> JOHANN'S VOICE
> Do you think they are still waiting for us?

> JORDI'S VOICE
> Maybe.

CUT TO:

EXT. ROADSIDE, KENT -- DAY

Firebug taking a piss at lay-by. Hears a noise from the back of the trailer. All we hear is the traffic and then an 'aw' sound.

Firebug zips up and looks quizzically at the trailer. He marches up to the horse-box and flings back the shutter to look inside. Furious horror spreads across his face.

EXT. KENT COUNTRYSIDE -- DAY

Jamie returns to the lads. Hair ruffled, buttons done up wrong.

> JAMIE
> Alright. You want the good news or the bad news? The good news is that I 'ad the most amazing shag...

> BACON
> Tha's terrible news...

> JAMIE
> Bad news is, I don't know where the 'orse is, but...

The others give Jamie some abuse.

> JAMIE (CONT'D)
> ... it's a small fairground, you'll find 'im –

> MOON
> You were meant to find 'im!

> JAMIE
> Look, I've got it sussed
> (To Bacon and Lee)
> You two find the 'orse an' get in there with 'im. One of you better get on 'im.

                              BACON
                 You what? I don't believe this.

                              LEE
               I'll take care of 'im. 'E knows me.

Pause.

                             JAMIE
        Moon, you get on the electrics, swap round a few cables, make
                       it go mental – alright?

                             MOON
                    Piece of piss, mate.

                             JAMIE
        Then I come along in the van, back it up, you ride the 'orse in
                  and Robert's yer Mother's brother.

                                                        CUT TO:

EXT. FAIRGROUND -- DAY

Firebug, Happy Jack, Derek, Michael and about a dozen other little Crusty kids.

                            FIREBUG
                  That is taking the piss, mate.

                          UNCLE DEREK
                   You bought him. Fair's fair.

All of them are staring at the donkey.

                            FIREBUG
            Fair's fair?! What part of Uranus are you from?

Firebug and Happy Jack pull guns on Derek. Derek changes tactics.

                          UNCLE DEREK
          Jesus bloody Christ! Alright, alright. It's just my little lad
               here, tryin' to be a bit clever and rip you off.

Derek grabs Michael and belts him repeatedly over the head.

                       UNCLE DEREK (CONT'D)
           Come here, you little fuckin' bastard! Look what you done!
                  You take a good look at those blokes...

                              73

He holds Michael in front of Firebug.

> UNCLE DEREK (CONT'D)
> These are proper London gangsters! They ain't blokes you
> fucks about with! Say sorry!

> MICHAEL
> Bollocks!

Uncle Derek hands Michael to Geraldine who keeps him at a safe distance.

> UNCLE BRIAN
> Don't take no notice of him, he's a bit of a saucy one.

Happy Jack lifts his gun to within a few feet of Brian's nose.

> UNCLE BRIAN (CONT'D)
> Fuckin' ass holes! Wouldn't like to get on the wrong side of
> you. Bet you're a bit handy with that gun too, eh?

> FIREBUG
> Jack here's the best shot in London. Ex-para.

> UNCLE DEREK
> Do you 'ear that Michael?
> (To Firebug)
> Listen... We hates bad feelin' in business. So I tell you what.
> I'll take back Aesop, give you that other horse. And I'll give
> you the chance to win your money back in the Shootin'
> Gallery – against my little lad.

Happy Jack looks at Firebug.

> FIREBUG
> We'll just 'av the 'orse, thanks.

> UNCLE DEREK
> (Quietly)
> Come on, mate. You'd be doin' me a favour – teach that little
> runt a lesson, won't it?

Firebug laughs.

EXT. FAIRGROUND -- DAY

Goldfish are hooked onto strings. Happy Jack inspects his air rifle.

UNCLE DEREK
Happy with that?

Happy Jack nods. Firebug grins – he's onto a sure thing.

Michael looks deadly serious as he loads his air rifle.

UNCLE DEREK (CONT'D)
Best of ten wins.

Happy Jack and Michael both hit their targets, goldfish explode. Re-load. Again, they fire, more goldfish splatter the back wall. As they're shooting, Derek drops a dodgy pellet into Happy Jack's pile. More shooting, more disintegrated fish. Even so far, tension mounting. They re-load again.

Happy Jack loads in the dodgy pellet. The goldfish rotate. Michael blasts, shooting his fish. Happy Jack aims. Finger squeezes trigger. Gun explodes in Happy Jack's face. He collapses on the ground, his face is a mess.

UNCLE DEREK (CONT'D)
Bloody Nora. Doesn't look too clever, does he? He's not dead
is he, boy?

Michael prods the still body of Happy Jack. Shrugs. Derek picks up Happy Jack's smoking air rifle. Firebug steps forward, gobsmacked.

FIREBUG
You rigged it, you...

Firebug pulls out Biretta. Without batting an eyelid, Derek whacks Firebug in the face with butt of air rifle. Firebug drops like a lead balloon. Uncle Derek disarms the two men and picks up Happy Jack, dragging him away.

UNCLE DEREK
Charlie, Michael, bring the other bastard.

Charlie and Michael begin to drag Firebug's body.

MICHAEL
Ah Dad, I coulda won 'im fair.

UNCLE DEREK
You don't need to be winnin' nothin' when you can cheat.

ACT FOUR

EXT. FAIRGROUND -- NIGHT

Establishing shot of fairground.

EXT. HILL OVERLOOKING FAIRGROUND -- NIGHT

Michael and Charlie digging graves. Loose earth lands on Firebug and Happy Jack lying half-conscious in a heap. Derek watches kids work.

EXT. HILL OVERLOOKING FAIRGROUND -- NIGHT

> UNCLE DEREK
> Right that's deep enough... get him in there.

Uncle Derek strides off back down the hill.

Michael and Charlie try to shove Happy Jack into grave. He groans and resists. The other kid joins in with the pushing.

> MICHAEL
> They should have bloody killed him properly.

> CHARLIE
> Whack 'im round the 'ead again...

Michael picks up the shovel again. At that moment Firebug struggles to sit up. Charlie tries to hit him with the spade but Firebug catches it in mid-air, swings it round. As he climbs unsteadily to his feet, Crusty kids run down the hill swearing.

CUT TO:

EXT. FAIRGROUND -- NIGHT

Moon walks through fairground casing it out. He pulls a cable out of the generator.

CUT TO:

EXT. FAIRGROUND -- NIGHT

All the lights on the hoop-la and the shooting gallery go out.

CUT TO:

EXT. FAIRGROUND -- NIGHT

Moon continues to doctor the electrics.

CUT TO:

EXT. FAIRGROUND -- NIGHT

The big wheel: sparks fly out of the middle, or along the middle somewhere; all the lights go out and the wheel stops.

CUT TO:

EXT. FAIRGROUND -- NIGHT

The candy-floss machine goes bananas, spraying pink sugar in every direction.

CUT TO:

EXT. FAIRGROUND -- NIGHT

Sherbet has come to a halt. Jamie leads the horse into the back with a bag of crisps. Lee cannot be removed.

EXT. FAIRGROUND -- NIGHT

Tots shriek hysterically as they are jerked around roughly in their noddy cars.

CUT TO:

EXT. FAIRGROUND -- NIGHT

The lads load Sherbet into the back of the horse-box.

EXT. FAIRGROUND -- NIGHT

Fairground chaos. Punters leaving in droves. Uncle Derek storms through the crowd carrying a shotgun.

CUT TO:

EXT. MOTORWAY -- NIGHT

Firebug drives, face grimy and psychotic. Happy Jack semi-conscious next to him, covered in blood and soil.

EXT. THE LOCK, THE YARD -- DAY

The two Dutchmen peer over the wall. They look exhausted.

> JORDI
> It's been nearly 24 hours. They can't still be there.

INT. THE LOCK BACK ROOM -- DAY

Bacon, Jamie and Moon conspire in hushed tones. Lee enters the room. They all stop murmuring, and pretend – badly – that they weren't talking.

> LEE
> What? What's goin' on?

> MOON
> Nuffin'.

EXT. THE LOCK, THE YARD -- DAY

The two naked figures of Johann and Jordi climb back over the wall. They approach the camper and Jordi opens the door. They creep into the back of camper. They shut the door. Subtitled.

> JOHANN'S VOICE
> Hello horse... nice horse... Shit!

> JORDI'S VOICE
> What!

> JOHANN'S VOICE
> He's nibbling my balls...

EXT. FAIRGROUND -- DAY

Derek stands looking into his empty horse-box. Crowd of Crusties behind him.

> UNCLE DEREK
> We'll kill him this time.

Looks down at the business card Firebug gave him.

> UNCLE DEREK (CONT'D)
> Looks like we're goin' on a trip to London...

EXT. THE LOCK, THE YARD -- DAY

Lads appear and walk towards the camper.

LEE
What do you wanna hide 'im at Nefarius's for?

JAMIE
If the Crusties show up at the pub we don't want them to see
the horse.

LEE
Nothing with four legs should go within' an' 'undred yards of
that kebab shop... or Kouros'll 'ave it spinnin' round with a
lemon on top.

They climb into camper.

MOON
'E'll be safe at Nefarius's locked in the back of 'ere.

LEE
Yeah well no funny business, right. Sherbet ain't gettin'
chopped up.

JAMIE
Course not, Lee... Bloody 'ell.

They start the camper.

JOHANN'S VOICE
Shit...

INT. HENLEY ARMS -- DAY

Firebug paces up and down, ignoring the activity in the background: a bloke lifts
a wok out of a box and shakes the polystyrene off it. Others give it a cursory
inspection and negotiate a price.

FIREBUG
Fuck this, I'm getting a choc ice.

Roy digs into his pocket for a coin.

ROY
Can you get us a creme egg?

FIREBUG
Not if I 'ave to watch you eat it.
(To Happy Jack)
'Ungry?

Smiler's jaw is bound up tight.

EXT. STREET, OUTSIDE HENLEY ARMS -- DAY

Firebug walks away, just missing a convoy of Crusty vehicles pulling up. Derek jumps out with his rusty old shotgun. Others follow with stakes, bottles, half-bricks and a pair of shears.

UNCLE DEREK
Let's show these Cockney bastards how to dance a jig.

EXT. TROJAN KEBAB SHOP -- DAY

The camper van arrives outside Nefarius's string of businesses.

BACON
Lee, go in an' sort us out some kebabs. We'll park this round
the back.

Lee looks at them all suspiciously.

LEE
No funny business, right?

BACON
Don't be so fuckin' paranoid.

Lee gets out. Camper drives around the back.

EXT. STREET, OUTSIDE CORNER SHOP -- DAY

Firebug exits corner shop. Wraps his lips round his choc-ice and breaks off a chunk. Sets off down the street. A lump of ice cream drops onto his suede loafer. He looks down at his ruined shoe – seethes. He could not be more pissed off. From a doorway, a chirpy *Big Issue* seller in a Liverpool shirt pipes up.

BIG ISSUE SELLER
Big Issue, Sir?

Firebug walks towards him.

INT. ROYAL TUNBRIDGE SOCIAL CLUB -- DAY

Air thick with bullets. Derek stands in the middle of the pandemonium blasting his shotgun at everyone. Someone is firing back but he doesn't seem to notice.

The Crusty with the shears is trying to stab Roy, who defends himself by swinging the wok.

Brian pummels a stricken figure on the floor. Happy Jack grabs him round the neck and puts a gun against his head. Pulls the trigger.

CUT TO:

EXT. STREET -- DAY

All we see of the *Big Issue* seller is his stretched Liverpool shirt in Firebug's fist. Firebug's other hand is twisting a rolled-up copy of the *Big Issue* into what can only be the vendor's throat. His head turns as he hears the gunfire coming from the direction of the Henley Arms. He drops the unfortunate vendor and heads back.

EXT. HENLEY ARMS -- DAY

Firebug turning the corner, pulls out his Biretta, just as Roy staggers out clutching his bleeding crotch. Firebug catches him before he falls.

FIREBUG
Who's in there? Who's doin' this to me?

ROY
My... my...

FIREBUG
Miami Vice? The bastard...

Firebug opens the door with his other arm. The gunfire escalates inside.

FIREBUG (CONT'D)
Is 'e in there?

ROY
No... no...

Firebug lets go of Roy as police sirens spring up. Roy finally gets out what he wants to say:

ROY (CONT'D)
My... balls.

But Firebug is gone.

INT. MIAMI VICE'S OFFICE -- DAY

SMITH, a dull and balding man, goes through the figures. Miami Vice sits behind his desk, glaring at all the paraphernalia of accountancy. Three Feet hovers by the desk, bored. Henchmen impassive at the door.

> ### SMITH
> ... you're due to pay £21,301.53 in VAT charges for the period
> from November to April this year. The £32,000 of Inland
> Revenue payments for the video import business I can hold
> back. That's for your European activities... not your Far
> Eastern ventures...

INT. HENLEY ARMS -- DAY

Carnage and destruction. Dead and wounded litter the floor. Uncle Derek stands in the middle of the room looking around. Is anyone left? Someone is gurgling somewhere but there is no sign of movement.

Happy Jack emerges from behind the remains of the wok boxes, covered in polystyrene. He fires.

Derek is hit in the thigh. He tries to stay up but sinks to the floor.

Happy Jack walks towards him, with his gun raised, but his arm trembling uncontrollably. As well as his bandaged jaw, he is suffering from a shoulder wound and drags one foot behind him.

Derek is sitting on the floor. He raises his shotgun and gets the shambling figure in his sights. Pulls trigger, click. Needs loading. He snaps the weapon open. Pats his pockets, looking for cartridges. Not in that pocket. Or that one. Happy Jack is only a few yards away. Even his shivering arm can't fail him now. Derek is out of ammo. He lowers his weapon and looks up at Happy Jack, preparing for the worst. Happy Jack stops, takes aim as best he can and... slides to the floor in a faint. His eyes roll.

Stillness.

INT. MIAMI VICE'S OFFICE -- DAY

Smith is still going.

> ### SMITH
> ... These figures I haven't been able to tally... as yet... but you
> see the hospitality costs for Fontwell were to be set against
> your... leisure investment, for which you don't seem to have
> got the appropriate documentation and... since the horse
> wasn't insured, I don't think we'll be able to recover anything
> on the investment.

> ### MIAMI VICE
> Is that the best you can do?

Smith looks up.

MIAMI VICE (CONT'D)
I want better figures than that.

SMITH
Better... figures...?

MIAMI VICE
Get rid of all this crap. And come back when you've done me
some decent fuckin' numbers.

Smith looks round at all the assembled henchmen and then at Three Feet, who
tells him – with a jerk of his head – to clear up and clear off. Smith starts to
pack his stuff into his briefcase.

MIAMI VICE (CONT'D)
I'll get that 'orse back. Don't you worry. You know what
bugs me?

THREE FEET
The watch.

MIAMI VICE
The watch. My watch. Somebody's wearing it right now,
showin' it to people. Checkin' the fuckin' time on it...

Miami Vice trails off in mid-sentence as he spies something in Smith's briefcase:
tucked away between the laptop and a copy of *Accounting Law* is a video: *Muff
Godivas*. Miami Vice stands up and pulls it out. Smith's mouth falls open.

MIAMI VICE (CONT'D)
Where the fuck d'you get this?

SMITH
I-I've never seen it before. What is it?

MIAMI VICE
It's a film of ladies doing it with horses, now who did you
fuckin' buy it off?

SMITH
A... little Greek bloke.

INT. NEFARIUS'S WAREHOUSE -- DAY

Nefarius sits behind his massive desk. Moon, Jamie and Bacon stand in front
of him.

NEFARIUS
I can't make kebab outta 'alf a million poun' 'orse – issa crayzi.

JAMIE
We got no choice. We can't risk Miami findin' the 'orse cos
'e'll suss out it was us. Then we'll all be kebabs – know what
I mean?

Nefarius shudders at the thought. Presses an intercom button. Speaks at it.

NEFARIUS
Kouros. Step inta da back.

Pause. Nefarius sits back and glares at them resentfully.

NEFARIUS (CONT'D)
Wha' am I doin'? Dis is nuffin' to do wiv me...

JAMIE
You 'elped us paint 'im.

NEFARIUS
I di'n't know it was Miami Vice's 'orse!

BACON
Neither did we.

Kouros strides in, glistening with sweat.

KOUROS
Yes, boss.

NEFARIUS
Special delivery. Big 'orse. Set up the mincer.

KOUROS
'Orse? Grea'. Dey las' weeks.

BACON
The deal is you've got to gut 'im first.

KOUROS
Eh?

BACON
There's a very expensive watch in'm and if we don't get it back
we're fuckin' dead.

Kouros nods, disappears enthusiastically.

EXT. NEFARIUS'S WAREHOUSE, REAR -- DAY

The Dutchmen climb out the back of the camper, both covered in hay. Furtively look around. Jump into front of camper.

INT. NEFARIUS'S WAREHOUSE -- DAY

                    NEFARIUS
    After we done dis, I don' wan' you come roun' wiv enny
        business for a little while, alrigh'. Iss bad fa my 'eart.

Lee is standing in the doorway with four kebabs.

                    LEE
        After we done what? You're gonna do 'im...

                    MOON
    Don't be stupid. Nefarius's found an old 'orse's 'ome. In the
    country. They grow their 'air long, run round, 'ang out with
                    the other 'orses.

                    NEFARIUS
                (Startled, shifty)
                    Er, yeah.

                    LEE
    Bollocks. It's always the innocent pay the price, innit eh?

                    BACON
            Lee-ee... trust us.

Lee looks at them uncertainly. Kouros puts his head round the door.

                    KOUROS
        I set up da mincer. Where's dis 'orse?

Lee drops the kebabs on the floor. Looks at them all.

                    LEE
            You... fuckin'... bastards.

Lee turns and runs out of the door. The other three charge after him.

EXT. NEFARIUS'S WAREHOUSE REAR -- DAY

Lee looks around frantically for the camper. A heap of used bricks, some cardboard boxes and a mountain bike chained to a drainpipe - no camper. It's gone.

The other three tumble out of the door.

> JAMIE
> Shit.

> MOON
> Shit.

> BACON
> Shit.

> LEE
> Good.

Sound of gear-box grinding on the other side of the building. They run round, see the camper van pulling onto the road. They run after it as it moves off down the road.

INT. CAMPER -- DAY

Johann drives down the street, trying to get through traffic. Both still naked.

> JORDI
> Chill out...

INT. MIAMI VICE'S OFFICE -- DAY

Smith's body is carried out. Miami Vice sits behind desk looking pretty pissed off. Three Feet sits opposite him.

> MIAMI VICE
> Do you think I got carried away?

> THREE FEET
> Ah, I wouldn't worry abou' it Guv'. You 'ad t'let off steam
> sometime. Can't bottle it up, y'll get an ulcer.

> CUT TO:

EXT. CINEMA -- DAY

Firebug storms through the entrance of Miami Vice's cinema.

INT. CINEMA -- DAY

Firebug walks straight past the ticket desk towards the stairs. TICKET COLLECTOR pursues him.

> TICKET COLLECTOR
> Excuse me sir. Sir? You can't go up there. Excuse me.

Ticket Collector comes galloping back trying to put out his blazing tie.

INT. STAIRS -- DAY

Firebug is still incensed as he walks upstairs. He mutters to himself:

> FIREBUG
> OK Miami Vice, takin' the piss. I'll dice an' fry you sunshine.

CUT TO:

INT. MIAMI VICE'S OFFICE, WAITING ROOM -- DAY

Barbie's desk. Firebug emerges from the lift.

> BARBIE
> (On the phone)
> Mmm... I don't think I'll be able to fit you in...

> FIREBUG
> Where is that ugly little toe-rag?

> BARBIE
> (On the phone)
> ... what about next week?

> FIREBUG
> Where's Miami?

> BARBIE
> (Indignantly)
> Would you mind just holding on a minute please – I'm on the phone! ... I'm sorry about that, where were we?

INT. NEFARIUS'S WAREHOUSE -- DAY

Miami Vice is sitting in Nefarius's chair, behind his desk.

> MIAMI VICE
> So let me get this straight Nefarius... You're saying you got me vids from the lads down at the Lock...?

NEFARIUS'S VOICE
(Under some sort of strain)
Yesssss.

MIAMI VICE
You sure?

NEFARIUS'S VOICE
Yessss... I dun wan no trouuublllle.

Kouros stands in the background nervously.

INT. MIAMI VICE'S OFFICE -- DAY

Firebug walks out of shot to reveal Barbie. Her hair smoulders.

EXT. STREET -- DAY

A BMW thunders down suburban street with Firebug at the wheel.

INT. CAMPER -- DAY

Johann and Jordi look at an on-coming BMW. Recognition on faces. Jaws drop open as BMW heads straight towards them.

JOHANN
It is the madman.

JORDI
Shhhhit!

They manage to steer out of the BMW's way. Straight off the road.

EXT. STREET -- DAY

BMW looks like a write-off. Johann tries to start the camper van. Firebug opens door and points gun at Johann's balls.

FIREBUG
I need a lift. Unless you two wanna go back to Krautland as a
pair of sopranos.

Johann slams on accelerator.

ACT FIVE

INT. NEFARIUS'S WAREHOUSE -- DAY

The lads enter, running towards Nefarius's desk. Miami is still sitting in his chair – his back to them.

> BACON
> Hey Nefarius! We need a car... Nefarius? ... What's
> that banging...?

> NEFARIUS'S VOICE
> Myyyy heaaaaad...

Lads stop and stare at the swinging figure of Nefarius hanging upside down. Miami turns the chair to face the lads.

> MIAMI VICE
> 'Ello boys...

Lads slowly turn to face Miami Vice.

> MIAMI VICE (CONT'D)
> Three Feet, cut 'im down. I got myself a new angle.

EXT. NEFARIUS'S WAREHOUSE REAR -- DAY

Firebug holds a gun to Jordi's head, as Johann drives.

> FIREBUG
> They're all gonna die...

Camper pulls up outside back entrance to abattoir. Firebug cracks the Dutchmen's heads against the windscreen. They collapse unconscious. There is a neighing sound coming from the back. Firebug twigs.

INT. NEFARIUS'S WAREHOUSE -- DAY

> MIAMI VICE
> Nefarius 'ere tells me that he bought some vids of mine offa
> you lads.

Miami Vice pauses. Lads are not sure how to play this one. Nefarius creeps his way towards the abattoir.

> MIAMI VICE (CONT'D)
> Course, they don't call him 'that fuckin' lying bastard Nefarius'
> for nothing. But... I believe 'im.

> MOON
> We sold 'im some vids. Didn't know they was yours.

> MIAMI VICE
> Whoever nicked my vids, nicked my watch.

> JAMIE
> We bought 'em. Looked like a regular bitta knock-off, dinnit?

Nefarius is about to enter the abattoir when Miami spots him.

> MIAMI VICE
> Oi Nefarius... come 'ere.

Nothing.

> MIAMI VICE (CONT'D)
> Three Feet, bring 'im back.

Three Feet goes after Nefarius.

INT. ABATTOIR -- DAY

Nefarius waddles towards the back door, terrified. Fumbles with the handle.
Ker-Bam. Door is kicked open. Nefarius is sent flying across the floor, knocking
over a bucket of blood that goes all over him. He doesn't get up. Firebug stands
in the doorway, looking round.

INT. NEFARIUS'S WAREHOUSE -- DAY

Miami Vice decides to cut the crap. Moves closer, speaks fast.

> MIAMI VICE
> Who did ya get 'em off?

Other lads stare at Lee.

> LEE
> ... Firebug.

This stops Miami Vice in his tracks. He wasn't expecting this. Miami Vice still has
the gun pointed at the four lads.

> MIAMI VICE
> Firebug? Douglas Fairbrass? That jumped up little prick who
> runs a spill full of dodgy action men?! Him?!

> LEE
> 'E said 'e nicked 'em just to fuck some geezer off. Never
> thought it would be you.

> MIAMI VICE
> Well fuck me. I need to have a little think about this.

Silence as Miami Vice ponders.

INT. ABATTOIR -- DAY

Three Feet hurries through the abattoir with a sawn-off shotgun, but then hears a sound. A side of meat hanging from a chain is sliding towards him. Whump. Knocks him backwards through the entrance to the walk-in freezer.

Firebug strolls forward with his lighter and a glint in his eye.

> FIREBUG
> Warm ya up a bit.

Squirts the gas canister. There is a roar of flame, Three Feet screams, cut short by the freezer door slamming shut.

INT. NEFARIUS' WAREHOUSE -- DAY

> MIAMI VICE
> Three Feet?! Fuckin' 'ell...

Miami Vice turns to Kouros - there's no-one else.

> MIAMI VICE (CONT'D)
> Oi, Rambo. Go find out wha's 'appened will ya?

INT. ABATTOIR -- DAY

Kouros walks into the abattoir. Sees wisps of smoke coming from under the freezer door, pulls it open. Cloud of smoke.

> KOUROS
> Uh?

He looks around for some explanation. Something catches his attention: Nefarius on the other side, covered in blood. Kouros lets go of the door just as a scorched and blackened Three Feet staggers towards it and sees it slam shut in his face.

Kouros throws himself on Nefarius's blood-soaked body.

> KOUROS (CONT'D)
> Noo!... Boss!

He cradles the unconscious man in his arms and throws his head back in melodramatic agony.

> KOUROS (CONT'D)
> Oh... no... Do-o-o-o-n't die... ple-e-e-ease.

INT. NEFARIUS'S WAREHOUSE -- DAY

> MIAMI VICE
> Well, I've thought about it lads, and... I reckon you're full of
> shit. Firebug Doug wouldn't have the bollocks.

A gun appears behind Miami Vice's head. He hears tick-tick, tick-tick... Without taking the gun off the lads, Miami Vice turns his head 180 degrees so that his forehead is against the gun, and he is staring straight at the watch on Firebug's wrist.

> FIREBUG
> Miami Vice, I've got fuckin' massive bollocks. Let me show you
> how big my bollocks are.

                                                        CUT TO:

INT. ABATTOIR -- DAY

Miami Vice looks up at Sherbet suspended in a harness above the mincer. Kouros's sobs are audible but no-one takes any notice of him.

> MIAMI VICE
> You got bollocks alright. Trouble is your bollocks are between
> yer ears.

> FIREBUG
> Oo, is that the time?

Firebug looks at 'his' watch. Relishing the moment. Rubs it in with his lame gags:

> FIREBUG (CONT'D)
> No wonder I'm 'ungry. Think I'll start off with racehorse. Then
> I'll 'ave er... bit of the Miami Vice... and for dessert... these
> sweet little lads.

Looks round for Kouros.

> FIREBUG (CONT'D)
> Eh, meathead, get the mincer going.

Kouros looks up from the blood-stained body of Nefarius.

> KOUROS
> He's... dead.

> FIREBUG
> (Extremely casual)
> That's right. I think I killed 'im on the way in, now how d'yer
> switch this on? I wonder which button it is – the red or
> the green?

There is a wail of primal agony and Kouros comes charging across the room with a meat cleaver over his head.

> KOUROS
> Aaa-ooouurgh!

Everyone freezes. Cleaver swings down – chop.

C.U. – FIREBUG'S FACE

... as he realises...

Firebug's hand, holding the gun, wearing the watch, flies through the air. Miami catches them.

> MIAMI VICE
> Well, there's got to be a gag in here somewhere.

Firebug looks in disbelief before Miami Vice points the hand and gun at Firebug and empties the chamber into his body. The lads grimace.

> MIAMI VICE (CONT'D)
> (To lads)
> Get my 'orse down will yer?

Miami Vice removes the watch and places it lovingly on his own wrist. Relaxes.

Nefarius wakes up.

> MIAMI VICE (CONT'D)
> Jesus. Look at that – he was tryin' to defend us from Firebug,
> I expect. What, you just 'ad a spine transplant?

Kouros looks round.

> ### KOUROS
> You're ali-i-i-i-ve...

He throws his arms round Nefarius's ankles. Nefarius kicks his way out of the embrace.

> ### NEFARIUS
> Arghh, geddoff me... you homo.

Miami Vice turns to the lads.

> ### MIAMI VICE
> You lot born under the same lucky star were you?

Lads laugh nervously.

> ### MIAMI VICE (CONT'D)
> You know, I got a feeling that you boys know a little more
> than you're letting on... But I'm in a good mood... and I'm
> gunna let this one go...

Looking at his watch.

> ### LEE
> Ah thanks...

> ### MIAMI VICE
> ... This time... Now piss off before I change my mind.

Lads exit. Miami looks at his watch.

> ### MIAMI VICE (CONT'D)
> Where is Three Feet?

EXT. CAMPER -- DAY

The naked Dutchmen are on their way to freedom. Johann drives. Jordi leans out of the window and shouts at bemused passers-by.

> ### JORDI
> We goink back to ze Hook of Holland and neffer comink beck
> zis fuckink shitty country.

Jordi pulls his head back inside and grins at Johann.

CUT TO:

INT. ABATTOIR / CORRIDOR -- DAY

Look of relief on lads' faces.

> JAMIE
> Ah, that was a close one?

Bacon pulls out the wad of money they tried to pay Firebug back with.

> BACON
> Not a bad result though eh?

> MIAMI VICE'S VOICE
> Oi!

Miami appears again behind them. He's just remembered.

> MIAMI VICE
> You still owe me for those vids.

Miami's eyes light up when they land on what Bacon is holding. They all look at the wad of cash in Bacon's hand. They can kiss goodbye to that.

> END

EPISODE 2

LOCK, STOCK... & TWO HUNDRED SMOKING KALASHNIKOVS

by Bernard Dempsey and Kevin McNally

ACT ONE

INT. TROJAN KEBAB SHOP -- DAY

A lazy day at the shop. Two men are sitting with mezzes and a plate of water melons playing backgammon. Kouros, who is wearing his bandanna, is stripping away slices from the donner kebab stack which is rotating by the window and filling the storage trays with donor meat. Kouros wears his bandanna with pride. A young black man is at the counter. He is dressed sharp. He holds up two fingers for two skewers of kebab. Kouros takes two spits from the cabinet and puts them on the grill. He tosses a pitta bread onto the grill beside them. The man turns from the counter and saunters over to the backgammon game. He takes out a toothpick and begins to poke at his teeth watching the game. The two men glance up at him. Behind him the door opens and a young man in motor-cycle jacket and dark visored motor-cycle helmet comes into the shop, carrying a large pizza tray. Kouros looks back from the donner stack.

> KOUROS
> Dis is kebab 'ouse. No pizza 'ere ... You get ouda 'ere.

The pizza boy opens the lid of the pizza box, takes out a gun. He fires it in the direction of the young black man. In the shock that follows the pizza boy is out of the door and aboard his moped/bike. Kouros snatches up a lethal-looking knife and vaults the counter, tears open the door and is after the boy.

CUT TO:

EXT. TROJAN KEBAB SHOP -- DAY

Kouros emerges from the shop only to see the pizza boy disappearing round a corner at speed. He turns and hurries back into the shop.

CUT TO:

INT. TROJAN KEBAB SHOP -- DAY

Kouros comes back into the shop. He sees the two backgammon players staring down at the stricken man. There is a pool of blood staining his shirt and the surrounding floor tiles. Kouros shouts to the backgammon players.

> KOUROS
> Get a whassname... ambulance!

He kneels to the victim. Nefarius appears from the back of the shop.

> NEFARIUS
> This is the start innit!

CUT TO:

OPENING TITLES.

CUT TO:

EXT. LONDON STREET -- EVENING

Sound of gun shot. We see a biker accelerate away. A crowd gathers round the wounded man as his friend tries to staunch the flow of blood from his wrist. A woman runs up the street for an ambulance.

CUT TO:

EXT. LAPLAND -- EVENING

The brightly lit Lapland frontage. Beneath the neon sign a queue of punters file into the interior as the music throbs inside.

CUT TO:

INT. LAPLAND. BAR -- NIGHT

A busy Saturday night crowd. Lee, Jamie, Bacon and Moon are sitting at a table which has several empty bottles of champagne littered across it. They are all heavily focused on an attractive woman near by.

> MOON (V.O.)
> It was the usual Saturday night. Good turnout of skirt, sweep-
> stake up and runnin', Jamie on one. No reason to think it was
> about to go tits up.

> LEE
> I'll have fifty on Jamie.

He chucks a fifty note over to Moon, then punches Jamie encouragingly on the arm.

> LEE (CONT'D)
> Go on, my son...

Jamie gets to his feet and arranges his tie. The lads watch as he walks, a little unsteadily, towards the bar.

From the lads' P.O.V. we see Jamie approaching a pretty young girl sitting alone at the bar. Jamie shakes his hands from side to side in the hackneyed gesture for 'do you want to dance?'

BACON
'E's fading fast...

LEE
Bollocks. 'E's on the 'ome straight.

They see the girl lean over and whisper in Jamie's ear.

LEE (CONT'D)
Get in Jamie. By a length.

But Jamie only bows politely to the girl and weaves his way back to the lads.

LEE (CONT'D)
Shit.

Jamie sits and drains a glass of champagne.

MOON
Well?

JAMIE
Two words, three effs. She's got to be a Velcro?

LEE
All bets're off if she likes fuzz on fuzz...

MOON
Stand back you amateurs. The favourite is at the gate and offering evens...

He stands straightening his jacket. Lee snorts and takes out his wallet and throws money on the table. Bacon and Jamie follow suit. Moon squares himself up and saunters over to the bar.

MOON (V.O.) (CONT'D)
Course the bird in question was a ringer. I fished 'er out the local corner shop, gave her the spiel, a cut and a bottle of bubbly. Must say, she did scrub up well.

Moon has reached the bar. He orders a drink, taking his time. He looks at the girl who smiles shyly. He shoots a look back to the lads at the table.

MOON (V.O.) (CONT'D)
Three hundred notes for a dance. My check-out girl was gunner do me proud. These boys were easy meat when they'd had a few...

He slides his drink onto the bar then moseys over to the girl.

MOON (V.O.) (CONT'D)
When all of a sudden... there's a whiff of Paco Rabanne... and...
Dis - aster ... The shoes were Kenzo... The suit was Armani...The
shirt was Turnbull and Asser.

A young man in a designer jacket cuts in front of Moon and pushes a drink over
in front of the girl. The girl smiles at the interloper.

The man leans into the girl's ear and whispers. She glides from her seat and they
move onto the dance floor. Moon stands dumbstruck. He looks back towards the
lads who are grinning and waving the winnings at him.

MOON (V.O.) (CONT'D)
The penny dropped. The favourite had been nobbled. Robbie
Rossie. A donkey turned thoroughbred. Back in school he
used to pay girls cola cubes for a ten-second tongue job. Now
look at him ... got dragged off to Scunthorpe with his old
man's firm ... comes back from Kuala Lumpur five years later.
Loaded. Now Leytonstone's own Casanova.

JUMP CUT TO:

Robbie is now sitting at the table with Lee, Jamie, Moon and Bacon. They are
sharing out the winnings as they laugh at Lee.

MOON (V.O.) (CONT'D)
In short - a right flash bastard.

Back at the table, Robbie has been joined by his oppo, Kerry Dowd.

MOON (V.O.) (CONT'D)
The little bloke, the Greaseball? Kerry O'Dowd. Robbie always
liked a posse ...

Kerry helps himself to champagne.

MOON (V.O.) (CONT'D)
As an arse-licker Kerry could've licked for England.

Robbie pours himself a glass of Champagne and smiles at Moon, eyebrows raised.

ROBBIE
OK you saddoes it's London, it's Saturday night, we're
all wedged 'up. We gonna sit around these prick-teasers
all night?

                         JAMIE
                 What do you have in mind?

                        ROBBIE
                 Your gaff. Vodka Derby...

He points his finger straight at Bacon's forehead.

                     ROBBIE (CONT'D)
                 ...him versus the sheepshaggers.

Moon and Jamie break into huge grins.

                                                    CUT TO:

EXT. THE STREET -- NIGHT

The rider roars off up the street as a dark-haired shopkeeper runs after him.

                          LEE
                 Not a satisfied customer...

                         JAMIE
                 Best get off before the flies arrive...

                         MOON
                       Too right.

They hurry off along the street. The pizza bike spins round at the end of the road
behind them, trying to shake off the dark-haired man and shoots back past the
lads, nearly taking out Kerry.

                         KERRY
                 What the fuck is going on?

                                                    CUT TO:

INT. MIAMI'S OFFICE -- NIGHT

Sirens in the street below. Miami is at the window craning to see what is going
on in the area. He is munching on a bacon and egg roll.

                         MIAMI
                 What the fuck is going on? It's like Beirut out there.

Three Feet is standing beside him, looking concerned. Miami turns to Three
Feet suddenly.

MIAMI (CONT'D)
Who's my Community Liaison Officer just now?

THREE FEET
Trevor Truscott.

MIAMI
Well get the tosser 'ere.

INT. MIAMI'S OFFICE -- NIGHT

Trevor Trusscott, Miami's Community Liaison Officer, face sweating as he faces Miami.

TREVOR
I haven't got a clue, Miami...

MIAMI
That is not good enough Trevor. You are paid to know what is goin' on. You're fuck-all use for anythin' else.

TREVOR
I've got all my feelers out.

MIAMI
Feelers? You're not a ant. There is a war on my manor. Why?

TREVOR
Word is that it's something to do with Eddie the Diamond.

MIAMI
The what?

THREE FEET
The Diamond. The spade who runs the clubs down Walworth...

MIAMI
Diamonds, clubs, spades? Have we drifted into an 'and of poker, here?

Trevor and Three Feet exchange uncomfortable looks. Miami catches the look and is instantly suspicious.

TREVOR
It, er, ain't his real name.

MIAMI
You amaze me. So what's 'is kosher 'andle?

103

TREVOR
It's Eddy Bunden.

Miami sinks to his chair as if Trevor had stuck a dagger in his heart.

MIAMI
Eddy Bunden?! Eddy Bunden 'as opened a club on my manor?!

TREVOR
It's a tuppenny 'a'penny gaff, Miami, full of twelve-year-olds
smokin' waccy baccy... don't even pull in pocket money...

MIAMI
EXCUSE ME, TREVOR... Are you trying to tell me that cockroach
has opened a maggot-'ole on my patch and you have done
fuck-all about it! I now have pizza delivery boys driving up
and down my high street making colanders out of each other.
Get round to that fucker's gaff tonight and tell him that as of
tomorrow he is out of the club business.

THREE FEET
We're not goin' to look too clever leanin' on a bunch of
juveniles, boss.

MIAMI
I don't care if they're fuckin' foetuses. Get round there and
slap a few arses.

He rounds on Three Feet.

MIAMI (CONT'D)
Eddy fuckin' Diamond. I am going to have to have a serious
word with you, son...

CUT TO:

INT. THE LOCK -- NIGHT

Bacon is seated facing a large moustached New Zealander across a table upon
which are lined up two rows of vodka shot glasses alternating with pints of
Guinness and the occasional 'fence' of a tumbler of spirits.. Robbie, Lee, Moon
and Jamie stand behind Bacon. Behind the New Zealander a bunch of Kiwis are
giving a drunken rendition of the Hakka, which reaches its ragged climax. Robbie
watches it unimpressed.

MOON (V.O.)
Vodka Derby's was Robbie's favourite.

> ROBBIE
> Yeah, lads, lovely...Right, are you ready?

> MOON (V.O.)
> Robbie was a champion in his youth, but you know what they
> say - if you wanna box really smart, send some other geezer
> into the ring.

The crowd press in. Last minute side bets are laid. Lee and Moon are running the book handing out markers.

> ROBBIE
> No spittin', no spillin', no barfin'...

He faces Bacon and the Kiwi.

> ROBBIE (CONT'D)
> Three, two, one... Go!

> MOON (V.O.)
> Now Bacon is a sponge. An' if the dosh is right, he'll soak it
> up by the barrel...

The Kiwi chugs back a shot of vodka to the cheers of his support then begins to suck on a Guinness. Bacon takes it slowly, eyeballing the Kiwi.

The Vodka Derby gets under way with the Kiwi drawing ahead. Lee finds Robbie by his side drawing him off to one side by the elbow. Moon, cheering on Bacon, clocks as Robbie begins whispering into Lee's ear. He then clocks Kerry who gives him a knowing grin. Robbie's doing business again. Lee and Robbie sit foreground. Robbie is leaning forward speaking in a low voice as the Vodka Derby proceeds behind them. Kerry hovers behind Robbie and Lee, earwigging their conversation.

> ROBBIE
> I'm not talking a suitcase here, Lee. I'm talking quality
> shmutter.

> LEE
> What you got? Girl Power t-shirts an' leather flying jackets?

> ROBBIE
> It's not Petticoat Lane shit, Lee, it's top of the food-chain gear.
> Here...

He extends his coat sleeve out in front of Lee. Lee looks at it.

ROBBIE (CONT'D)
'Undred per cent silk. Double-stitched, designer...

He opens the breast of the jacket to display the maker's name.

ROBBIE (CONT'D)
There's probably only a rail full these in the entire universe.

LEE
Original?

Robbie nods firmly.

ROBBIE
As good as.

Lee's eyes narrow. Robbie smiles and slips off the jacket and hands it to Lee. Lee is impressed despite himself as he examines the jacket.

LEE
You tryin' to tell me this is Mickey Mouse?

ROBBIE
We got a Chinaman out there who can imitate any cut, any material. We give him a pot of tea, an' a bowl of speed, an' he turns it out the next day.

LEE
OK. I'm mildly impressed.

ROBBIE
Yer fuckin' interested. In a few days I'll 'ave a truck-load of this stuff.

Jamie comes lurching over to their table.

ROBBIE (CONT'D)
Jamie boy, 'ow's it 'angin'?

JAMIE
The Kiwi's a fuckin' fish.

Robbie shakes his head and winks.

ROBBIE
Final fence...

Back at the Vodka Derby. The Kiwi has half pint of vodka and one pint of Guinness to go to Bacon's three and two vodkas. His supporters scent victory. Bacon stares at the Kiwi with a grimace on his face. The Kiwi gets to his feet and reaches over for his final half pint of vodka, smirking in victory. As he drains the drink in one he is suddenly stopped in his tracks. He stands blinking, immobile.

Pull focus to Lee, Jamie and Robbie who are looking on.

> ROBBIE (CONT'D)
> Say goodnight, matey...

Like a felled tree the Kiwi pitches forward and then falls to the floor.

> JAMIE
> The final fence?

Robbie takes out a bottle of Turpentine from his pocket.

> ROBBIE
> Splash of paint thinner ... makes all the difference.

Jamie runs over to Bacon who stands like a cross-eyed boxer and raises Bacon's hand in triumph. The action makes Bacon stagger back. There is some pushing and shoving.

> LEE
> So what do you want from us?

> ROBBIE
> There's a certain amount of, er, interest in gear of this quality
> from the Church boys...

> LEE
> Church boys?

> ROBBIE
> C of E.

Lee still looks puzzled. Robbie rolls his eyes.

> ROBBIE (CONT'D)
> Anyone speak English? Customs and Excise. Kuala Lumpur
> Customs is reasonable men, with a reasonable price. Back 'ere
> they think it's a religion. You gotter be a bit clever.

By now all hell has begun to break loose as the Kiwis suspect their man has been got to. An argument is breaking out with Moon and Jamie in the thick of it,

Kerry keeping out of it. Lee and Robbie look on unconcerned as they negotiate their deal.

> LEE
> Alright, cut to the chase.

> ROBBIE
> What I need from you is a truck, a driver and somewhere to
> lodge the gear 'til I line-up me buyer.

> LEE
> Do-able.

Kerry grins slyly.

> ROBBIE
> Plus twenty up front to pay off the captain of the boat.

> LEE
> Twenty large?

> ROBBIE
> All refundable with interest.

> LEE
> How much interest?

> ROBBIE
> 'Undred and fifty per cent.

> LEE
> You got yourself a deal then ain't yer?

Robbie takes his hand. A body lands heavily on the table before them. Lee and Robbie get to their feet and begin swinging punches.

INT. THE LOCK. KITCHEN -- MORNING

Breakfast. Moon is at the range frying up breakfasts. Jamie is flitting around the kitchen assembling vegetables and fruit for his daily vitamins drink, nursing a raw steak over one eye. Throughout the scene Bacon is ferrying crates of bottled beers from the yard into the bar with a bandage round his head. Lee is sitting at the table with a notebook of figures. He is trying to talk business despite the hectic atmosphere of the kitchen.

> LEE
> It's a bit of an outlay given our present cash flow...

Moon bandage on nose, dumps a plate in front of Jamie who looks at
it suspiciously.

                    JAMIE
              What's this?

                    LEE
        ...but the profit margin more than compensates for
                    the cough...

Bacon comes through with a couple of crates. Moon points with his fish slice at
Jamie's breakfast.

                    MOON
        That is a bagel, that is smoked salmon...

                    LEE
        ...injecting much needed funds into our accounts. Now...

                    MOON
        And that is an egg. They come from 'ens.

                    JAMIE
        And what's this yella shit on top of it?

                    MOON
        That is 'ollandaise sauce you peasant...

                    LEE
        Will you two put a dummy in? I'm trying to explain
                    business 'ere.

Bacon crosses with empty crates heading for the yard.

                    BACON
              You tell 'em, Lee.

                    LEE
        We are about to expend a considerable outlay of foldin'.
              I'd appreciate a bit of attention.

                    JAMIE
        We're buying some threads from Robbie. Where's the drama?

                    LEE
        It's that simple is it? First, we gotta find somewhere to house
                    the gear...

Moon calls over his shoulder from the range.

                         MOON
        We can stick 'em in my Mum's back room.

Lee nods, the wind taken from his sails a touch. Moon lays a plate of breakfast
before Lee.

                          LEE
           Second, we need to rent a truck...

                         JAMIE
      Kerry the Greaseball said he could do us a cheap rental.

                          LEE
    ...And we got to find a driver who can 'andle a two-tonner...

Bacon is crossing carrying two more beer crates.

                         BACON
              I've driven two-tees.

                          LEE
    When in flyin' fuckland 'ave you driven two-tonners?

                         BACON
      When I left school I had a job delivering 'taters.

He goes through into the bar. Moon is back at the range, Jamie is loading his
juicer. Lee looks at his plate tetchily.

                          LEE
        Right. OK. I raise the capital... What's this yella shit?

EXT. STREETS -- DAY

                       MOON (V.O.)
        Now this world is divided into two sorts of people, on the
        one hand those you would happily touch for a bob or two,
        on the other hand there are those suffering from advanced
                      psychotic tendencies.

Barry Blue emerges from a doorway (Betting Shop?) followed by Lee. Barry
is counting out fifty pound notes into Lee's hand with excessive if not
compulsive concentration.

                          LEE
      You're a life-saver, Barry, we'll pay you back by the end of the week.

BARRY BLUE
And I'm going to make a profit?

LEE
Yeah...by the end of the week.

Barry catches him by the elbow.

BARRY BLUE
So, you'll pay me back? 'Cos I need that money...I've got
big plans.

LEE
Er...that's great, Barry.

He tries to leave but Barry holds his arm, tightening his grip.

LEE (CONT'D)
Barry, that's beginning to hurt a bit...

BARRY BLUE
You won't let me down. Not like the others.

LEE
Er, who's been lettin' you down Barry?

Barry gives him an intense look.

BARRY BLUE
The pigeons.

He gives him a knowing look then releases Lee's arm.

INT. THE U4EA CLUB. CAMBERWELL -- DAY

Three Feet and Trevor appear at the entrance to the bar, accompanied by a couple
of handy looking goons. They all wear long coats except for Trevor who looks
slightly out of place. Three Feet catches the barman's eye and waves him to
come over. The barman carries on cleaning glasses. Three Feet looks to Trevor
who casts his eyes to heaven, disapproving of the whole expedition. Three Feet
gestures once again, more demonstratively. The barman sees him but chooses to
ignore him. Three Feet suddenly slaps his palm on the bar, causing a momentary
silence in the bar. The barman resignedly saunters over to Three Feet.

BARMAN
Ja man.

111

> THREE FEET
> I'm 'ere to see Eddy the Diamond.

> BARMAN
> Ja wanna drink?

> THREE FEET
> I wanna see Eddy the Diamond...

> BARMAN
> T'ain't 'ere.

The barman wanders back up the bar and continues cleaning glasses. Three Feet angrily sweeps some glasses off the bar crashing them noisily to the floor. The bar falls silent. The barman saunters back to Three Feet.

> BARMAN (CONT'D)
> Tut. T'ain't no need for dat bone, man.

> THREE FEET
> I wanna see Eddie the Diamond...

> BARMAN
> You's treadin' on fire fool.

Three Feet whips out a sawn-off shotgun from his coat. He bellows at the bar.

> THREE FEET
> I ain't fuckin' askin' you!

Almost simultaneously the two goons behind him also whip out pump action shotguns and legs apart take a cowboy stance. It is a tense moment... Even the barman has produced a large long-barrelled pistol which is trained on Three Feet's temple. As Three Feet raises his eyes he sees more guns trained on them from upstairs galleries.

It is a forest of firearms. Trevor licks his lips nervously. Eddy comes out of his office and leans over the banisters and smiles a brilliant white smile. He speaks a ludicrous patois.

> EDDY
> Me say you boys truly in de lion mout', uh? De Gospel eye an
> eye preach tain't good for sinners. De 'erb is de root t'Zion an'
> you' tain't got de flow in ya veins. Ja want amends, ja say low
> down de peace pipes, Bloodclot.

The crowd cock their weapons.

TREVOR
Nice one, Three Feet...

INT. MIAMI'S OFFICE -- DAY

Miami sits behind his desk smoking a large cigar. Robbie is in full flow.

ROBBIE
I'm not talking a suitcase here, Mr Vice. I'm talking quality shmutter. 'Undred per cent silk. Double-stitched, designer...

He opens the breast of the jacket to display the maker's name.

ROBBIE (CONT'D)
There's probably only a clothes-rail of these in the entire universe.

MIAMI
Cut the crap, son, what's the price?

ROBBIE
Hundred grand. The lot.

MIAMI
Listen, son. There are one or two ground rules we've got to establish here. Nobody but nobody operates on my patch. But you've got bollocks, son. And I like to give a young lad a chance so let's call it charity shall we? I'll pay you fifty. Now sling your hook. And meet me back here when you've done the drop.

CUT TO:

EXT. THE LOCK -- DAY

Lee emerges from the Lock with Kerry.

KERRY
If you have to ditch it, it was reported knicked last Thursday. Keep the keys, they're bloody murder to replace. Oh and if you have the time, rip the radio out. Always a nice touch.

Lee wanders over to the lads. A two-ton truck is parked on the fore-court with its hood up, Bacon fiddling with the engine. Moon is leaning against the wheel arch leafing through a London A-Z. Jamie's boots are visible hanging out of the truck's passenger window as he naps.

113

                              LEE
                          Any problems?

                             BACON
            Just trying to override the guvnor. Give us a bit of poke.

Lee grabs his arm.

                              LEE
             For fuck's sake, we don't want a pull for speedin'.

                             BACON
                It's a joke. I'm checkin' the oil, dipstick.

He holds the dipstick up to Lee, smiling.

                             MOON
                     Come on lads, I'm driving.

                             BACON
                           Fuck off.

                             MOON
                          Watch me.

Moon smiles and jangles keys.

                              LEE
                Let's get goin' - we got a meet with Robbie.

                                                        CUT TO:

INT. U4EA CLUB -- DAY

Three Feet and Trevor talk to Eddy the Diamond.

                             EDDY
            Ting is ja breakin' me bone wit' holler verb. Dis is ma
                 playgroun' an eye an' eye 'as de t'rone.

                          THREE FEET
                    The fuck you talkin' about?

                             EDDY
         Ja ain't got no sting in de tail 'ere nigger. Mi blood start
                            to boil ...

                              114

                    THREE FEET
    Trevor. You got any idea what 'e's tryin' to say?

Trevor very slowly shakes his head.

                       EDDY
    Raas man you's a blind dog pissing up de wrong tree.

                    THREE FEET
    Look, do you even know why I'm 'ere Diamond?

                       EDDY
    All eye an' eye knows is wha' jah knows an' he say you's in de
                    shit now ... blood.

                                              CUT TO:

INT. MIAMI'S OFFICE -- DAY

Three Feet and Trevor are sitting on a couch. Three Feet has a large fabric
bandage stretched over a plainly fractured nose and a black eye. Trevor has
his arm in a sling. Miami is in a carpet-chewing rage, pacing up and down
the office.

                       MIAMI
            And they knew you was from me?

                    THREE FEET
    I think so guv. I did say it. 'I am 'ere in the name of
                    Miami Vice.'

                    THREE FEET
    Then the fuckers set about us with baseball bats.

                       MIAMI
    Right, then - they've had it. I cannot be doing with this. That
    fucking club is history, finito, kaput, fucked. I don't care how
            you do it - dynamite the gaff if you have to.

He calms down enough to see Three Feet tentatively nursing his jaw.

                  MIAMI (CONT'D)
            You had that looked at?

                    THREE FEET
            I'm OK, boss...

MIAMI
Don't argue. Get it looked at.

Three Feet nods and goes out of the office. Miami, still in a pet, lights a calming cigar. Trevor sees he may be calm enough now to listen to reason.

TREVOR
You know who's really responsible?

MIAMI
Surprise me.

TREVOR
The Russians.

Miami tries to get his head round this one.

MIAMI
I may be being obtuse, Trevor but I thought the Cold War
was over.

TREVOR
I'm talking about the émigrés. Russki Mafias.

MIAMI
What is this 'reds under the beds' bollocks?

TREVOR
It's the Muscovite Black Market. They're floodin' the streets with shooters.
Ever since that wall came down anyone with a fiver can pick up all their army
surplus shit.

MIAMI
And why would the ex-commies be snuggling up with the pill-
popping funny haircuts?

TREVOR
They'll sell to anyone.

Miami digests this information.

MIAMI
Anyone? Trevor, get me a Russian.

CUT TO:

EXT. THE LOCK -- DAY

Robbie's car pulls up outside the pub where the lads are waiting for him. Lee holds out a large envelope which Robbie takes. Bacon wearing hat.

                              LEE
                       Twenty thousand.

                             ROBBIE
            You lucky bastards are getting money for jam. All right, let's
                       earn some fuckin' money 'ere.

Robbie gets map out and unfolds it.

                        ROBBIE (CONT'D)
            You pull up at pier 17. You give the captain his whack
            and load the gear. Now I've got a buyer, so you deliver to
                              this address.

Lee takes the piece of paper offered by Robbie.

                        ROBBIE (CONT'D)
            Meet me back here in two hours and I'll have the divvies.

                             BACON
                             Sweet.

Moon, Bacon and Jamie head off for the truck. Robbie starts to leave.

                              LEE
                       Who is the buyer?

                             ROBBIE
                 Bit of a nutter but I got a good price.

INT. TROJAN KEBAB HOUSE. NEFARIUS' OFFICE -- DAY

Hard cut to close up of Miami. He and Three Feet sit opposite Nefarius. Three Feet has a bag on his lap. Nefarius is dressed in a topcoat and scarf with a hat on his head suffering from a heavy cold. He is pouring shot after shot of Metaxas as he speaks.

                             MIAMI
            Nefarius, you're confusin' me with someone who gives a fuck.
                 Today is Wednesday and Wednesday is your flag day.
                          Now cough up.

                            NEFARIUS
            All I'm askin' is a couple of extra days... Dere's dese guys.
            Bleedin' Turks. Dey openin' frickin' mezze shops all over the

          knobbin' place. Four on the High Road this month.
                 Now dey're leanin' on me.

                  MIAMI
You wouldn't believe 'ow pissed off this kind of bollocksin'
                 makes me...

               NEFARIUS
I gotta see the manager down the bank a'n' I?

                  MIAMI
The time and the amount is not, was not and never will
               be negotiable.

               NEFARIUS
               Two days...

                  MIAMI
               Three Feet...

               NEFARIUS
             No, pliss, Miami...

Three Feet reaches into his bag and pulls out a large pair of pliers and a mouth
clamp from his bag.

            NEFARIUS (CONT'D)
          Miami, pliss, I BEG YOU!

                                    CUT TO:

INT. TROJAN KEBAB HOUSE -- DAY

Kouros, wearing his bandanna, and a waiter are outside Nefarius' office listening
intently. Suddenly from within the office comes the noise of pitiful screaming.
Kouros and the waiter exchange concerned looks. The screaming stops. Kouros
and the waiter spring back from the door as Miami and Three Feet emerge from
the office and walk by them without a word. Kouros looks at the waiter. He
opens the door slowly.

                                    CUT TO:

INT. TROJAN KEBAB HOUSE. NEFARIUS' OFFICE -- DAY

Reverse. Kouros' head appears round the door. Nefarius is distraught, but he looks
unscathed. He looks up to see Kouros. As he smiles sarcastically at Kouros he
reveals a large bloody gap in his front teeth.

NEFARIUS
Frickin' knock before you come in 'ere innit?
Not enough I'm bin put out of frickin' bushinesh by the
frickin' Turksh now my office ish a frickin' washname...
open houshe.

Kouros signals apology and withdraws.

NEFARIUS (CONT'D)
Bashtadsh.

CUT TO:

EXT. THE LOCK -- DAY

Moon is at the wheel getting his bearings on the instrument panel. Bacon sits beside him, with Jamie occupying the passenger seat. Lee gets in.

LEE
Remember, no speedin'.

Moon glances at Lee.

JAMIE
So 'e's got a buyer already?

LEE
Apparently.

MOON
Who is it?

LEE
He didn't say.

CUT TO:

EXT. THE LOCK -- DAY

We see a cable van opposite the Lock. Robbie and Kerry are at the doors of the Lock. Robbie turns and looks towards the cable van and makes a gesture which is not seen by the Lads. The van follows the lads.

CUT TO:

EXT. TROJAN KEBAB HOUSE -- DAY

Miami and Three Feet emerge from the shop and wait on the pavement for their car to appear. Miami draws Three Feet to him confidingly.

> MIAMI
> What's happening to you?

Three Feet shuffles uncomfortably. His face is aching badly.

> THREE FEET
> Sorry boss, Nefarius insisted on seein' you personal...

> MIAMI
> It's like having a dog and having to shit in the park yourself.

Nefarius appears at the door of his shop behind them.

> NEFARIUS
> Miami, I'm goin' now. Down the bank I get your money, yeh?

Miami turns away disinterested.

There is the distant high-pitched whine of an engine and a moped swings round the corner with a pizza delivery boy riding.

SLOW-MOTION

Three Feet is the quickest to realise the danger as the delivery boy swerves to the kerb, stops the bike and reaches into the pannier for a pistol. Three Feet runs towards Miami in slo-mo. The pizza boy levels the gun at Miami (or is it Nefarius behind him?). There is a puff of pistol smoke from the barrel of the gun followed by a sharp retort. Three Feet heroically dives in front of Miami and collects a bullet in the chest. Miami is rooted to the spot in shock as Three Feet hits the pavement and bounces at his feet. Miami's car happens to appear from round the corner and speeds to his assistance. The pizza boy hurriedly mounts his moped and pulls away.

END OF SLOW-MO

The car speeds to Miami's side and men jump out of the car surrounding Miami like a presidential bodyguard. The car mounts the pavement and speeds after the pizza boy only to see him escape down a narrow alleyway. Miami stares wild-eyed at the red-stained pavement under Three Feet's body.

> MIAMI
> They got Three Feet. The bastards got Three Feet...

The minders hustle Miami towards the car and decant him into it. The car speeds away. One of the minders checks on Three Feet's body lying on the pavement. In the background Nefarius, wide-eyed, inches along the wall 'til he can dive back into his kebab shop.

                                                                    CUT TO:

END OF ACT ONE

ACT TWO

INT. MIAMI'S OFFICE -- DAY

Miami is sitting by at his desk looking at a very dated framed picture of Three Feet with the inscription 'Hapy Crismas Bos from Three Feet.' Miami has a look in his eye of hunted, distant planning. Trevor is agitated, trying to get Miami to listen to the voice of sweet reason.

                          TREVOR
          Miami, we don't have the teams to hit all his clubs in the same
                     night. That's not a hit, it's a ground war.

                          MIAMI
               We draft men in. We've done it before. It's not exactly
                            a skilled job.

                          TREVOR
            I can't send 'em in with baseball bats. These kids are seriously
                            tooled up.

Miami lowers at him.

                          MIAMI
            You'll 'ave your firepower. Did you send the get well card?

                          TREVOR
                      Course Miami.

                          MIAMI
                    What you put in it?

                          TREVOR
               'Get well soon, regards Miami.'

                          MIAMI
               Hardly fucking Shakespeare is it?

                            121

Miami looks down on Three Feet' photo. The clock on the wall ticks loudly.

> MIAMI (CONT'D)
> I got him Christmas, Eighty eight. He used to work for Greasy
> John. He came to me and he said, 'Give us a start, Miami. I
> won't let you down'. And do you know, he never has?

Silence. Trevor shuffles.

> TREVOR
> Er... Miami...

Miami holds up his hand imperiously.

> MIAMI
> Shut the fuck up, can't you see I'm having a moment here?

Trevor holds up a placatory palm. Miami searches for his thread.

> MIAMI (CONT'D)
> And what does he get for all his loyalty? A bullet in 'is
> pancreas from that scumbag Eddy The Diamond.

CUT TO:

INT. TRUCK CABIN. LONDON ROAD. CONT'D

Bacon holding at the lights. Lee beside him. Moon and Jamie still asleep.
Moon stirs.

> MOON
> Are we nearly there yet?

> BACON
> Bin there, done it, bought the fuckin' tee-shirt, son.

Moon sleepily looks out into the wing-mirror of the truck to see the car behind
them.

> MOON
> Nice one. Did the Captain get his whack?

> BACON
> He'll be in fish fingers for the rest of his natural.

> MOON
> Sweet. When did we pick up the tail?

                    LEE
                    What?

                    MOON
          A van with two geezers in it.

Jamie springs from his sleep and looks in the mirror.

               MOON (CONT'D)
     Bin with us for the last five minutes... What we going to do if
                    it is a tail?

Jamie and Bacon crane round.

                    JAMIE
          Chill out. Mr Paranoia...

EXT. ARMS WAREHOUSE -- DAY.

Miami's Rolls Royce approaches the gate. As the car approaches a guard whips
out a double barrelled shotgun and levels it at the windscreen of the car. The car
brakes sharply.

                                                    CUT TO:

INT. MIAMI'S CAR. ARMS WAREHOUSE -- DAY.

The two hoods reach into their pockets and take out hand guns. The goon in
the back throws himself across Miami to shield him. Miami struggles to free
himself, annoyed.

                    MIAMI
     We are meeting an International arms smuggler. I think we
     can expect to come across the odd fuckin' firearm you tit...

Exasperated Miami snaps down the electric window as the goons sheepishly look
at each other and ship their weapons back into their holsters. The man in leather
approaches the rear window of the car. Miami hands him a letter of introduction
which the man glances at, opens the gate and waves the driver through with the
butt of his gun. The car pulls forward.

                                                    CUT TO:

INT. TRUCK. LONDON ROAD -- DAY

Bacon is looking into his wing mirror.

                              BACON
                         I can't see them.

Jamie looks into his wing mirror.

                              JAMIE
         It's okay, they seem to 'ave got snarled up at the lights.

                              BACON
           Some fuckin' tail... You're a right wind up Moon.

                                                           CUT TO:

INT CUSTOMS VAN. -- DAY

Robbie plus two very officious-looking hoods.

                             ROBBIE
         Sweet. Give them an hour to drop the stuff. Then put stage
                         two into action.

                                                           CUT TO:

INT. ARMS WAREHOUSE -- DAY

Miami is walking side by side with Sergei, his Chechnayan arms contact. Slightly
behind them are Trevor and Miami's minders and one of Sergei's 'salesmen'.

                             SERGEI
         What sort of terrain are you seeking to... pacify?

                             MIAMI
           Mainly interiors, with occasional street work.

                             SERGEI
                         Urban or rural?

                             MIAMI
                       Urban, very urban.

                             SERGEI
                       Is noise a factor?

                             MIAMI
           The noisier the better, put the wind up the fuckers.

Sergei smiles, or at least tries to.

                              SERGEI
                  And the degree of skill of the end user?

                              MIAMI
                        Come again, Serge?

                              SERGEI
              Who will be operating the ordnance? Are they trained?

                              MIAMI
              As a matter of fact a lot of the end users will be as thick as
              turnips, so we're lookin' for something you point, pull a
                        trigger, end of manual.

Sergei gestures forward one of his 'salesmen' who is carrying a long case.
Sergei opens the case and takes out a Kalashnikov rifle.

                              SERGEI
              The AK-47. Rapid fire assault Kalashnikov. Clip loading, wide
                 arc of fire. An infantry man's weapon, requiring little
                        expertise or training.

He hands the gun to Miami who feels the weight with satisfied appreciation.

                              MIAMI
                     I'd like to see it in action.

                              SERGEI
                           For sure...

He gestures for Miami to hand the gun to the 'salesman' who fits a clip of ammo
into the breach loader. He walks forward and indicates a cardboard soldier target
standing at the end of a firing range. Miami nods his approval.

                                                              CUT TO:

INT. FIRING RANGE. END OF ARMS WAREHOUSE -- DAY

Pull focus from Miami to the target. There is a burst of automatic fire and the
soldier target disintegrates in the wilting fire in a deafening volley of noise. As
the gunfire ends the target keels over and drops to the ground.

                                                              CUT TO:

INT. ARMS WAREHOUSE. CONT'D. -- DAY

Pull focus back to Miami who regards the mayhem with a happy smile.

                                125

MIAMI
I'll take four dozen...

There are trestle tables laid out with small arms and grenades. It is something like a lethal car boot sale, with each table manned by one of Sergei's 'salesmen'. Behind Miami are his two goons and Trevor, who is trying to keep up while writing down Miami's purchases in a notebook. Sergei pauses at a table and holds up a hand pistol from a selection on the table.

SERGEI
For hand weapons the Walther has no equal. Light, portable
and doesn't jam.

He hands the gun to Miami who points it at Trevor and clicks the trigger. Trevor flinches.

MIAMI
It's not loaded, you tosser. Put me down for a score, Serge.

CUT TO:

INT. TROJAN KEBAB. NEFARIUS' OFFICE -- DAY.

Nefarius and Kouros are gaffer tapped to their chairs. Opposite them sit two heavily built Turkish goons. When Nefarius speaks it is apparent that he has lost yet another of his front teeth.

NEFARIUS
Ok, boys. I think I understand your offer. You take my
business and I frick off back to Cyprus or you cut my shaggin'
knob off?

The head Turk smiles and nods. The other heavies get up and leave the office leaving Nefarius and Kouros alone.

KOUROS
Blimey. Talk about a hostile takeover bid, innit?

CUT TO:

EXT. MIAMI'S WAREHOUSE -- DAY

The lads get out of lorry in front of the Warehouse.

CUT TO:

INT. MIAMI'S WAREHOUSE -- DAY

The Warehouse doors are opened by two tough looking hoods. The lads drive into the warehouse. Lee and Jamie get out as the hoods begin to circle the truck suspiciously. One of the hoods pauses and looks at Bacon in the driver's seat. Bacon returns his stare.

> BACON
> That is a very attractive 'aircut you got there.

The hood says nothing but takes out a handgun and points it in Bacon's face. Bacon looks to heaven then gets out of the cabin followed by Moon. The lads stand with their hands raised as the second hood goes to the back flap of the truck and peers inside. Under the covering gun of the first hood Jamie speaks from the side of his mouth to Lee.

> JAMIE
> I take it the buyer is not Fortnum an' Masons?

The second hood has finished his examination and nods to his oppo.

> LEE
> We was thinking we'd just drop off the goods and fuck off.

Pause. The hoods smile.

> LEE (CONT'D)
> If that's alright by you?

The hoods break into a grin then jerk their heads to the door. Needing no second invitation the lads leg it as fast as they can out of the place.

EXT. THE LOCK -- DAY

The lads are getting out of a cab.

> JAMIE
> Okay, so they weren't the most polite people we've ever dealt
> with. It's still thirty grand for an afternoon's work.

CUT TO:

EXT. THE LOCK -- DAY

Bacon, Lee and Moon are standing outside the pub. Street deserted.

> MOON (V.O.)
> At least that was the plan. Except Robbie seemed to 'ave
> forgotten our appointment ...

127

BACON
Where the fuck is he?

Lee looks at watch. Jamie comes out of pub door.

JAMIE
'E moved out of his flat this mornin', owin' two months' rent,
no forwardin' address.

LEE
The dirty fucking toe-rag.

BACON
He always did have the potential for being a slimy little git.

Lee is on his feet.

JAMIE
Where you off?

LEE
To find the bastard.

CUT TO:

INT. ARMS WAREHOUSE -- DAY

Miami is pacing along the trestle tables of weapons.

MIAMI
I think we 'ave met our requirements.

SERGEI
Now. All our merchandise is packed in grease to protect it in
transit so you must clean each...

Miami stops him with a hand as his attention is caught by something on a
nearby table.

MIAMI
What's that?

Sergei turns and looks. There on the table is a five foot red and white rocket
missile with Cyrillic lettering along its slim sides.

SERGEI
This is a Soyuz Ifgeny PP904. An anti-tank surface to surface missile.

                         MIAMI
            Look at that Trev. We'll 'ave one of them.

Sergei's eyebrow raises in surprise. Trevor tries to get Miami's attention quickly.

                        TREVOR
        Er... Miami... what do we want with a missile?

Miami rounds on him.

                         MIAMI
        I want a missile and I am goin' to get a fuckin' missile.
                        So button it.

Sergei looks worried. He's met some mad dictators in his time but Miami
is taking the biscuit. Miami turns to him.

                     MIAMI (CONT'D)
        We'll 'ave one of them and whatever it takes to fire
                        the bastard.

                        TREVOR
        Guv...I know you're upset about Three Feet...

                         MIAMI
        Fuck Three Feet. Who do you think Eddy the Diamond was
        aiming at? Me! So I'm goin' to put my fuckin' rocket up the
            cunt's jack an' danny. Now put a bun in it.

                                                        CUT TO:
INT. CAR. STREETS -- DAY

Kerry Dowd is about to get out of his pride and joy, a C reg Ford Granada, when
he notices Moon and Lee in front carrying light sledge hammers. Behind the car
are Jamie and Bacon.

They pull Kerry out of the car. Jamie and Bacon hold him whilst Lee and Moon
stand over the car with their hammers.

                          LEE
                 Where is Robbie Rossie?

                         KERRY
        How should I know? Haven't seen him for days.

Almost before the comment is from his lips Moon has swung his hammer and
smashed Kerry's offside headlight.

> **KERRY (CONT'D)**
> What the fuck?!!!

> **MOON**
> Wrong answer. Now, there's an easy way and there's a
> hard way...

> **KERRY**
> No lads please not my Granada. I've just had it MOT'ed. I don't
> know I tell ya!

The rear lights are smashed in rapid succession, the first by Moon, the second by Lee.

> **KERRY (CONT'D)**
> You fuckin' loonies...

> **LEE**
> Personally I'd 'ave gone for the easy way...

Moon lays into the car with his sledge hammer. As the other Lads look on with a distraught looking Kerry.

INT. MIAMI'S OFFICE -- DAY

Miami is sitting behind his desk watching as Trevor who sits on the front of his desk explains their forthcoming sanctions against Eddy's clubs, to two uniformed high ranking police inspectors who sit before him in comfy chairs with large brandies in their hands..

> **MIAMI**
> Gentlemen, as you know I've always worked very hard for this
> community. I've taken a pride in making sure this is a place
> where decent hard working people can bring up their kids in
> peace. I was saying to the chief constable just the other day.
> How pleased I was that he had decided to work with me on a
> more efficient drive for law and order. And now this fucking
> toe rag, Eddie the Diamond, jumps up out of the woodwork
> and starts brandishing shooters at our little ones on the street.
> So I've had a word with the chief, who as you know is fully
> behind a policy of zero tolerance for scum like that. And
> we've decided on one big whack, large scale over a large area.
> All 'is clubs simultaneous. A limited engagement. A one night
> stand. Monday mornin', business as usual...

The policemen look on stone faced.

> MIAMI (CONT'D)
> Course there'll be adequate compensation for the inevitable
> bollocks you lads will be getting' from the media.

The policemen look at each other then nod their assent minimally. Miami takes
out a pair of brown envelopes and throws them on the desk. The policemen
collect their packages and slip them into their coats. They nod in deference to
Miami then slip out of the office. As soon as the door closes Miami is on his feet
spraying air-freshener around his office.

> MIAMI (CONT'D)
> Fuckin' filth...

> TREVOR
> They don't say much do they?

> MIAMI
> Sheer animal cunnin'...

He opens the drawer of his desk and switches off a tape recorder.

> MIAMI (CONT'D)
> But I'll get the fuckers on tape one day...

EXT. STREET -- DAY

Kerry's car is now only fit for the crusher. Moon is still raining down blows all
over the battered bodywork.

> KERRY
> Alright! Alright!

Moon stops his assault on the car.

> KERRY (CONT'D)
> Robbie's on the Limehouse Lag...

> MOON
> Lime'ouse Lag?

> BACON
> What the fuck is the Lime'ouse Lag?

> KERRY
> You paid Robbie up front for the gear you was buyin'? Yeah?

JAMIE
Twenty long 'uns.

KERRY
And I expect the buyer did and all.

JAMIE
You what?

KERRY
Robbie gets you to pay his mark for some knock off shummter.

LEE
Yeh, which we are meant to sell on at a nice little profit.

KERRY
So you drop the goods and wait for your readies. Only Robbie
and his mates are clearing the warehouse of the stuff posing
as Customs and Excise.

MOON
Leaving us and the buyer well out of pocket.

KERRY
And Robbie quids in. Then 'e fucks off to Leeds or Newcastle
and looks for another bunch of greedy, none too clever
wankers... And that in a nutshell is the Limehouse Lag.

CUT TO:

INT. MIAMI'S OFFICE -- DAY

Miami is at his desk reading a pamphlet, puffing on a cigar... Laid across the desk
before him is the SAM missile. Trevor comes into the office and sits across from
Miami, staring at the missile unhappily.

MIAMI
It says 'ere that the PP904 missiles 'ad mixed success in Afghanistan.
Fuck knows what it'll do to Eddy the Diamond's office.

He laughs delightedly as he puffs on his cigar, then sees Trevor's unhappy face.

MIAMI (CONT'D)
What's the matter with you?

TREVOR
Miami, I know your mind is made up and that is why your sit
in the big chair...

132

MIAMI
Speak your mind Trevor.

TREVOR
The guilty parties have got to be got, that's common sense.
But if we were to be seen as knockin' off a substantial number
of erm...less guilty...

MIAMI
Innocent...

TREVOR
...parties.

MIAMI
What's yer point?

TREVOR
It needs careful handling.

MIAMI
Which is why there's only one man I trust to lead the hit on
Eddy's clubs.

TREVOR
Who?

MIAMI
You.

TREVOR
Me? When?

MIAMI
Tonight.

Trevor is suddenly ashen. Miami comes round the desk and lays a hand on
his shoulder.

MIAMI (CONT'D)
Don't get flaky. You won't be on your own. Barry Blue and
Toxic'll be right by your side.

Trevor tries to fight down his nausea.

TREVOR
I... I thought Barry was still in Broadmoor.

133

Miami smiles encouragingly.

CUT TO:

EXT. STREET -- DAY

Lee, Jamie, Bacon and Moon are clattering down the street.

> BACON
> You gotta admit, it's got a touch of gold about it. He rips the
> arse out of our bank account, gets us takin' all the risks, then
> walks off with all the soft centres an' we're none the wiser.

> LEE
> Actually, I didn't get the money from the bank on account of
> there bein' nothing in there. I 'ad to arrange a borrow to
> facilitate our cash flow.

> JAMIE
> A borrow from who?

> LEE
> Barry Blue.

A bell tolls.

> JAMIE
> Excuse me, would that be the same Barry Blue who is
> undergoin' electro-convulsive therapy for a clinical inability
> to control 'is violent emotions? The same Barry Blue who
> strangled 'is pet rotweiller because it was lookin' at 'im in
> a funny way?

> LEE
> We was desperate.

> JAMIE
> That's not desperate. That is suicidal.

Another bell tolls.

> MOON
> Fuck this, fuck Robbie and fuck the buyer. We're going round
> there now to nick the van. Come on.

END OF ACT TWO

ACT THREE

EXT. REAR OF MIAMI'S WAREHOUSE - NIGHT

Lee and Jamie are standing at the warehouse doors. Jamie takes out a pair of bolt cutters and snaps the padlock on the doors.

> JAMIE
> You call this a plan?

> MOON
> It's a sight better than lendin' twenty grand off
> Broadmoor Barry...

Moon takes out a jemmy and levers into the warehouse doors. He freezes as there is a sudden sound coming from the shadows behind them.

> MOON (CONT'D)
> Shit.

Moon and Jamie press themselves against the doors as two figures edge along the side of the warehouse. It is Bacon and Lee.

> BACON
> Moon? Jamie?

Moon emerges from the shadows, livid.

> MOON
> What are you two doin' 'ere? You're supposed to be
> keeping watch.

> LEE
> You better be quick. We've got problems. It's like Brick Lane
> market, round the front.

> BACON
> Virtually every face in the district is pilin' in.

Moon thinks furiously. This isn't the plan.

> MOON
> Well keep an eye on them. When me and Jamie 'ave got the
> van we'll give you three flashes. Get your arses over there
> treble quick.

CUT TO:

INT. MIAMI'S WAREHOUSE -- NIGHT

The two hoods who took the consignment from the lads are in the back of the two ton truck. One is ferrying out the designer gear and stacking it on the pallet in the warehouse, while the other is struggling with ammunition cases and loading them into the truck. As they cross, one of the hoods freezes and listens.

> HOOD 1
> What was that?

They freeze and peer into the darkness.

> HOOD 2
> Probably just a rat.

The first hood drops his load and takes out his gun. He begins blasting away indiscriminately into the darkness.

                                        CUT TO:

INT. MIAMI'S WAREHOUSE -- NIGHT

Moon and Jamie are pressed hard into a stack of wooden palettes.

> JAMIE
> I do not want to depart this world bein' mistaken for a rodent.

> MOON
> Shut. The fuck. Up.

                                        CUT TO:

INT. MIAMI'S WAREHOUSE -- NIGHT

Trevor in the warehouse. On his right side is Toxic, a large scarred, old foot - soldier of Miami's and on his left is Barry Blue. Dwarfed between the two, Trevor looks like a condemned man, sweating freely. Men are filing into the warehouse, the detritus of violent London of every shape and age. As they pass before Trevor they are being given cloakroom tickets by Toxic, from a series of different coloured pads before him.

> TREVOR
> Malcolm Prior. You worked with Three Feet on the Canada Square job?

Prior nods. Trevor sweatily runs a finger round his collar.

> TREVOR (CONT'D)
> You'll be with Barry Blue.

Prior takes his ticket and takes a seat. The next man comes to the table.

> TREVOR (CONT'D)
> Dave Cousins, one of Danny Carter's boys? You'll be with me
> an' Toxic again the U4EA club.

Dave collects his ticket. The next man comes forward.

> TREVOR (CONT'D)
> Larry the Lip with Barry...

Trevor turns to Barry Blue beside him.

> TREVOR (CONT'D)
> You all right, Barry?

Barry stares ahead of him, chewing the inside of his cheek.

> BARRY BLUE
> The geezer in the check jacket. He keeps lookin' at me.

Trevor closes his eyes. Trevor turns to Toxic.

> TREVOR
> Toxic, Barry's on the turn again. You finish off here, I'll get
> him some air.

He gets up from the table.

CUT TO:

INT. MIAMI'S WAREHOUSE -- NIGHT

The dark shape of the Rotherhithe hire truck. Two figures sidle along the side of the truck and fiddle with the door. They are delighted to find that the door is open. As they let themselves into the cabin of the truck the cabin light picks out Jamie and Moon. In slight panic at the light they quickly close the driver's door, extinguishing the light.

CUT TO:

INT. MIAMI'S WAREHOUSE -- NIGHT

The two hoods have returned to their card game. In the background one half imagines that he has seen the cabin light of the truck go on but dismisses it as a trick of the light.

CUT TO:

INT. TRUCK. MIAMI'S WAREHOUSE -- NIGHT

Moon and Jamie are in the cabin of the truck. Jamie is fiddling with the wires in the steering column of the truck with a bank of taped torch batteries, in preparation for hot wiring the motor.

> JAMIE
> The key's in the ignition.

Suddenly the passenger door of the truck opens putting on the cabin light once more. Jamie and Moon curl into foetal positions expecting the worst.

> BACON
> We 'eard shooting...

Moon lunges at Bacon and drags him and Lee into the cabin as Jamie fights to extinguish the cabin light. They freeze, barely breathing.

> MOON
> Bacon, when I tell you open the bloody doors of
> the ware'ouse...

CUT TO:

INT. MİAMI'S WAREHOUSE -- NIGHT

The two hoods are in their pool of light gorging on pot noodles. Hood 1 stands as he unquestionably sees a flash of cabin light in the shadows. He draws his gun again and walks towards the truck, followed by a puzzled Hood 2. They stop as they hear the gentle sound of the engine purr into life. The Hoods look at each other unsure of themselves. The truck's headlights suddenly come on full beam and the truck begins to inch towards them. Suddenly there is a squeal of tyres and the truck hurls towards them at speed. They dive for cover as the truck careers past them, to the doors. As they get to the doors they swing open and they drive out of the warehouse, the door swinging closed behind them. The Hoods get to their feet covered in pot noodle. Have they had a close encounter? They stand in the warehouse staring after the truck for some seconds. Suddenly the door-within-a-door opens and Trevor, Toxic and Barry Blue come into the warehouse and approach the hoods.

> TREVOR
> Right. Where's the truck?
> (BEAT)
> Oh shit.

CUT TO:

INT. TWO-TON TRUCK -- NIGHT

Lee, Bacon, Jamie and Moon are crammed into the cabin of the truck, all laughing and cheering fit to burst their lungs. They eventually get it out of their system and fall silent.

LEE
So. What now?

BACON
We get rid of this shit as quick as possible.

CUT TO:

INT. MIAMI'S WAREHOUSE -- NIGHT

The hoods sit around smoking in the empty warehouse which is now lit with overhead main lights which cast long shadows onto the walls. Trevor is sitting at the Hoods' card-table, staring ahead of him wondering at Fate. Giving him a wide berth are Toxic and Barry Blue, who stand at a distance. The door-within-a-door of the warehouse opens and Miami enters with two minders. The atmosphere is sombre, almost funereal.

Finally Miami finishes his handshaking and goes over to Trevor. He takes him by the elbow and leads him away from the earshot of the others. He speaks to him quietly, almost gentle.

MIAMI
Want a fag?

He proffers a packet. Trevor shakes his head.

MIAMI (CONT'D)
You've made a cunt of me, Trev, you know that don't you?
You filled this warehouse with some of the hardest bastards
this side of Bosnia and still you let some fucker run off with
my shooters.

Trevor nods his head, tears just below the surface.

MIAMI (CONT'D)
Anybody you want to blame?

Trevor considers then shakes his head. Miami pats him on the back.

MIAMI (CONT'D)
Good lad.

He walks away from Trevor and nods imperceptibly to Barry Blue. Via the shadows on the wall we see Barry walk over to Trevor, hold out his arms in apology, then take out a cosh and deal Trevor a single vicious 'thwock'.

>   TREVOR (O.O.V.)
>   Ahhhhh

He goes down like a sack of coal. The shadows on the wall show Barry Blue dealing Trevor a frenzied kicking. When he's finished Miami summons him over.

>   MIAMI
>   Take as many men as you need. Money no object. Find out
>   who did it. I want that fuckin' truck.

>   BARRY BLUE
>   You got it, boss.

                                                      CUT TO:

EXT. TROJAN KEBAB HOUSE -- MORNING

The two-ton truck is parked outside Nefarius' shop. The lads are pursuing Nefarius around the truck as he tries to get away from them.

>   MOON
>   Nefarius, just listen...

>   NEFARIUS
>   Get that thing ouda here. I'm tellin' you boys I'm
>   not int'rested.

>   JAMIE
>   Jus' two minutes...

>   NEFARIUS
>   Between you an' me I'm packin' in the whole gaff innit? Goin'
>   back 'ome. For one thing I can't afford the frickin' dentist
>   bills. Some country you got 'ere boys...

>   MOON
>   We are practically giving the stuff away...

>   JAMIE
>   A once in a lifetime, yours for thirty grand...

>   NEFARIUS
>   I ent got thirty pence to give away. Fuckin' Turksh is squeezin'
>   my pips. I ent got money for buyin' clothes.

MOON
Nefarius, 'ave we ever steered you wrong? I promise you with
the gear in the back of this van you can make a real killing.

JAMIE
Just take a look. That aint gonna hurt ya.

Jamie dangles the keys in front of him. Nefarius wavers then seizes the
keys. He waddles to the back of the van and opens the back. The lads wait
in anticipation.

Nefarius appears wild eyed from the truck. He quickly closes the door. He grabs
Jamie and Moon by their collars. He speaks hoarsely.

NEFARIUS
Come into my office. We do business.

He almost frog-marches the lads to the shop looking wildly about him to make
sure he is not being watched.

Moon and Jamie are mystified but pleased.

CUT TO:

INT. THE LOCK -- DAY.

All the lads are sitting around the bar, plainly in high spirits.

MOON
We have just recovered our entire outlay - plus a little
healthy profit.

JAMIE
Cash, already in the bank.

EXT. RESTAURANT -- DAY

C.U of a large restaurant window with the words Pasha's Mezze Restaurant
written on it in Turkish style lettering. A canvas covered truck edges into the
kerb opposite the restaurant. From the passenger side Nefarius emerges looking
well hard as he lights a Clint Eastwood cigarillo. He stares flinty-eyed at the
restaurant. He grins to reveal two gleamingly restored front teeth. He suddenly
raises his hand above his head and barks an order in Greek. The canvas sides of
the truck is thrown open to reveal Kouros, still wearing his bandanna, with a
couple of other Greeks who are aiming Kalashnikovs at the resturant. Nefarius
drops his hand and the Greeks open fire obliterating the window of the
restaurant. Everyone looks on stunned. When it ends there is a profound silence.

Nefarius chucks away the cigarillo and climbs back into the truck. As the truck pulls away...

                                                             CUT TO:

INT. MIAMI'S OFFICE -- DAY

Miami is on the phone.

                              MIAMI
              You what? ... That little Greek toe rag.

INT. TROJAN KEBAB HOUSE. Nefarius's OFFICE -- DAY

Hard cut to Nefarius's desk upon which are some freshly pulled teeth and the now familiar pliers. Miami is seated in Nefarius's chair.

                              MIAMI
           I'm sorry Nefarius who did you say sold you my shooters?

Cut to Nefarius mumbling in extreme agony.

                            NEFARIUS
                       The lads from The Lock

                                                             CUT TO:

INT. MIAMI'S OFFICE -- DAY

Lee, Bacon, Moon, Jamie and Trevor are gaffer-taped onto chairs in a semi-circle in the office. In the daylight the extent of Trevor's injuries are apparent. He has been well pasted by Barry Blue.

                              MIAMI
          There's no point in beggin'. You're all dead already.

                              MIAMI
       But bein' a student of 'uman nature, I'd like to know why you
           lads broke into my ware'ouse and nicked a truck load of
                              assault rifles.

The boys look between them.

                              JAMIE
                          Assault rifles?

                              MOON
                          Oh my God.

                              MIAMI
          Fucking up in the process, I may say a carefully orchestrated
              plan, which thanks to you cunts now lies in tatters.

Miami pauses.

                          MIAMI (CONT'D)
          What is it with you lot? A death wish? Didn't you think I'd
           notice that one hundred grands worth of eastern weaponry
           had gone walkies? I'm not accustomed to this type of lunacy.

As Miami is speaking Lee is looking on at Miami's desk. He notices a piece of
paper with 'import and export' written on it. The combination of this and Miami
saying 'accustomed' cause Lee to suddenly blurt out.

                               LEE
                             Customs.

They all look at Lee.

                          LEE (CONT'D)
                          Yeh, customs.

                              MIAMI
                           You what?

                               LEE
                    We were just following orders...

Lee is desperately trying to come up with a story.

                              MIAMI
                    What are you talking about?

                               LEE
          We heard your warehouse was about to be raided... by the...
                      anti terrorist squad... posing as...

The three lads look at Lee in disbelief.

                          LEE (CONT'D)
          ... Customs officers. So Trevor told us to get the gear out of
                      your spill ... didn't you Trevor?

The focus swings to Trevor who is none the wiser.

Miami turns to Trevor.

> MIAMI
> Is this true?

Trevor thinks then nods (what the hell, it's better than nothing).

> MIAMI (CONT'D)
> Why the fuck didn't you tell me?

Trevor racks his brain.

> LEE
> How could he? He didn't want to alert the geezer who
> shopped you to them. The mole in your organisation.

Miami is appalled. Moles are his secret fear.

> MIAMI
> We got a mole, Trev?

Trevor considers then nods, definitely.

> MIAMI (CONT'D)
> Who is it Trevor? Who is the mole?

Trevor thinks hard but is at a total loss for a name. Lee looks over to Trevor.

> LEE
> It's too late to protect the bastard, Trev.

Lee turns to Miami.

> LEE (CONT'D)
> It was Barry. Barry Blue...

The phone rings Miami picks it up. He listens.

> MIAMI
> That was Toxic. The warehouse just got raided. They said they
> were Customs.

CUT TO:

EXT. STREET -- DAY

The lads walk along having lived to scam another day.

> LEE
> Well that was a bit of a result.

JAMIE

Yeh. Mind you I wish you had mentioned all the other fuckers we owe money to an' all.

INT. STREET CORNER -- DAY

Barry Blue is eating chips out of a bag in a shop doorway. He looks up in surprise to see Toxic standing before him. He is even more surprised when the rope comes round his neck from behind him and the big man in the black suit strangles him.

CUT TO:

INT. MIAMI'S OFFICE -- DAY

Miami is sitting at his desk, smoking on a cigar. Trevor, now pristine, sits opposite him.

TREVOR

Apparently the Turks have been moving in trying to get a stranglehold on the Greeks' catering business. They were taking out contract killings using pizza boys.

MIAMI

So they were 'avin' a pop at Nefarius not me when Three Feet copped it?

Trevor nods. Miami smiles.

MIAMI (CONT'D)

You 'andled yourself like the Duke of fuckin' Wellington in this business Trev, I take my 'at off to you.

TREVOR

Just doin' the job, Miami.

Miami picks up the phone and dials.

MIAMI

So strictly speakin', Eddy the Diamond is totally innocent of all this bollocks?

TREVOR

Pretty much.

Miami is connected. He speaks into the phone.

MIAMI

Has Toxic left yet?... Okay, never mind...

He hangs up the phone.

                          MIAMI (CONT'D)
                        Minor fuckin' detail...

                                                              CUT TO:

INT. U4EA CLUB -- NIGHT

Eddy the Diamond is bouncing into his night club. His eyes are taken by a large
wooden case on the bar. He's even more choked on opening it, to reveal Miami's
surface-to-surface short range nuclear missile.

C.U. of Eddy's face.

As he takes a step towards it he has little time to regret his carelessness as the
timer goes off and the missile blows up. Cut to white screen.

                                                              CUT TO:

INT. THE LOCK -- DAY

Jamie is having a game of darts with Bacon while Moon is settling down to
a Sunday roast.

                           MOON (V.O.)
                So that was that. We was in Miami's good books for quite a
                while after that. Oh, yeah... there was one other little thing...

The door opens and Miami walks into the bar, Three Feet in tow, on metal
crutches, carrying a brown paper wrapped package. Miami wanders to the bar
and leans against it.

                            MIAMI
                I been thinkin'. Them anti-terrorist boys. The ones who
                claimed to be customs... They impounded a load of designer
                gear I had at the ware'ouse. Why the fuck would they do such
                a thing? Been puzzlin' me for days. But you know what it put
                             me in mind of?

                            JAMIE
                    What's that then Miami?

                            MIAMI
                    The Lime'ouse Lag.

Moon chokes on a mouthful of lunch.

MIAMI (CONT'D)
A fifth-rate losers scam run by a tosser called Tommy Rossie
back in the eighties. I had to run 'im out of the manor. He
fucked off to Scunthorpe I believe.

He gestures to Three Feet who throws a bag on the counter. Lee slowly pulls out
a blood-stained designer jacket from the bag.

MIAMI (CONT'D)
Like father like fuckin' son. I don't know what the fuck you
was up to but then neither do you, probably. So we'll let the
kippin' dog kip. This time.

Miami and Three Feet stride from the room.

MOON
What a bummer. That was a beautifully cut jacket.

He tosses the jacket into the rubbish bin. Bacon and Jamie go back to their darts
and Moon back to his lunch.

END

EPISODE 3

LOCK, STOCK... & A FIST FULL OF JACK AND JILLS

by Chris Baker and Andrew Day

ACT ONE

EXT. BUILDING SITE -- DAWN

Close-up of black stretch limo followed by a black Merc. They pull over. Close-up of doors opening, black boots on concrete. We pull back to see El Torro and his henchmen all in black leather coats. They walk in slow motion, leather coats blowing in the wind. Camera pulls back even further to reveal a wasteland scattered with building materials.

A sign: 'Larry Harmless Construction - The Best of British'. There is a lone portacabin.

INT. PORTACABIN -- DAWN

Typical portacabin interior: a knackered old metal filing cabinet topped with trays overflowing with paper, the inevitable nudie calendar on the wall, and hard hats on a row of coat hooks. Other odds and sods like luminous tape, a tool box and a broom.

LARRY HARMLESS is in good physical shape - apart from his face, which has a squashed nose and battered eyebrows. He is still a frightening figure to behold. He sits behind a cheap desk.

Larry's henchmen, MARS BAR (40s, face covered in scars), and DOORFRAME (the biggest man you'll ever see) stand on either side of him.

All three men look down at photographs laid out on the desk for their benefit:

first photo shows the facade of a glitzy casino called The Lucky Lady. A neon woman with flashing nipples invites passers-by to enter. Second photo shows the facade has collapsed and the neon woman points towards a pile of rubble and rooms open to the street. Harmless seems to show genuine concern:

HARMLESS

Yeah, looks like an earthquake to me. One of them localised ones. Pretty rare, but this shows they do 'appen.

Now we see who he's talking to. Eight solidly built Latin men in very expensive suits. Something about them says they are drug barons. EL TORRO steps forward, (he has one blind white eye, and a thick Andalucian accent).

EL TORRO

There was no earthquake, Harmless.

El Torro lays out a third photograph. It is a close-up of a collapsed portion of wall. The broken concrete reveals crushed-up old oil cans.

150

HARMLESS
Bloody hell ... look at that, lads. That is shockin'.

Passes photo to henchmen.

HARMLESS (CONT'D)
I knew we shoulda used our own boys. Didn't I say that, lads ?

MARS BAR
Shouldn't never trust something like this to a bunch of bloody
foreign scum -

HARMLESS
(Interrupting hastily)
Yeah, yeah, so you want me to send out one of these two to
track down the cowboys who tried to save on concrete ?

EL TORRO
No need. They are saving concrete underneath our new casino
in Malaga.

HARMLESS
Quite right. So it's a re-building job you're 'ere about, right ?

EL TORRO
You're not goin' anywhere near our new casino.
We want compensation.

El Torro slides a sleek attache case onto the desk.

HARMLESS
Compensation ?!

EL TORRO
Your company is responsible.

HARMLESS
(Confidently)
Well I fink tha's a complicated legal -

The lid of the case flips up and El Torro pulls out a gilt-edged hatchet.

EL TORRO
One million. By the end of the week. Or I will gut you like a
fucking pig.

El Torro buries the hatchet into the table. Photos and splinters fly into the air.
Silence.

INT. LOCK. BACK ROOM -- DAY

Bacon takes the corner of a dustsheet which is covering a table in his hands.

Moon, Jamie and Lee exchange sceptical looks.

> JAMIE
> What is that?

> BACON
> Under 'ere is a magic bucket. Every time a punter walks past,
> he'll stop and bung 'is cash in it.

> LEE
> You been talkin' to the pixies again?

> BACON
> Don't believe me?

Bacon pulls the sheet back ceremoniously to unveil a roulette table.

> JAMIE
> (Sarcastic)
> Now why didn't I think of that?

> MOON
> How do you work it?

Bacon demonstrates:

> BACON
> Spin the wheel, bung in the ball bearing, and ...

As the ball rattles round, Bacon picks up a miniature wooden rake used
by croupiers.

> BACON (CONT'D)
> (Miming)
> ... rake it in.

> LEE
> It's got potential but you'll need a magnet.

> MOON
> A what?

> LEE
> Magnet. Otherwise the ball can land anywhere, can't it?

INT. PORTACABIN -- DAY

Mars Bar and Doorframe try to repair the desk with gaffer tape. Harmless bites his nails.

DOORFRAME
Cheeky bastards ain't they?

MARS BAR
Don't you wan' us to go roun' there an' give 'em a doing?

HARMLESS
You're fucking joking. Can't start a war with that lot. They got half an army backing 'em up, I knew them cans was too rusty, I told 'em to use new ones.

INT. LOCK -- DAY

AS ONE SCENE WITH EDIT BREAKS.

The lads are still getting the hang of the roulette table. Johann and Jaap (Johann's brother, jittery, wired) make a big entrance:

JOHANN
Hey, hey, are zere any leds in here?

JAAP
Any leds who are wantink to heff time of life ?

BACON
(Pointing at Jaap)
Who's he?

Johann and Jaap assume brotherly pose.

JOHANN
Zis is Jaap. Brozzer of me. I sink maybe you knowink za name DJ Whizz from Amsterdam, jah? Famous DJ of Euro Techno ent speed Garage.

JAAP
MTV are votink me number one DJ of Benelux country.

JAMIE
What happened to your mate?

JOHANN
Jordi? Jordi is stayink in Hook of Hollant for restink mind.

Johann points to his head.

                              JAMIE
                  What's the matter with his mind?

                              JOHANN
            Jordi mind is suffer from za culture shock of drifink many time
                   to Inklant ent goink beck, ent go again.

                              JAAP
            Now he liffink in special hospital in Hook of Hollant for za
                       people who are freak out.

Reminded of his good friend, Johann pauses a moment. He shares a tragic look
with Jaap.

EDIT BREAK 1

Johann's sad face, contrast to before.

                              JOHANN
               Za poor guy. I am always blame myself.

                              BACON
                    So, what've yer got for us?

Back to business - Jaap removes the top of the box: pills.

                              LEE
              We don't know anyone with a headache that bad.

                              JOHANN
           Come on, zese are za pill for makink happy and dance around.

                              BACON
              What are you two muppets doing with all these pills ?

Bacon picks one up and looks at it. It has two luscious lips stamped on it.

                              JOHANN
             Is good shit, guys, pure MDMA. We are callink Two-Lips ...

                              JAAP
                   Like Two-lips from Amsterdam.

                              BACON
                Yeah we get it. Not really our area, mate.

Bacon throws the pill back in the box.

> JOHANN
> You not interestink in makink money ent keepink pill for you
> and giffink to girlfriend?

> JAAP
> Are zese za guys you told me were so tough and cool
> London geezer?!

> JOHANN
> Come on, guys.

> BACON
> Nah, we don't want it.

It's their final answer.

> JOHANN
> OK, OK, you are not drinkink zis cup of tea.

> JAAP
> We have anuzzer kind of pill.

> JOHANN
> Completely different kind of one. You are luffink ent you can
> sellink so easy.

They lift the lid off another box. It is full of plastic medicine bottles. Johann
hands Jamie a bottle.

Close-up of plastic medicine bottle, labelled 'VAGIRA for Impotence Problems -
Twenty tablets'.

Jamie takes out one pill, puts it on the table.

> MOON
> You made it?

> JAMIE
> In your lab?

Bacon picks the pill up.

> JAAP
> In zese pills we are puttink somesink special extra. We are
> mixink powder body-builder are eatink for buildink muscle.

155

> BACON
> It works though, right?

> JOHANN
> Guys, zis one is perfect formula.

> JAAP
> Me, I take and heffink so amazink hart-on.

No-one wants to hear this.

> BACON
> Yeah alright, that'll do.

Bacon puts the pill down again. The lads look at each other.

> LEE
> It might sell.

> JAMIE
> Alright, we'll take some of your Jack and Jills.

The Dutchies are confused by this.

> JOHANN
> Ah, you are talking zat cockney rhymink slag, jah ?

> JAAP
> Zese guys.

> MOON
> We'll take three hundred.

The Dutchies hesitate, looking at each other.

> JOHANN
> OK guys, now is time for askink favour.

> JAAP
> Business favour.

> BACON
> Business favour ? Ain't no such thing boys.

> JAMIE
> Gotta be something in it for us.

JAAP
Oh, jah, jah ... we just needink help wid dose Gadaffi Broder.

JOHANN
Dey giffink to us bodder.

JAMIE
Told you to keep clear of them. They're shot away - big time.

LEE
What they do to you ?

EDIT BREAK 2

JOHANN
We don't want to talk about zat.

JAMIE
What you want us to do ?

JAAP
Just droppink zese to factory and collectink payment.

Shows them the first box of pills.

BACON
How's it worth our while ?

JAAP
For you we trow in anuzzer twenty Firility.

MOON
To deal with the Gadaffis ? That's peanuts.

JOHANN
Ent five per cent also.

BACON
You mean ten per cent, doncha ?

JAMIE
Danger money.

JOHANN
Jah, OK, OK, ten per cent.

LEE
You came to the right people.

CUT TO:

INT. ASYLUM -- DAY

(TO BE INCORPORATED IN BREAK 1)

Jordi lies on bed strapped down.

CUT TO:

INT. SWEATSHOP -- DAY [FLASHBACK]

THE CALIPH chases the Dutchies towards the sweatshop door with a machete.

CUT BACK TO:

INT. PORTACABIN -- DAY

Harmless is on the phone. Mars Bar and Doorframe are in attendance.

> HARMLESS
> Listen you Swiss bastard ... no, I don't care. That car better be
> in London tomorrow or you'll be counting notes with your
> fucking toes ... Thank you.

Puts phone down. His wife, Sylvia, enters.

Harmless's expression changes. This is an unexpected visit.

> HARMLESS (CONT'D)
> Alright darling. Nice surprise.

Sylvia has no time for pleasantries.

> SYLVIA
> We need a big box of impotence pills. Today.

Harmless glances at Mars Bar and Doorframe and explains:

> HARMLESS
> For your clients at the massage parlour you mean?

> SYLVIA
> Listen, I got a coachload of Japanese booked in for the
> weekend. Don't want 'em to blow their cookies in the first
> five minutes and refuse to pay for the whole hour.

> HARMLESS
> Tha's fine babe, but today is a little bit ...

Sylvia goes up a gear.

> SYLVIA
> Larry, it's a small thing to ask, and it'll make a big difference
> to business - to my business. But maybe you think I should
> take second place to a bunch of brick-layers.

> HARMLESS
> Alright, alright ...

> SYLVIA
> We went over all this before we got married.

> HARMLESS
> We did. I'll sort it.

Sylvia is all sweet again.

> SYLVIA
> You're an angel. I thought we could have lunch in that new
> restaurant in Wapping that some of the girls has been talking
> about. Bye bye.

Taffy enters, passing Sylvia on her way out.

> TAFFY
> Oh, hello Mrs Harmless.

> HARMLESS
> Taffy. How are you ?

> TAFFY
> Not bad, I've 'ad a few things goin' on with -

> HARMLESS
> (Interrupting)
> Yeah, never mind all that. The auction starts at eleven. You
> go there, keep away from the bar, buy the old motor and drive
> it away, got it ? Lot number firteen.

Harmless hands Taffy the catalogue.

> TAFFY
> Piece o' cake.

> HARMLESS
> This car is coming all the way from Switzerland for a reason.
> It might look like an old banger, but it is worth a fuck of a lot

of money - to me. And I'm counting on that car to get me
out of a very nasty financial mess.

TAFFY
Do I get a cut ?

HARMLESS
Yeah, just above your Adam's, now piss off.

CUT TO:

INT. LOCK -- DAY

BACON, JAMIE and LEE counting out pills from a heap in the
middle of the table. They count aloud up to nineteen, and
then put the top on the bottle of 'twenty'. The dialogue is
muttered between the numbers.

MOON
(Into phone)
The lads are batchin' 'em up, as I speak.

BACON
... eleven, twelve ... Who's that, Moon?

MOON
(Covering receiver)
Larry 'Armless.

LEE
Six, seven ... Nice one.

MOON
(Into phone)
Not bodgin' 'em up, batchin' 'em up Mr Harmless, yeah. We'll
bring 'em over tonight.

Moon puts phone down.

JAMIE
... Eighteen, nineteen. 'Ow many's 'e want?

MOON
Said we gotta talk to 'is wife.

JAMIE
I volunteer for that job.

LEE
(Finishing a batch)
Right, tha's for the Pleasure Zone.

MOON
An' I left a message for Moira at Lapland. These are right up
her street, I reckon.

BACON
This stuff is really shiftin', innit?

MOON
Guys who can't fuck want to fuck. Guys who can fuck want
to fuck more.

INT. AUCTION HOUSE -- DAY

Taffy has his feet up in the bar, reads *The Racing Post.*

AUCTIONEER (O.O.V.)
Lot number 13, an Armstrong Sidley...

Taffy sighs and looks at his watch. Puts the *Racing Post* down. Picks up the
catalogue and turns to Lot 30: a 1972 Alfa Romeo GTA. He rings the photo
with a biro.

A WOMAN stands right by his shoulder. He looks round and stares at her arse.
Lifts his drink and sits back contentedly.

EXT. SWEATSHOP -- DAY

Lads pull up outside sweatshop in Jamie's car. Bacon leads the way.

BACON
Le's do some business, then.

The others are a lot more wary.

LEE
They still owe us, don't they ? For those Lacostes that fell
apart.

JAMIE
Best we don't mention that. If the Caliph's off 'is medication.

CUT TO:

EXT. STREET. AGAINST WALL -- DAY (FLASHBACK)

The Caliph is held down on the pavement by two security guards. He struggles wildly.

> GUARDS
> Hold him ! Hold him down !

> CALIPH
> Aaaagh

The Caliph's body is partially obscured, only his screams can be heard.

CUT BACK TO:

INT. SWEATSHOP -- DAY

> JAMIE
> There ain't no tellin' what's gonna happen.

INT. SWEATSHOP -- DAY

Ali is talking to a KID of about eleven.

> ALI
> Tell yer social worker you can't go to school because it's an
> Islamic 'oliday.

> SWEATSHOP KID
> She's Muslim ... I wanna go, it's football practice tonight.

> ALI
> You selfish little bastard. You wanna go school and play
> football instead of earnin' money for your granny ? You sit
> there and finish them Chanels or I'll 'ave you in the skinnin'
> shed with yer sister.

Pushes kid back behind sewing machine. Sees the four lads.

> ALI (CONT'D)
> Well fuck a duck. Ain't seen your ugly mugs round 'ere lately
> ... you been 'idin' ?

The Caliph emerges from another door, behind the lads. Doped up to the eyeballs.

> THE CALIPH
> Ugly ? Nah, they're quite cute from the back.

                    BACON
             We got a delivery for yer.

Mehmet appears from nowhere and joins Ali.

                   MEHMET
         Sweet. Who you runnin' errands for?

                    LEE
         We got happy pills, from the Dutchmen.

                    ALI
         Aaah, ain't they bringing it theirselves ?

                    MOON
         They're of a nervous disposition.

                   MEHMET
              An' you're not ?

                    LEE
                    No.

Lee puts the box of pills on the table. Ali checks the contents. Breaks one pill,
grinds into his palm, smells it, tastes it.

                   BACON
                 Five large.

                   MEHMET
                   Four.

                   BACON
         We ain't 'ere to piss about.

                    ALI
              Four an a half.

Pause. Then Bacon nods.

                ALI (CONT'D)
            Mehmet, sort them out.

Mehmet steps forward. Lads unsure what 'sort them out' means in this case...
until Mehmet produces a roll of dosh from his jacket pocket.

INT. HEAVENLY RELIEF -- EVENING

Bacon and Jamie sit in the Reception area. A row of girls in white coats sit opposite. Silence speaks volumes. One of them smiles at Lee.

> JAMIE
> (To Bacon)
> You. Didn't bring any dosh wiv yer, did yer ?

> BACON
> No.

> JAMIE
> Me neither.

Jamie tries to strike up a conversation with Sam, a blonde.

> JAMIE (CONT'D)
> That natural your hair ?

Blonde looks up from her paper with a bored:

> SAM
> Yeah.

> JAMIE
> Looks nice.

Blonde goes back to her paper. End of conversation. Bacon takes the piss:

> BACON
> Smooth bit of work there mate.

INT. LAPLAND, DRESSING ROOM -- EVENING

Smoke-filled room. Barbie stands in front of a coffee-table. On the coffee table is a gold bag and around the bag is an array of dildos, vibrators, love-eggs, crotchless knickers, something with a feather on it and a whip. She is holding up a vibrator with a revolving head. She turns it off and shrugs.

> MOIRA
> If y'ask me it's just a gimmick, really. but they do sell. People
> like the novelty, I think.

There are about eight women in the room, including Moira and Tanya. There are glasses, bottles and fags everywhere.

> BARBIE
> (Suspicious)
> Revolvin' head, it's like something out of The Exorcist. 'Ave you tried it?

MOIRA
Oh yeah, I tried 'em all.

BARBIE
And?

MOIRA
Well with this one you do get a funny feelin', you could call
it a thrill, but it's nothing' like sex.

TANYA
Unless yer ole man's got a revolvin' helmet...

BARBIE
The thing is, if I'm gonner take a load of 'em up to Holloway, I
need something straightforward to sell.

MOIRA
Well, yeah. To be honest with yer, Barbie, if yer lookin' for
somethin' to do a job, you go for the bendy dildo at £12.99,
and yer won't regret it. But girls, if yer lookin' to pamper
yerself, y'know ... what yer want is the Ivory Tusk.

She produces a white dildo out of her bag. As well as the usual erect and
crumpled penis, there is a clitoris-massager that arches over the top. Gasps
of wonder from around the room.

MOIRA (CONT'D)
I tell yer what. Whoever made these things knew something
that God didn't.

INT. LAPLAND -- DAY

Moon and Lee stand outside the door.

LEE
Ever been to one of these dos ?

MOON
Lee. They're for women. Look, we just go in sell the pills.
Easy.

LEE
This will be a right touch.

They knock on the door and open it. In front of them is Moira and the women
surrounded by dildos etc. Moira is holding the ivory tusk. The boys are
dumbfounded.

> ### MOIRA
> Hello. What can I do for you boys?

Lee and Moon look at each other.

> ### MOON
> Um ...

Lee tries to take over, but there is a tremble in his voice.

> ### LEE
> Actually we got some merchandise for you.

> ### TANYA
> Oh yeah?

Pause.

> ### MOIRA
> Well don't just stand there, give us yer spiel.

> ### LEE
> 'Ave a look at these.

He produces a bottle of pills from his pocket and pours a few onto the table-top. The girls peer down at them.

> ### LEE (CONT'D)
> Get yer old man to pop one of these and you won't 'ave no complaints about 'im.

> ### MOIRA
> They work ?

> ### MOON
> Think of a rocket taking off.

> ### TANYA
> How would you two know ?

> ### LEE
> Eh ?

> ### TANYA
> You taken 'em ?

> ### LEE
> (Offended)
> Nah, course not.

166

BARBIE
Nothin' in this room gets sold without a demonstration.

MOIRA
Moon ... you know our Tanya quite well, don't yer ?

MOON
What ?

MOIRA
Well down one of them and take Tanya round the back.
She can tell us if there's anything... extra.

Lee feels he should step in here and stick up for his mate. Opens his mouth
to speak, but Moon reaches down and picks up a pill:

MOON
(Casually)
Yeah, alright.

EXT. HEAVENLY RELIEF -- DAY

Harmless, Mars Bar, Doorframe and Taffy are all looking at a rust-bucket of a car
- an old Italian Formula One. Taffy looks pleased with his work.

TAFFY
I can see why you wanted her, Guv.

HARMLESS
What the fuck is that, Taffy ?

TAFFY
'S your car.

Mars Bar whacks Taffy in the kidneys and he falls to the floor.

HARMLESS
No Taffy that ain't my car.

HARMLESS
My car is big, silver, and British. That is red, rusty and Italian.

TAFFY
But that was it... Lot firty.

HARMLESS
Lot firty, eh ? I'm sure it was lot fuckin' firty. But I didn't
want lot firty, I wanted lot fir-TEEN, you dozy cunt, fir-TEEN.

167

MARS BAR
Deaf as well as dumb.

TAFFY
No ... no ... I'll make it up to -

HARMLESS
(Interrupting)
Yes Taffy, I know you're very sorry... but sorry ain't no bloody
fucking good to me...

Nods at Mars Bar. Mars Bar knocks Taffy out. Passers-by in the street look away
and keep walking. Harmless tries to keep calm.

HARMLESS (CONT'D)
(To Doorframe)
Get on the blower and find out who's bought my car.

INT. LAPLAND, DRESSING ROOM -- EVENING

There is music playing now, the bartering session is over. Lee relaxes, turning
a glass of whisky in his hand. A couple of the girls are listening to his patter.
Muffled scrapings and bangings from the next room.

LEE
Yeah, I've never been a 9-to-5 kind of geezer, I'm too ... too
free. Like an eagle... a bit.

Moira walks past.

MOIRA
'ow long's it been?

LEE
(Proudly)
This is long, even for 'im. Told you they worked.

INT. HEAVENLY RELIEF -- EVENING

Sylvia enters from a back room.

SYLVIA
Hello boys. Nice of you to come so quickly.

Jamie and Bacon stand up.

BACON & JAMIE
Mrs... Harmless.

SYLVIA
You look well, Jamie.

Jamie blushes.

JAMIE
Thank you very much Mrs...

SYLVIA
Sylvia.

JAMIE
Sylvia.

SYLVIA
(Teasing)
If only I was ten years younger. Have you got my magic
pills, then?

BACON
Duracell strength, these little beauties.

Hands Sylvia a shoe-box. Just then Harmless walks in with Mars Bar who
is dragging the unconscious Taffy behind him.

HARMLESS
S'cuse us.

BACON & JAMIE
Mr Harmless...

SYLVIA
Larry, I told you not to conduct your business from this
building. How am I supposed to keep up a respectable
image ? This is a brothel not a ... Sorry girls.

Taffy is dragged and rolled across the room.

HARMLESS
We'll be out of you're 'air in a jiffy darlin' ...

SYLVIA
(Angry)
Mars Bar, don't spill any claret on the linoleum this time...

MARS BAR
Right you are, Mrs Harmless.

Mars Bar and Doorframe drag Taffy out of the other door.

> SYLVIA
> (To Harmless)
> I've got some very important clients in there. You're paying
> for them.

Harmless's expression changes: you what ?

> JAMIE
> Right well, we gotta shoot.

> SYLVIA
> Why don't you stay and have some fun?

> HARMLESS
> Who's down there ?

> SYLVIA
> See Larry about your payment.

They look at Harmless but his attention is elsewhere now.

> HARMLESS
> Sale or return, eh ?

Lads look annoyed. But Harmless exits the way Mars Bar and Doorframe went.

EXT. HEAVENLY RELIEF -- EVENING

> BACON
> We coulda stayed. Run up a tab or something.

Jamie looks at him.

> BACON (CONT'D)
> What ?

INT. HEAVENLY RELIEF, DRESSING ROOM -- EVENING

Sauna door, steam. Benches against wall. El Torro's honchos in white towels.
Mars Bar and Doorframe stop and look at them. Enter Harmless, sees the Spanish.
El Torro appears from the sauna in a gush of steam, with two massage girls.
Everyone looks down at Taffy except Harmless and El Torro.

> EL TORRO
> Thanks for the hospitality.

                    HARMLESS
                    S'alright.

Pause. El Torro decides to notice Taffy now.

                    EL TORRO
            Everything going according to plan ?

                    HARMLESS
        Oh, yeah, yeah. It's all sorted. Wheels are in motion.

EXT. BUILDING SITE -- NIGHT

Huge concrete mixer rolls around. MR SKIN and MR BONE finish digging a grave
of cosy proportions under a half-finished building.   Harmless, Mars Bar and a
trussed-up Taffy watch.

                    MR BONE
        Right choice, the Gravedigger. Perfect place for it, too.

                    HARMLESS
            Yeah ? The Postman always seems more fittin'.

                    MR BONE
        Oh no... they suffer a lot with the Gravedigger. They can last
                    hours. They got time to think.

Harmless nods. Taffy is trying to speak. Mars Bar kicks him. Doorframe appears
from the portacabin, with a scrap of paper.

                    DOORFRAME
        Some poncey Duke bought it. Reckons it was 'is first car back
        in the firties, used to use it to chase debs - whoever she was.

                    HARMLESS
                    (Impatiently)
            Doorframe... which Duke?

                    DOORFRAME
                    Duke of Pewsey.

Mr Skin and Mr Bone drop Taffy into the grave.

                    HARMLESS
        Can we get old Sharpy on the case? 'E's on the out ain't 'e?

                    DOORFRAME
        Just finished a two-stretch, Guv. Lookin' for work.

Deftly, Mr Skin and Mr Bone whip off Taffy's gag, ram a long plastic tube in his mouth, and pass the tube to Doorframe to hold. Taffy's moans come up the tube. Doorframe places his palm over the end of the tube to muffle the sounds of mortal fear.

MARS BAR
(To Skin and Bone)
Want a hand ?

Mars Bar helps them wheel the mixer to the edge of the grave. They tilt the barrel of the mixer and in pours the concrete. Harmless and Doorframe walk back towards the portacabin.

HARMLESS
Send Sharpy round to Sylvia's. Full works, on the house.
Ugly fucker prob'ly needs a good seein' to.

Concrete comes up to the brim of the grave. The tube pokes out the top.
Mr Skin and Mr Bone start patting down the concrete with shovels.

INT. PUB -- NIGHT

Moon and Lee walk into pub.

LEE
That was a right touch. Moira was well impressed.

Moon looks drained.

MOON
Yeah. I'm a bit stiff.

LEE
You alright? Don't want you endin' up like old Jordi...

MOON
No chance of that.

Moon holds out his hand. In his palm is the pill he didn't take.

LEE
'Ang on... 'ow did you keep goin' for...

Looks at his watch, starts to work out how long Moon was in there.
Moon interrupts his calculation with a knowing grin.

MOON
One day, I'll tell you all I know.

INT. HEAVENLY RELIEF -- NIGHT

Harmless, Sylvia and SHARPY (40, tracksuit and trainers, very short, very skinny).

SHARPY
This is very kind of you, Mr Harmless.

HARMLESS
Don't you worry Sharpy. You get my motor back an' I'll make
sure all the top blags start comin' your way again.

Harmless pats Sharpy on the back. Sylvia hands Sharpy a small silver tray with a
handful of pills scattered on top.

SYLVIA
Extra staying power.

SHARPY
After two years inside it'll be a miracle if I last ten minutes.

HARMLESS
Well, don't keep 'er waitin' boy. She's in there.

Sharpy exits into other room. Harmless's smile disappears.

HARMLESS (CONT'D)
I want 'im out in an hour.

SYLVIA
If he's not, I'll send Maxine in with them. She'll finish 'im off.

INT. NIGHTCLUB -- NIGHT

On the dance-floor, teenagers who should be loved-up are standing swaying on
the spot like zombies, or Goths. A kid is puking up right by the bar. The Gadaffis
are getting stick from about five or six very pissed-off lads. One PUNTER,
gagging on his own vomit, is shouting at them:

PUNTER
You listen. I just spent an hour puking my guts up an' another
hour tryin' to remember what my name was. I want a fuckin'
refund for all that shit.

Gadaffis are seething. Mehmet pulls the Caliph aside.

MEHMET
You're comin' off the sedation for a while. Here's a couple of
Red Dragons to perk you up.

173

Evil grin spreads across the Caliph's face.

INT. LOCK, BACKROOM -- NIGHT

Roulette wheel spins. A handful of PUNTERS watch closely. Lee stands over the wheel and Bacon is on the far side. Ball comes to a halt on black.

> LEE
> Black is the winner... again.

Rakes in the bets. Punters groan. Lee winks at Bacon.

> BACON
> Tha's his holiday gone.

> MOON
> Tha's his wife gone too, innit ?

Jamie walks up to Lee.

> JAMIE
> Lee, that magnet.

> LEE
> Works a treat, dunnit ?

> JAMIE
> Yeah, but just go easy on it. Yer meant to let 'em win sometimes.

> BACON
> Tha's Nutty Harris, a man with a breakin' point.

> LEE
> Chill out, I can see in their eyes 'ow much punishment they
> can take.

INT. NIGHTCLUB CORRIDOR -- NIGHT

The Gadaffis march down the corridor purposefully. The Caliph is transformed: the dopey look has gone, and he is totally fired up, about to kick off at any moment. Another disgruntled clubber appears and tries to remonstrate with them.

> CLUBBER
> I wanna know what you lot are gonna -

Without looking at the clubber, the Caliph grabs him by the skull and smashes him against the wall. The Clubber crumples to the floor. The three men stride on.

INT. HEAVENLY RELIEF -- NIGHT

Camera pans from Sam to a shocked Sylvia to an angry Harmless. They are all looking down at something.

> HARMLESS
> Fucking hell.

Sharpy lies dead on the bed. The impotence pills spilled on the floor beside him. His face is frozen in a grin.

> HARMLESS (CONT'D)
> How many did 'e 'ave ?

> SAM
> One.

> HARMLESS
> One ?! Right.

INT. LOCK -- NIGHT

The roulette wheel is bashed in and blackened. Lee looks down at it forlornly.

> JAMIE
> We said go easy with the magnet.

> BACON
> A man like Nutty Harris can only stand so much bad luck.

> LEE
> So it's my fault 'e's a nutter, is it ?

> MOON
> It's your fault 'e 'ad such bad luck.

Phone rings and Jamie picks up. Jamie says nothing at all - just turns a whiter shade of pale. Puts phone down. The others wait for an explanation.

> JAMIE
> Harmless... 'e ain't too pleased with us.

END OF ACT ONE

ACT TWO

EXT. BUILDING SITE -- NIGHT
Lads sit in the car.

> MOON
> Maybe... we... should've met 'im somewhere else ?

> LEE
> Yeah, no-one goes down to Harmless's building site in the middle
> of the night, not unless they want an underground nap.

> BACON
> Relax. We blame the Dutchies.

Car headlights appear.

> JAMIE
> (Firmly)
> Right lads. Let me do the talking.

>> CUT TO:

INT. PORTACABIN -- DAY

The four lads stand in the cabin, flanked by Mars Bar and Doorframe. Harmless
stands in front of them.

Jamie splutters pathetically:

> JAMIE
> But Mr Harmless.

> HARMLESS
> But what ?

> JAMIE
> Nothing.

> HARMLESS
> Listen. Normally, I wouldn't trust you clowns to pick up my
> laundry. But right now I got a problem. An' I ain't got time
> to dick about. Which is lucky for you cos now you got a
> chance to make it up to me.

> LEE
> Don't worry Mr Harmless, we'll -

HARMLESS
Shut up. If I don't see an Armstrong Sidley on my doorstep
tomorrow morning... you're all gonna have to learn to wank
with the other 'and... Doorframe, give 'em that Duke's address.

Doorframe hands Jamie a scrap of paper.

MOON
No problem, Mr Harmless.

BACON
Consider it done.

LEE
We're very sorry about Sharpy.

Harmless has turned his back on them.

MARS BAR
Mr Harmless wants you to leave now.

INT. DUTCHIES' VAN -- DAY

Speed garage playing. Johann is reading a book called *The Miracle of The Mind*.
Draws his open palm towards the flame of a candle.

JOHANN
Mind over matter... Watch, Jaap. Jaap?

Jaap is spinning imaginary decks, eyes half-shut, fidgeting about.

JOHANN (CONT'D)
Look.

Puts hand into flame. Pulls it straight out again.

JOHANN (CONT'D)
Ah ! Shit !

Heavy knock on the door. Jaap stands up.

JOHANN (CONT'D)
Jaap! It could be the gypsies again.

Jaap gives Johann a dismissive look and sidles over to the door. Opens it. A hand
reaches in and grabs Jaap by the collar.

BACON
Right, you're coming with us.

The four lads stand outside.

EXT. STATELY HOME -- NIGHT

On the fringes of the surrounding parkland, in a small copse, a van rolls to a halt. Lights out.

CUT TO:

The lads and Dutchies in van.

JAAP
I em sinkink maybe is better you guys go for car ent we drifink fen.

JOHANN
Jah, jah, because I em feelink so sick.

LEE
Got a note from yer Mum 'ave yer ?

JOHANN
Really I heff pain in stomach area!

BACON
You ain't gettin' away with poisonin' our clients while we carry the can. You're gonna redeem yourselves.

JAMIE
Tell us again what you 'ave to do.

JOHANN
Walkink to garage, ent comink beck quick, ent not to makink noises.

JAMIE
And checkin' if the car is in there - don't forget.

JOHANN & JAAP
Jah, jah.

Johann and Jaap speak in Dutch, which is sub-titled as throughout when they are alone:

JOHANN
I've got terrible gas building up. I just want to lie down.

178

JAAP
If anything goes wrong, we'll just run away and hide.

JAMIE
Stop pissin' about you two, an' get on with it.

JOHANN & JAAP
OK, OK.

The Dutchies get out of van.

LEE
Fifty quid says they'll fuck up.

No takers for this.

EXT. STATELY HOME -- NIGHT

Dutchies run across lawn.

EXT. STATELY HOME -- NIGHT

The Dutchies peer through a window: THE DUKE OF PEWSEY sits snoring in his armchair, a decanter and glass on the side-table. Sounds of Television X in front of him.

EXT. STATELY HOME -- NIGHT

Johann notices the puppies.

JOHANN
Jaap... look.

JAAP
Pretty.

JOHANN
Pretty angry.

A large dog stands in front of them, then walks towards them.

The Dutchies back away carefully, Johann assuming one of his martial arts positions.

CUT TO:

INT. VAN -- NIGHT

The lads sit in van.

> MOON
> I spy with my little eye something beginning with SH.

The lads look at Moon.

EXT. STABLE BLOCK -- NIGHT

Johann and Jaap run round corner into shot.

> JOHANN
> I think we lost it.

> JAAP
> Bastard bit me.

> JOHANN
> It's always you, isn't it?

> JAAP
> Oh, and mummy's little favourite, my perfect brother never
> gets hurt.

They are about to have a fraternal row when suddenly Johann sees the car in the stables. Points throught the window. Jaap gives him the thumbs up, then clenches his fist.

> JOHANN
> Wait, there might be...

Smash. Too late. Johann's arm has broken the window. Alarms go off.

> JOHANN (CONT'D)
> ... alarms.

CUT TO:

INT. STATELY HOME -- NIGHT

The Duke sits bolt upright. Eyes bloodshot.

> DUKE
> Poachers !

EXT. STATELY HOME -- NIGHT

Floodlights spark into action. Whole place lit up like a Christmas tree.

CUT TO:

INT. VAN -- NIGHT

The lads look with disbelief. Moon puts his head in his hands. Jamie starts
the van.

INT. STATELY HOME -- NIGHT

Duke takes a pike off the wall. Catches the eye of one of his ancestors staring
down from the wall.

DUKE
Run 'em back to the village with an extra arsehole, eh Gran'pa ?

Charges out.

INT. STABLE BLOCK -- NIGHT

Jaap is trying to open stable doors. Johann sits in the car, revving up.
 Jaap shakes the doors with all his might, gives up and turns to Johann with
a desperate shrug. Johann gestures for Jaap to move out of the way.

JAAP
(In Dutch)
Wait !

Johann puts his foot down. Car jerks forward.

JAAP (CONT'D)
Aaah !

Jaap leaps out the way. Car smashes through the wooden doors. Disappears into
the night.

At that moment the Duke smashes through a back door, pike in hand.

JAAP (CONT'D)
Jesus Christ !

Jaap runs out after car. Duke charges after Jaap.

DUKE
Rrra-a-a-a-ar !!

INT. VAN -- NIGHT

Jamie puts his foot down. The other three look back. The Silver Shadow comes into view, pursued by Duke.

LADS
They got it ! They got the car !

EXT. STATELY HOME -- NIGHT

DUKE
I've got the bugger Gran'pa, I've got 'im !

Duke lunges at Jaap's arse with the pike. Jaap jumps onto the running-board.

Johann is looking over his shoulder as he drives straight between the gate posts...

JAAP
Look out!

Johann turns round again, sees that he is just about to crash into the dog who is standing in front of them, swerves at the last minute to avoid the collision (but has gone off in the opposite direction to the lads).

Duke is left behind, bellowing Etonian oaths into the night.

INT. VAN -- NIGHT

BACON
They've gone the other way!

JAMIE
Eh ?... Shit, we better turn back.

MOON
No fucking way. Did yer see that geezer with the spear ?

EXT. SILVER SHADOW -- NIGHT

Johann stops the car. Jaap is high on adrenaline and rummages through the glove compartment and finds leather gloves and goggles.

JAAP
Johann, check this out.

Puts the gloves and goggles on. Johann is not especially interested.

JAAP (CONT'D)
I feel like I'm in a movie. Maybe a porno movie. Maybe we'll
see some hitch-hikers !

Jaap tries to put the goggles on Johann, who has had enough.

> JOHANN
> What's the matter with you ?

> JAAP
> Me ?

> JOHANN
> Yeah. You are pushing everything too far. You shouldn't take
> so many drugs - especially our drugs.

> JAAP
> I thought you'd changed, but no you're still a total square.

> JOHANN
> I blame Mum for breast-feeding you 'til you were three.

> JAAP
> You're so square you should wear a tie.

This is the ultimate insult. Johann is furious.

Jaap folds his arms.

Johann steps out of the car and walks round to Jaap's side.

Johann opens Jaap's door and grabs Jaap.

> JAAP (CONT'D)
> Get off ! Hey ! Are you going mad?

They struggle. Johann tries to lift Jaap out of the car.

> JAAP (CONT'D)
> You're crazy.

Jaap grabs the lining of the roof and the steering wheel. Johann pulls at
Jaap's feet.

> JAAP (CONT'D)
> Help.

Johann leans back and pulls on Jaap's legs with all his might. The roof
lining rips...

Bank notes fall out of the roof lining. Hundreds of them. The Dutchies freeze.

183

EXT. LOCK -- NIGHT

A shot of the Gadaffi brothers at the door. Ali bangs on the door. The Caliph paces up and down madly.

                                                              CUT TO:

INT. VAN -- NIGHT

The lads are down the road, watching from inside the van.

                          LEE
           Looks like the Caliph's off his sweeties.

                         MOON
                  What do they want ?

                        JAMIE
              More drugs, knowin' them.

                        BACON
        Yeah, well they can fuck off. Let's get out of 'ere.

Jamie puts the van into reverse.

                        JAMIE
                  Where to, lads ?

                         MOON
        Lapland don't shut for another half an hour.

                         LADS
                          No.

                        BACON
    Might as well just go and crash at the Dutchies' place. They'll
                  turn up sooner or later.

INT. HARMLESS'S KITCHEN -- NIGHT

Harmless stands looking out of window, sweating, hair sticking up.
Sylvia walks into kitchen.

                        SYLVIA
                You want some hot milk ?

> HARMLESS
> (Hoarsely)
> I want my fucking car.

Sylvia looks at him blankly. What's he talking about ?

> HARMLESS (CONT'D)
> The fuckin' money's in it !

> SYLVIA
> In the car ?

> HARMLESS
> Sewn into the fuckin' roof.

Sylvia shakes her head in weary disbelief.

> SYLVIA
> Oh, Larry...

> HARMLESS
> Weren't that bad an idea.

EXT. WAREHOUSE -- DAWN

Johann and Jaap, carrying a bag, follow a fat old man in a dressing gown and slippers - FUNNY MONEY. Funny Money has a pit-bull on a leash, and love–hate tattoos on his knuckles.

> FUNNY MONEY
> Who give yer my name then ?

> JOHANN
> Effrybotty say you are number one guy for printink money.

> FUNNY MONEY
> Hmm, well you're in luck anyway. We just printed off a new
> batch. We got this new geezer in, knows how to beat the
> ultra-violet scan.

They arrive at Funny Money's garage. Funny Money opens the many different locks. The Dutchies lapse into their native tongue, which is sub-titled.

> JAAP
> Maybe we can buy an island. One of those Polygamous islands.

> JOHANN
> You mean Polynesian Islands ?

                         JAAP
No, Polygamous. A place where we can have lots of wives.

                        JOHANN
                    (Condescending)
                Is that really spiritual ?

                         JAAP
                     (Muttering)
                    Who cares ?

Funny Money lifts the door of the garage, revealing printing machines, an old
computer, and a drawing board. Piles of cash. The Dutchies follow him in.
Funny Money turns his back for a second and, quick as a flash, Jaap takes a wad
of cash off a pile and slips it into his pocket. Johann nudges him, the Pit Bull
growls. Funny Money turns round:

                     FUNNY MONEY
                How much do you want ?

                    JOHANN & JAAP
                        Fill it !

They hold up an empty bag.

INT. DUTCHIES' VAN -- MORNING

Lads are crashed out around the camper. Moon is snoring.

                        BACON
                    Put a sock in it.

Lee picks up a Dutchie tennis sock and starts to lower it into Moon's gaping
mouth. Stops as he hears the two Dutchies arrive.

                                                            CUT TO:

EXT. DUTCHIES' VAN -- DAWN

Jaap reaches for a bag marked with a cross. Johann reaches for a bag with a zero
on it. Jaap points to Johann's bag:

                         JAAP
                No, the one with the zero is fake.

Johann points at Jaap's bag:

>   JOHANN
> The circle represents oneness. Truth. The cross is a symbol
>   of conflict and falsity.

>   JAAP
> I made up a rhyme to help remember: 'The real money is
> marked with a cross, Johann is not my fucking boss.'

>   JOHANN
>   (Scornful)
>   Very funny, Jaap.

>   JAAP
>   You sure that's the real money?

>   JOHANN
>   (Patronisingly)
>   I marked the bags.

They take the bag with the zero on it over to the van and throw it onto the
passenger seat. They go back to the car and carry the bag with the cross on
it round to the back of the van, singing:

>   JOHANN & JAAP (O.O.V.)
> Money, money, money... Aaaah all the things I could do, if I...

INT. DUTCHIES' VAN -- DAY

Dutchies open the door, turn the light on and stop singing.

All the lads are sitting up.

>   JOHANN & JAAP
>   Aaah !

They drop the bag, and cash spills out. Lads clock this.

>   JAMIE
> Where the... if you've sold that fucking car I'll kill you.

>   JAAP
>   No, no, za dough was in za - za...

>   JOHANN
>   ... in za car, en' za car is outside.

Lee runs his eye over the cash.

187

LADS
Must be about a million.

EXT. BUILDING SITE -- MORNING

The Spanish mobsters, led by El Torro are standing listening to Mars Bar, who is doing his best to remember his lines:

MARS BAR
Er, he's not here... he's gone to pick up some money... for some
Spanish blokes... who he's givin' the money to tonight.

El Torro looks at his colleagues. No-one believes that Harmless is not there, but it doesn't matter.

EL TORRO
Tell him to come to my hotel at six o'clock. Any later an'
I'm gonna -

His next few words are drowned out by the scream of a pneumatic drill starting up, making Mars Bar jump.

EXT. LOCK, YARD -- MORNING

Lads van arrives back. Silver Shadow is already there, Moon leaning on the bonnet as if he owns it.

LEE
What took yer ?

Bacon, Jamie and Moon climb out of the van. Jamie tosses the keys up and down in his palm.

BACON
Sorted ?

LEE
Shoulda seen 'ow many looks I got. This is a babe magnet,
mate, I'm tellin' yer. We might be able to keep it.

BACON
Yeah, right.

LEE
It's obvious - Harmless only wanted the dosh that was inside of it.

JAMIE
Ask Harmless if 'e'll let you 'ave it for yer birthday.

                         MOON
                 I can smell somethin'.

                          LEE
                         What ?

                         MOON
        Double egg, sausage, bacon, mushrooms, beans and fried
                  bread. Tea with two sugars.

Instant agreement from everyone.

                         BACON
                       Le's do it.

INT. PORTACABIN -- MORNING

Mars Bar enters portacabin. Harmless and Doorframe are waiting for him.

                        HARMLESS
                       Spics gone ?

                        MARS BAR
                         Yeah...

Mars Bar looks pale, wipes his brow.

                        HARMLESS
                  You alright Mars Bar ?

                        MARS BAR
        That bloke with the funny eye... e's a bit... sick in't 'e ?

                        HARMLESS
            Yeah, they do get a bit emotional, that lot.

                        MARS BAR
                    Bit too emotional.

Mars Bar sits down.

                        HARMLESS
               Right, I better go pick my car up.

INT. DUTCHIES' VAN -- DAY

Jaap and Johann staring at the money with the zero on it. Smoking out in
a big way.

                    JOHANN
    See? All through history... the circle symbolised truth.

                    JAAP
                 (Not interested)
                    Yeah?

                    JOHANN
    Yeah. And the cross, symbolised, y'know, all the fucked-upness
                    of life.

                    JAAP
                 Like money.

                    JOHANN
                Yeah, like money.

                    JAAP
        So the cross symbolises money.

                    JOHANN
                  It can...

                    JAAP
    So why have we got a bag with a zero on it?

Contemplative silence becomes uneasy silence.

                    JOHANN
                    Jaap?

They look at each other.

                 JOHANN & JAAP
            This ain't the real money...

Jaap sits bolt upright, wide awake.

INT. LOCK KITCHEN -- DAY

Moon is tucking into his fry-up. The others have teas and coffees, and peruse
the papers. Idle atmosphere.

                    LEE
              That'll keep you awake.
                    MOON
                (With mouth full)
              Will it bollocks.

                    190

BACON
I am gonna sleep like a baby.

JAMIE
Jokin' int yer ? We got to get that car to Harmless.

BACON
Yeah well that ain't exactly the difficult bit is it ?

JAMIE
I ain't gonna relax 'til I see Harmless standing in front of 'is
car, with that bag in his hand and a big smile on 'is face, sayin'
'Nice one lads, you're off the hook.'

BACON
Chill out Jamie. After breakfast we'll get the bag of cash out
the safe, stick it in the motor, and drive it over to Harmless's.

A look of extreme anxiety crosses Lee's face. Jamie clocks this.

JAMIE
Fuck off Lee, you can't wind me up that easy. I know there is
no way you woulda left that bag in the back of the motor -
where any old mug could just walk past and pick it up.

Lee stands up and rushes out.

JAMIE (CONT'D)
Oh my God.

Jamie and Bacon run to the door, then Bacon runs back to grab Moon -
who hasn't moved yet - and drag him away from his plate.

EXT. LOCK, YARD -- DAY

Johann and Jaap climb over the wall with the bulging bag.

EXT. LOCK -- DAY

Harmless pulls up in his Jag. Steps out.

EXT. LOCK, YARD -- DAY

Johann and Jaap look into the Silver Shadow. They see the other bag just sitting
there on the back seat. Jaap gives Johann an I-told-you-so look:

JAAP
See? 'The real money is marked with a cross. Johann's not my fuckin -'

191

JOHANN
Shhh...

There are footsteps. Jaap quickly swaps the bags around. Sound of someone rattling the gates to the yard. Scratching sound of lock being attacked.

HARMLESS (O.O.V.)
Ah, fuck it.

END OF ACT TWO

ACT THREE

EXT. LOCK, YARD -- LATER

Panning shot of the lads' reactions to the sight of Harmless on the deck. Moon is cool under pressure. He crouches over Harmless's body then stands, holding up a vanity mirror without any condensation on it.

MOON
Dead, alright.

He throws the mirror aside.

LEE
What is goin' on ?

BACON
We got a dead man lyin' in our yard, in broad daylight...

JAMIE
A dead man who has a lot of nasty friends.

Moon checks the car.

MOON
Whoever done Harmless didn't know about the cash.

BACON
'Ang on, that means we are seriously up on this deal...

LEE
We could disappear with this.

JAMIE
Wake up lads, if anyone sees this old fart pegged out in our

yard, we'll disappear for free. Now 'ow we gonna get rid of
him and his stupid car ?

                    MOON
        What about that land-fill site in Romford ?

                    BACON
            He'll be in good company there.

                    JAMIE
            Nice one. Give us a hand.

Stoops to pick up Harmless. Bacon picks up his feet.

                    BACON
            Christ, what's he made of ?

Moon opens the boot of the Roller and they bundle Harmless in. Moon shuts the
boot.

                    JAMIE
        From now on, we keep the money with us at all times.

They all jump into the Roller and Moon reverses out. A big Audi with tinted
windows blocks their way. Moon leans out of the window to dish out abuse.

                    MOON
            Move yer fat arse, pal, I'm comin' out !

Three figures step out of the Audi.

                    MOON (CONT'D)
                    Oh, shit.

EXT. STREET -- DAY

Johann and Jaap walk down the street, pleased with themselves. They stop
outside a tobacconist. Jaap reaches into his pocket and pulls out a £50 note.

                    JAAP
        Let's get some big fat cigars and celebrate. Listen Johann, I'm
            sorry I've been a pain in the arse.

                    JOHANN
        You're just over-excited. It's your first business trip to England.

                    JAAP
            Yeah... brothers shouldn't argue.

They embrace, then Jaap goes into the shop. There is a shout from inside, and then Jaap comes tearing out. Holding the bank-note in his hand. He grabs Johann by the shoulder and pulls him along.

> JAAP (CONT'D)
> Come on.

EXT. LOCK, YARD -- DAY

The lads are all out of the car. The Gadaffis stand facing them. This is a big scene for the brothers but the lads are irritated, they haven't got time for this.

> ALI
> We were gonna kill you.

> JAMIE
> Oh, right.

> ALI
> The Caliph still wants to kill you. But I am being nice today.

> JAMIE
> What're we supposed to 'ave done ?

> MEHMET
> You... have made us look like fools. You peddled us dodgy gear.

> BACON
> Weren't our kit, mate.

> MEHMET
> You were sellin' it.

> MOON
> It was the Dutchies' gear - you know that.

> ALI
> We like your car.

> LEE
> Nah, that ain't ours.

> JAMIE
> (Interrupting)
> Hang about, Lee.

> ALI
> We'll take your car, and call it quits.

194

The other lads realise what Jamie is thinking and pretend to find this hard to swallow.

                              JAMIE
                    I dunno... that's a bit harsh.

Ali laughs, then goes dead serious.

                               ALI
                       We'll take the car.

The Caliph opens the car door.

                              BACON
                 Better just get me bag out yer way.

The Caliph pulls out machete.

                          BACON (CONT'D)
                    Jesus... no worries, eh ?

Bacon steps back again. Ali puts his hand on the Caliph's shoulder.

                               ALI
                You don't know how lucky you been today.

Mehmet gets into the back. Ali gets into the front. The Caliph gets into the Audi. They drive off.

                              JAMIE
                    Well, that was lucky.

                               LEE
                          Lucky ?!

                              JAMIE
           No-one's gonna come lookin' for us while they got Harmless's
                  car with Harmless's body in the boot.

                              BACON
                  And all Harmless's cash...

                              MOON
            Yeah, what about the bloody cash, Jamie ?

Jamie walks off.

                              JAMIE
                  Some people are never happy.

INT. SWEATSHOP -- DAY

Ali drives the Silver Shadow into the delivery bay and the door closes behind
it. Mehmet is already standing there. As Ali and the Caliph climb out, Mehmet
notices the bag on the back seat and hauls it out.

                              ALI
                       Allah be praised...

Mehmet looks inside. A whoop of delight. Ali turns to show the Caliph, who
does a weird dervish dance across the factory floor. Kids at machines stop work
and stare at the three overlords, celebrating.

The Sweatshop Kid leans over to his neighbour:

                         SWEATSHOP KID
                  You ever seen them smile before ?

The other kid shakes his head. They both look terrified.

The Caliph has danced all the way down the aisle. He swings his machete round
his head and plunges it into the MDF wall.

                              ALI
                     It's your day off, kids.

                            MEHMET
                     Go on, take the day off !

All the kids sit behind their machines, petrified.

                              ALI
             What's the matter with you ? Get up, get out, go on.

                          THE CALIPH
                           Get out !

The Caliph shoos them away. They get the message and scuttle off the
factory floor.

                              ALI
                     Let's get some girls in.

Mehmet picks up the phone and dials.

MEHMET
What do we want ?

ALI
Three blondes. And tell 'em to bring some downers for the Caliph.

INT. LOCK -- DAY

CLOSE-UP of a £50 note held up to the light.

JOHANN
Zis is real ?

Lads and Dutchies look down at the note.

JAMIE
No it bloody ain't. Now wha's goin' on ?

CUT TO:

INT. SWEATSHOP -- DAY

The boot of the Silver Shadow is banged open. An arm and a leg loll out.

Harmless clambers out like a zombie from the grave. Holds his head. Looks around him. Hears sounds of celebration. Peers through onto factory floor and sees the Gadaffi brothers. Reaches into pocket for mobile. Speaks in hushed voice. Backs out carefully towards the door.

HARMLESS
Mars Bar... Round up the boys. Kit 'em out. Meet me round
the back of the Gadaffis' place... NOW, Mars Bar, NOW.

CUT BACK TO:

INT. LOCK -- DAY

Johann and Jaap are struggling to explain the bank note being held in their faces.

JOHANN
Is case of going little crazy, jah?

JAAP
Jah, is take too much da pill an' freak out...

JOHANN
Jah, jah...

197

JAAP
Mush... mush...

JOHANN
Jaap brain is mush.

BACON
Get to the point.

JOHANN
Is fake.

JAMIE
We know it's fake, where did you get it ?

JOHANN
Zis guy zey are callink Funny Money is sellink to us fake
money ent we are makeink exchange wiz real money for
keepink ent liffink life of millionaire.

JAAP
But we are puttink in car real money ent keepink fake money,
ent forgettink and confusink two times ent.

The lads are well pissed off. They start pushing the Dutchies.

LEE
Do you know what would've 'appened if we gave Harmless a
sack of fake notes ?

JAMIE
We'd be dead.

BACON
I should deck the both of yer.

Johann and Jaap are close to tears.

JAAP
We are feelink to you so sorry !

JAMIE
Stop snivelling.

The lads turn away from them in disgust.

MOON
We should go an' nick the money.

                    BACON
                  You what?

                    MOON
    The real money. We should just go and get it back off the
          Gadaffis, we got nuffin' to lose.

                    LEE
              'Cept our lives.

                    JAMIE
        'Ang about... 'ang about. Moon's right.

We see the van turn off the street.

                 JAMIE (CONT'D)
    We'll pretend to be Harmless's mob. We get tooled up, steam
    in there, get the money off 'em an'... easy life, 'ere we come.

Van pulls up outside the sweatshop.

                                                    CUT TO:

INT. VAN -- DAY

Two Dutchies sit in front of van. Four lads in the back. They wear tracksuits and
balaclavas and carry sawn-offs.

                    JAMIE
    Jaap, you keep the engine runnin' an' the doors open, right ?

                    JAAP
                Dead right.

                    LEE
          Don't use that word.

                    BACON
                (To Dutchies)
        You boys keep yer minds on the job, right ?

Johann and Jaap point to the cans of Mad Cow they are drinking and nod firmly.

                    LEE
                (To Jamie)
        You sure this is gonna go alright ?

                        JAMIE
                   Nah, not at all.

                         LEE
                        Fine.

                        BACON
                Le's jus' do it then shall we ?

Everyone nods. Jaap fires the engine. All lads take deep breaths.

                   BACON (CONT'D)
                     Go, go, g -

                        MOON
                  'Old on, 'old on...

Jaap brakes.

                        BACON
                       WHAT ?!

                        MOON
                Me gun's got caught on something.

EXT. STREET OUTSIDE SWEATSHOP -- DAY

Harmless's van pulls up. Mars Bar, Doorframe and three other henchmen wave
to Harmless. They have automatic weapons and also balaclavas.

                      HARMLESS
                Right let's sort those bastards out.

Harmless climbs into the van.

EXT. SWEATSHOP -- DAY

Two vans reversing towards each other. Doors of both are flung open. Everyone
freezes. Everyone wears a balaclava and holds a gun. Panic on both sides.

                        JAMIE
                   Who are you?!

                      HARMLESS
                   Who are you?!

                        LADS
                Put the guns down!

HARMLESS
Put the guns down? I say put the fucking guns down!

Everyone is shouting at once. Guns waggle back and forth. Harmless takes a decisive step forward and silences the melee.

HARMLESS (CONT'D)
Who the 'ell are you?!

JAMIE
(Disguising voice)
Back off pal, we're working for Larry Harmless.

Pause.

HARMLESS
Is that right, sunshine ?

Harmless pulls off his balaclava.

JAMIE
Shit, we thought... we thought we'd... give you a hand !

HARMLESS
You what ? Who are you?

LEE
It's us, innit lads ?

They lift up balaclavas to show their faces.

BACON
We came 'ere to get your car back.

HARMLESS
(Sceptical)
Shot anyone lately 'ave yer ?

Harmless pulls his balaclava down.

HARMLESS (CONT'D)
You lads stay at the back. And take it easy. I don't wanna get shot up the arse with any of your friendly fire, alright ?

Lads nod, and pull balaclavas down.

INT. SWEATSHOP -- DAY

Ali and Mehmet are sitting at a table. They are putting money back in the bag.

> ALI
> (Shouting)
> Caliph, I told you not to mix tea an' tequila.

> MEHMET
> He's gonna be too sick to do anything to a girl, innit?

> ALI
> We won't let her go to waste.

Mehmet laughs. We hear retching in the background.

EXT. SWEATSHOP -- DAY

The Balaclava mob stand poised by the door, guns cocked and checked.
Moon whispers:

> MOON
> This is a bit serious.

> LEE
> Maybe we should, y'know...

> MOON
> Run ?

> JAMIE
> Bit late now.

INT. SWEATSHOP, TOILETS -- DAY

The Caliph lifts his head up from the bowl. He looks awful.

INT. SWEATSHOP -- DAY

Ali closes money bag and puts it to side of room.

EXT. SWEATSHOP -- DAY

> HARMLESS
> (To his firm)
> Ready.

His firm all nod.

HARMLESS (CONT'D)
(To the lads)
Ready.

LADS
Er... yeah.

Mumbles, throat-clearings - they don't sound too confident.

INT. SWEATSHOP -- DAY

Doors burst open. Ali and Mehmet jump up. Harmless and his mob steam in.
The lads follow up. Harmless fires a warning shot.

INT. SWEATSHOP, TOILETS -- DAY

The Caliph hears the shot. Pulls out two Colt 45s. Still looking pretty sick.

INT. SWEATSHOP -- DAY

Seen from lads P.O.V:

HARMLESS
Don't you fuckin' move. Don't you fuckin' move.

Ali and Mehmet look blankly at the mob. They start stepping back. Their guns
are behind them on another table.

Jamie and Bacon glance at each other.

MARS BAR
Take one more step, an' your brains are gonna be sprayin' the walls.

INT. VAN -- DAY

The Dutchies are nervous. So nervous that they are unable to speak Dutch.

Jaap is rubbing his gums with speed, he is totally off his tits.

JAAP
Let's go ent take money ent swappink again.

JOHANN
You total crazy...

JAAP
Jah is crazy! We live on edge of life! Come on, we are only
live once!

203

JOHANN
We are only live five minute if we go in zere! Jaap? Jaap?!

Jaap is already running towards the sweatshop. Johann runs after him - to stop him rather than to follow.

INT. SWEATSHOP -- DAY

Ali is grinning. The atmosphere is tense.

HARMLESS
What... are you grinnin' at ?

ALI
You're makin' a big mistake.

Harmless has to laugh at this.

HARMLESS
Is that right ? D'you hear that, lads ? We've made a mistake.

MARS BAR
(Mock worry)
Oh no, guv, what we gonna do ?

HARMLESS
We'd better say sorry, hadn't we ?

Jamie does not share their confidence. Through-out this section the Dutchies edge towards bag of cash in back of shot.

JAMIE
Er, Larry...

HARMLESS
Sorry, son, you say something ?

JAMIE
The er... Caliph is not here.

HARMLESS
That's always good news isn't it?

JAMIE
Just wonderin' if he might be y'know, around somewhere.

HARMLESS
(Dismissive)
Looks like he's too scared to come out. Come on lads, hurry up.

The Caliph charges in from the side shooting. Mars Bar and Harmless fire at him as he runs up between the sewing machines. He eventually falls.

Doorframe is pointing his gun at Mehmet and Ali. They are unable to move.

The Caliph, before he dies, manages to aim his gun at Doorframe and shoot him. Ali and Mehmet use this opportunity to dive into their office.

Harmless and Mars Bar see Doorframe being shot, they turn and start to fire at Ali and Mehmet. They do a gangster-style Tommy-Gun shoot up of the office.

During this the Dutchies run in, alongside the car, behind Harmless and Mars Bar and exchange the bags by the table. And run back out.

CUT TO:

EXT. SWEATSHOP -- DAY

The Dutchies run out of sweatshop with bag. Johann is snivelling. Jaap is punching the air in triumph, totally ecstatic.

JAAP
I am alive! I am alive!

JOHANN
(sobbing)
I was nearly die...

JAAP
That was a sign... zat I am indestrucible, choosing by God.

JOHANN
You so wrong. Zat was sign of chaos ent... ent... violence in za
crazy head of us.

They climb into car and drive off.

INT. SWEATSHOP -- DAY

Harmless and Mars Bar stop firing. The office is riddled with holes, broken glass etc. Paper floats gently down, and wisps of gun smoke envelope the office. The two occupants are spectacularly dead.

Harmless is extremely pleased with this scenario.

> HARMLESS
> Al Capone... you are nothing.

> MARS BAR
> Shame about the office.
> (Looks around)
> Shame about Doorframe.

> HARMLESS
> Ah well, never mind. Let's get the cash and get out of here.

Mars Bar grabs the cash - glancing at Doorframe's body he is aware that his own death would get just about as much sympathy.

The lads stand up, taking off the balaclavas. Sweaty brows, hair sticking up. Very shocked. Lee wobbles as if he might have been shot in the legs.

> LEE
> Something wrong with me knees.

Harmless and Mars Bar lead the way out, the lads follow.

EXT. SWEATSHOP -- DAY

The lads look at the space where the van is not. Two cans of Mad Cow on the ground.

> BACON
> Those bloody Dutchies.

> JAMIE
> Er, Mr Harmless ?

Harmless turns around.

> JAMIE (CONT'D)
> Can we 'ave a lift ?

Harmless looks at him suspiciously.

CUT TO:

INT. VAN -- DAY

Dutchies drive away, a bit frantic.

                           JAAP
Zat was better zan best orgasm I am ever heff. Multiply times million!

Jaap shoves his hands deep into the sack of cash.

                      JAAP (CONT'D)
Times t'ree millions! T'ree million Gild -

Freezes, stares at the paper in his hands.

                      JAAP (CONT'D)
Is fake... Is fake, Johann, is fake, what happen?

                          JOHANN
I am not care.

                           JAAP
You not care? Is t'ree mill -

                          JOHANN
Is real, is fake, so what? Today I nearly die...

                           JAAP
No, no, no...

Jaap starts rummaging round in the glove compartment, looking for his speed.

                      JAAP (CONT'D)
Johann?

                          JOHANN
I need spiritual guidance. I need to get back to the
Karmarama Lodge and meditate like fuck.

                           JAAP
I need to meditate but I just want to take some more Speed.

                          JOHANN
Is finish.

Jaap roars with frustration.

INT. HARMLESS'S VAN -- DAY

The lads are in the back of the van with Mars Bar. Harmless is up front with the
driver. Van pulls up outside a hotel. Harmless and the driver get out and walk
round to the back.

HARMLESS
You lads, stay here.

Harmless and Mars Bar haul the bag out. The driver goes with them into
the lobby.

The lads all breathe a huge sigh of relief.

INT. HOTEL ROOM -- DAY

The Spanish are watching Harmless intently.

HARMLESS
You see ? P'raps you doubted me. But there is, as they say,
honour amongst businessmen. Mars Bar ?

On cue, Mars Bar drags the bag of cash forward and the two of them lift it up
onto the coffee table. El Torro nods approvingly. He reaches in and pulls out a
note. Looks at it. Looks at Harmless. Holds the note up and then looks at
Harmless again, his face full of fury.

EL TORRO
You are takin' the piss out of me.

EXT. DUTCHIES' VAN -- DAY

Johann builds a bonfire with the 'fake' money.

JOHANN
(Contemptuously)
Goodbye material world.

INT. VAN -- DAY

The lads in the back of the van hear:

HARMLESS (O.O.V.)
Noooooooo !

The lads hear a loud thud on the roof of their van. Then Harmless' face appears
at the top of the windscreen and slides down followed by the rest of his body.
Notes flutter down on top of him. He seems to be staring at them upside-down.

HARMLESS
Er... fuck.

Dies. Lads look at one another.

                              BACON
                         Those bloody...

                               LADS
                           ...Dutchies.

EXT. DUTCHIES' VAN -- DAY

Johann is trying to light his bonfire but the match keeps blowing out.

                              JAAP
                          What is zis?

                             JOHANN
          I startink new life. You sink this money is fake?
                         (pause for effect)
                       ALL money is fake.

Johann and Jaap stare at each other, pondering the incredible deepness of this
last comment. Johann lights a match. Mobile phone rings in van. Jaap goes
back to the van.

EXT. STREET, NEAR HOTEL -- DAY

Lads walk down the road with Jamie on the phone.

                              JAMIE
                  C'mon, c'mon, answer it you twats.

INT. DUTCHIES' VAN -- DAY

Jaap picks up the mobile.

                              JAAP
          Yo. No, no, zis is Jaap. Jordi is in mental institution in Hook
                          of Hollant...

EXT. STREET, NEAR HOTEL -- DAY

The lads stand waiting on tenterhooks as Jamie tries to get the message across.

                              JAMIE
             Johann, whatever... that money you got is real.

EXT. STREET, NEAR HOTEL -- DAY

Johann has now found a Zippo and a bottle of paraffin.

EXT. STREET, NEAR HOTEL -- DAY

Jamie tucks his mobile back inside his jacket.

> MOON
> What did 'e say ?

> JAMIE
> Sorted. Says they got it. Let's get round there.

INT. DUTCHIES' VAN -- DAY

Jaap goes white. Mobile drops from his ear to the floor.

EXT. DUTCHIES' VAN -- DAY

Jaap bursts out of the van. Johann's face is lit up with pyromaniac glee.

> JAAP
> Noooooo !

> END

EPISODE 4

LOCK, STOCK... & SPAGHETTI SAUCE

by Chris Baker and Andrew Day

ACT ONE

INT. UNDERGROUND GARAGES -- NIGHT

A garage door is lifted revealing a tied-up figure – BILL. He starts to squirm and his eyes open wide in fear. A shadow appears in the doorway. A naked bulb is switched on, and SPAGHETTI EDDY is revealed. A large man of about 45. He has earned his nickname by copying Italian gangsters: his Armani overcoat is draped over his shoulders, he chews on a cigar, top-dollar jewellery glints from his neck and knuckles, and his quiet speech is punctuated by small hand gestures. His henchman, TONY 'PEACEMAKER' GIBBS, walks in. He is carrying a workbench and a toolbox. He waits to be told where to put the equipment.

> SPAGHETTI
> Just there.

Spaghetti stoops and rips the gaffer tape off Bill's mouth.

> BILL
> Please, Spaghetti... I won't sell no more gear. I'll disappear,
> won't I? You won't 'ear nothing from me ever –

Tony picks up a hacksaw.

> SPAGHETTI
> Do it careful, Tony.

> TONY
> Don't worry boss, I've got CSE woodwork.

Tony drops the bench heavily.

Spaghetti turns back to Bill.

> SPAGHETTI
> Fing is Bill, this filthy business... is my filthy business. You was
> warned, an' you didn't take no notice.

Spaghetti pulls a videotape out of his pocket.

> SPAGHETTI (CONT'D)
> Your only hope is that I'm in a lovin' mood today.

He whacks Bill in the face with the tape.

SPAGHETTI (CONT'D)
I'm not. I never am.

Spaghetti nods at Tony who picks up the struggling Bill.

BILL
Wait, wait, wait, wait –

An oily rag is stuffed in his mouth. Tony brandishes a hacksaw.

TONY
Right...

SPAGHETTI
Tony... Use the mallet. We ain't got time to mop up.

Tony is disappointed. Swaps the hacksaw for a mallet as Spaghetti leans over Bill.

SPAGHETTI (CONT'D)
The porn world's under new management. Night, night.

Mallet comes down.

CUT TO:

EXT. OLD CHURCHYARD -- DAY

STYLISED SHOTS, JUMP CUTS: Back door of van swings open. Heavy-duty metal cases are slid out. BACON, JAMIE, MOON and LEE are in sharp suits, a couple of them smoking. They unpack all the equipment. Massive close-ups make it look like some kind of weapon they are assembling rather than what it is – a video camera and a few lights. The lads look very professional.

MOON
Right.

Moon hoists the camera onto Lee's shoulder.

LEE
Let's do the business.

SLOW MOTION as lads walk up the path – *Reservoir Dogs* style – to the church where a wedding party is gathering outside.

JAMIE (V.O.)
This is a lucrative little number... five hundred quid to turn up,
stand around, an' get pissed...

CUT TO:

EXT. OLD CHURCHYARD -- DAY

Camera tracks towards Jamie and an OLDER WOMAN.

JAMIE (V.O.)
An' of course... see what other perks are on offer...

Jamie is writing his phone number in biro on the inside of the woman's wrist.
It tickles, she giggles.

JAMIE
Nah, you look fantastic. Only thing missin' 's a pair of wings
on yer back... honest. That silk?

Strokes the sleeve of her dress. She nods.

JAMIE (CONT'D)
Suits you.

Camera whips round and we cut away.

CUT TO:

EXT. OLD CHURCHYARD -- DAY

Two families glare at each other. Atmosphere of unease. Comments are
beginning to be exchanged.

JAMIE (V.O.)
Mind you, we oughta get paid up front for some of these dos.

Camera turns and bears down on a heavily PREGNANT BRIDE looking
uncomfortable in her dress, staring forlornly at the two unhappy families.
Jamie, Lee and Moon try to jolly things along but it's not working.

JAMIE (V.O.) (CONT'D)
You know why they call 'em shotgun weddings? They can go off at any time.

A fight between two women breaks out.

CUT TO:

EXT. OLD CHURCHYARD -- DAY

Bacon is filming the bride sitting on the steps crying. BRIDE'S FATHER and
MOTHER try to comfort her.

                        JAMIE (V.O.)
        Sometimes there's even the opportunity to earn a bit on
                            the side.

                                                        CUT TO:

INT. CHURCH -- DAY

                        JAMIE (V.O.)
            But... there's usually an 'appy endin'...

Sound of bridal march. SEMI-CONSCIOUS GROOM is helped up the aisle by
Jamie, Moon and Lee. Jamie winks at the bride's father. Bride stands waiting in
front of the altar, smiling again.

                                                        CUT TO:

EXT. OLD CHURCHYARD -- DAY

BRIDE throws her bouquet high in the air above a throng of girls.

                        JAMIE (V.O.)
            Yeah... we're always willin' to do a bit extra...

Lee catches it.

                            LEE
            Alright, girls 'ow much you offering?

                                                        CUT TO:

EXT. OLD CHURCHYARD -- DAY

Moon's eye is jammed against the eyepiece.

                        JAMIE (V.O.)
            It's true, subtlety ain't our strong point...

                            MOON
    Yeah... yeah... that's right girls, give it to me, yeah... come on
                gimme a little more... that's right...

He's filming four tipsy BRIDESMAIDS hitching up their dresses to show garters.

                        JAMIE (V.O.)
            ... But we get into the spirit of it.

EXT. OLD CHURCHYARD -- DAY

JAMIE (V.O.)
... To make sure it all goes off with a bang...

At the back of the churchyard, the four tipsy bridesmaids are getting a seeing-to from the four lads.

CUT TO:

EXT. SAUCE TV STATION -- AFTERNOON

A black Merc pulls up. Tony climbs out and joins Spaghetti, who stands watching electricians erecting the Sauce TV logo. As they reach Spaghetti's side, Tony takes out a folded list.

SPAGHETTI
Done?

TONY
Yeah, we 'ad some fun with ole Porky. You was right about them jump leads.

SPAGHETTI
Yer not meant to 'ave fun, Tony.

Spaghetti and Tony walk into the building.

CUT TO:

INT. SAUCE TV STATION, RECEPTION AREA -- AFTERNOON

DIZZY BIRD on reception. Techies walk up and down. Security guards nod at Spaghetti as he passes.

TONY
Only one left is this Kraut bloke, Heinrich, or somefin'.

Spaghetti stops walking.

TONY (CONT'D)
He ain't been seen. Doubt 'e's in the country.

SPAGHETTI
'E's in the country... I know it.

CUT TO:

INT. BLACK MERCEDES -- NIGHT (FLASHBACK)

The car is stationary. Spaghetti is interviewing HEINRICH (about 40, mullet-haired, German, thinks he is incredibly cool) in the back of the Merc. Spaghetti speaks very softly. There is an atmosphere of creepy intimacy.

SPAGHETTI
Heinrich... every deal you do with one of my enemies, I lose
out. You're takin' money out my pocket.

HEINRICH
Spaghetti... a lot of guys want to make business with me...

SPAGHETTI
Next time you come and blitz London, you're gunner find
there ain't so many customers around.

HEINRICH
Come on, why not everybody just have a piece of the cake? It's cool.

SPAGHETTI
Don't give me that Euro hippy shit. This is England. Winner takes all.

CUT TO:

EXT. STREET -- NIGHT

The Black Merc screeches away as its door is pulled shut. Camera pans round to Heinrich, getting up off the floor, looking shocked.

CUT BACK TO:

INT. SAUCE TV STATION, RECEPTION AREA -- AFTERNOON

SPAGHETTI
Listen,'e's been makin' a dent in my business for two years.
Cos I fancied 'is 'Amburg connections, I gave 'im the chance to
come in. He didn't take it. That makes 'im a piss-taker.

Spaghetti turns away from Tony, who sighs – he's still got work to do.

CUT TO:

INT. STUDIO SET -- AFTERNOON

Tacky set. A naked GIRL IN A CHEF'S HAT is frying sausages. STUART, the Director, has a fatherly arm over her shoulder as he shows her how he wants her to fry them. Enter Spaghetti.

                    SPAGHETTI
          Fuck's sake Stuart, what are those?

Stuart follows Spaghetti's pointing finger all the way to the poor girl's tits.

                SPAGHETTI (CONT'D)
    They're not double-D. I want melons, not fried eggs. Where's
          the other bird, she got big ones?

Everyone gives him blank looks.

                SPAGHETTI (CONT'D)
    Oh for Christ's sake they're meant to 'ave a food fight at the
          end! With icing sugar... and chocolate!

Spaghetti picks up a sizzling banger without seeming to feel pain.

                SPAGHETTI (CONT'D)
    Sausages?! If that's your idea of sexy I pity your Mrs.

Spaghetti throws down the sausage in disgust and walks away. In wobbles
CANDICE, cheerfully.

                    CANDICE
          Saw the sign. Looks very professional.

                    SPAGHETTI
              Looks professional?

                    CANDICE
                    (Tutting)
                    Moody...

Spaghetti has caught sight of Stuart again, though we don't see what he sees.

                    SPAGHETTI
        Noooo you pansy... tell 'er to shake 'em.
                  (To Candice)
              You strippin' tonight?

                    CANDICE
          Miami's got me on the double shift.

                    SPAGHETTI
        Miami Vice... used to be a major face.

                    CANDICE
              'E ain't finished yet.

SPAGHETTI
'E just don't know it yet. 'E never 'ad a vision.

Suddenly Spaghetti sees that Tony is standing in the doorway on the other side, watching the girl.

SPAGHETTI (CONT'D)
Is 'Einrich from 'Amburg 'idin' in my studio?! Get after 'im !

CUT TO:

INT. MIAMI'S OFFICE -- DAY

C.U. – A cricket bat – brown, stained. MIAMI is about to total another ACCOUNTANT. THREE FEET, however, steps in.

THREE FEET
Guv, guv, guv...

Miami stops in his tracks and shoots Three Feet a glance.

THREE FEET (CONT'D)
Remember? The libel case? Squeaky clean?

Miami ponders. The accountant's life hangs in the balance.

MIAMI
Thank you, Three Feet. But I hate people telling me what
I should and shouldn't do. Y'know?

THREE FEET
Right, Guv.

Miami lowers the bat and returns to his seat. Accountant wonders if he might perhaps have got away with it.

MIAMI
Especially when it comes to money.

THREE FEET
Accountants always think they know best.

MIAMI
I mean, no-one goes on 'oliday to Monte on a budget. What's
more, if I'm gonna start up this dog track in Hong Kong... it's
not cash I need – you listening? ...

The accountant sits up straight.

MIAMI (CONT'D)
It's collateral. Johnny Chinaman has to see that I've got what
it takes. I need to show him... an empire.

He lays the bat down very softly.

THREE FEET
You, er... finished with Mr Pristy?

Miami nods and looks away, deep in thought. The Accountant breathes a sigh
of relief. Three Feet whacks him round the head, knocking him out cold.

THREE FEET (CONT'D)
Sean?

A huge heavy called SEAN enters.

THREE FEET (CONT'D)
Take him away. Do him over. Medium rare.

CUT TO:

INT. LOCK -- DAY

Three VCRs sit on top of each other. A tangle of wires spout out the back. Moon
is checking through it. The others are arguing with JOHANN and JAAP. Johann
sits down and skins up. Jaap dances to the music in his head.

BACON
It's 50p a tape.

JAAP
Before, yah, but now we are heffink to stick up.

JOHANN
Sefenty-fife.

LEE
Oh yeah, 'ow come?

JOHANN
Treffelink expenses.

LEE
Don't take the piss.

JOHANN
No, we are za guys which are go here ent zere for efrybody, all
za time – it's not fair.

MOON
But that's your job.

Pause, as Dutchies look over to Moon and back at the rest of the lads.

JAAP
OK, 50p, but next time 75. Efrybotty is takink us for liberties.

JAMIE
Well le's 'ave 'em then, we're in an 'urry 'ere.

JAAP
We, no. We not in hurry. Zis is time for take break ent smoke
out.

JOHANN
Shmoke o-o-out...

They light up.

BACON
Ain't you gotta be nowhere else?

JAAP
Sure, we make visit to Peepink Tom's. Our super big buddy
Heinrich is in London UK.

JOHANN
Heinrich is main man. He was teachink us how to sellink all
za gear...

JAAP
German yah, but so great guy.

LEE
Well give us the tapes and get down there to see yer bum chum.

JOHANN
We are not liking zose guys from Peepink Tom who are callink
Debbie ent Deep Trout... zey are likink... strange things.

JAMIE
Yeah, well we gotta do two hundred weddin' vids by teatime.
So, where's the tapes, in the back?

                              JOHANN
                          Yah, in za back.

Two Dutchies shrug. Johann hands Jaap the spliff.

                                                          CUT TO:

EXT. LOCK -- DAY

Jamie and Lee start unloading boxes of tapes. Jamie kicks door shut.

                                                          CUT TO:

INT. PEEPING TOM'S -- DAY

A fetish porn shop. Tacky. Full of bizarre sex aids. DEBBIE sits by the till. She is
about 40, and covered in piercings and tattoos. Long, dyed-black hair. She's
reading one of the fetish mags. HEINRICH is staring at her.

                             HEINRICH
              Hey, that's my favourite you're reading. Means you and me
                         got something in common...

                              DEBBIE
                         (Without looking up)
                          Don't talk to me.

                             HEINRICH
              Strange, isn't it? You hate me, but you fancy me at the
                            same time.

Just then, DEEP THROAT enters. Deep Throat is Debbie's husband, tall and nasty-
looking, with a hideous cut across his throat.

                           DEEP THROAT
               Oi, Heinrick. I told you not to talk to my wife. She don't
                            like you.

                             HEINRICH
                         How can I help it?

                           DEEP THROAT
              You'll help it, alright. If you wanna carry on 'idin' out 'ere.

Heinrich holds up his hands to say 'no offence'. Then flips open his attaché case.

                             HEINRICH
               You guys wanna see the future of pornography?

Heinrich spins the case round and lifts out a mechanical pussy, with wires attached, saying as he does so:

> HEINRICH (CONT'D)
> Prototype. They gonna make 'em in Taiwan. Or Thailand.

> DEBBIE
> Tha' your suicide masturbation kit?

> HEINRICH
> Internet pussy. Plug it in, an' link up to some chick at the other end. You can fuck pussy ten thousand miles away, man.

Deep Throat picks up the pussy.

> DEEP THROAT
> I like to see what I'm shaftin'.

> HEINRICH
> The face is on the screen, man, she's lookin' right at ya while ya give it to her.

> DEEP THROAT
> But I like the personal touch, y'know. What d'yer reckon Debbie?

> DEBBIE
> (Matter-of-factly)
> They'd sell...

She goes back to her mag.

> DEEP THROAT
> Yeah.

Heinrich gets his calculator out.

> HEINRICH
> How many you want?

> DEBBIE
> We'll take this one. Twenty-four hour trial.

> DEEP THROAT
> Free.

> HEINRICH
> Guys, that's the prototype.

DEBBIE
We're your favourite customers. You said so.

DEEP THROAT
An' from what I 'ear, you're runnin' out of other customers.
Live ones, I mean.

HEINRICH
OK, but I can hide here 'til the deal is done?

DEEP THROAT
Just don't jump on her again when she's on the khazi or she'll
break yer neck.

CUT TO:

INT. LOCK BACK ROOM -- AFTERNOON

The lads are dubbing the wedding tapes. Moon has headphones on, taking it a bit
too seriously. There are stacks of tapes knee-high on all sides.

JAMIE
I told yer... stick the labels on the ones we done.

LEE
Tha's what I told YOU to do.

BACON
Girls, it don't matter who told who, what, when. Fact is we
gotta go through and check 'em all again.

Moon takes the headphones off, pauses the picture.

MOON
There! He's done it again. I'm tellin' you that vicar keeps winkin' at the groom.

BACON
Is that important?

MOON
Wouldn't 'ave 'im for my weddin'.

JAMIE
Take that tape out, we gotta check these, find out what's
dubbed, what's blank.

MOON
You didn't label 'em?

226

Moon leans forward and ejects the tape.

> MOON (CONT'D)
> Amateurs...

CUT TO:

INT. PEEPING TOM'S -- EVENING

C.U. – Screen hisses and shows snow.

> DEBBIE
> What the fuck's goin' on?

> JAAP
> Maybe problem wiz machine.

> DEBBIE
> Honey... I think we got a problem.

> DEEP THROAT
> Nasty problem.

> JOHANN
> Hey, no, no nasty problem, guys.

> JAAP
> Zose stupid lads in pub are mixink tapes.

> DEBBIE
> What lads?

Johann looks at Jaap, who gives the 'Go on, tell him' look.

> JOHANN
> Za stupid guys are takink wrong tapes from fen.

> JAAP
> Zey are so stupid bastards.

> DEBBIE
> Well, we'd better get those tapes back cos I've got a couple of
> 'undred desperate perverts itching to cop off on 'em.

Heinrich enters. Goes straight over to the Dutchies.

> HEINRICH
> Hey, hey...

227

Dutchies nod sheepishly.

> HEINRICH (CONT'D)
> Now we can all go party, uh? Guys? Debbie? This pocket is
> full of sniffing snow and I'm one generous son of bitch.

> DEEP THROAT
> Oi you, shut up.

> HEINRICH
> (To Dutchies)
> Zese English, don't know how to let the hair do-o-own.

Debbie grabs Heinrich by the lapels and throws him back against the wall.

> DEBBIE
> The only reason we put up with your shite is cos you bring us
> the hi-tech from Hamburg, but I'm beginning to think it's not
> worth the GRIEF !

Debbie has her hand over Heinrich's throat.

> DEEP THROAT
> No more verbals, Heinrich.

> DEEP THROAT
> (To Dutchies)
> Get on the blower to those lads of yours. We'll 'ave them
> tapes back. Tonight.

CUT TO:

INT. LOCK. BACK ROOM -- EVENING

Lee puts the phone down. Nudges Jamie.

> LEE
> Those tapes... we dubbed the lot, yeah?

> JAMIE
> Yeah course, why?

> LEE
> Right. Shit.

CUT TO:

INT. PEEPING TOM'S -- NIGHT

The door is kicked open. Tony and a couple of heavies walk in. Debbie is behind the counter. Heinrich is trussed up in bondage gear with a dog collar and a rubber mask on. He sits on the counter like a trained monkey. The Dutchies kneel on the floor meekly.

> DEBBIE
> This is a private session.

> TONY
> We're looking for someone.

Deep Throat enters through the multi-coloured plastic strip curtain, with a steaming mug.

> DEEP THROAT
> You're looking for Heinrich from Hamburg. Spaghetti wants
> him dead, every fucker knows that.

> TONY
> We're gonna find him, Deep Throat.

> DEEP THROAT
> Better get out there lookin' then. You walk into this shop
> again, and I'll open you up like a tin of sardines.

Tony sneers.

> TONY
> Next time I walk into this shop, it'll be a fuckin' newsagent.
> Your days are numbered.

Tony leads his boys out. The door clangs shut. Debbie unzips Heinrich's mask.

> DEBBIE
> Now then Heinrich, say 'Thank You Debbie'...

CUT TO:

INT. PEEPING TOM'S -- NIGHT

Dutchies look at the floor like naughty schoolboys. The lads glare at them. Debbie holds a bull-dog clip in front of Heinrich's nipple, making the jaws open and shut. Heinrich squeals. In the other hand she has a lit candle.

> JAMIE
> You must be Deep Throat.

Deep Throat does not acknowledge this.

JAMIE (CONT'D)
I'm Jamie. Moon, Bacon, Lee.

DEEP THROAT
Remember them names Debbie, when you order their gravestones.

Debbie turns around.

DEBBIE
(To the lads)
Put the tapes on the counter.

JAMIE
Thing is... we didn't know there was anyfin' on 'em.

DEBBIE
So...

JAMIE
So we, er...

MOON
Copied over 'em.

JAMIE
By accident.

DEBBIE
You copied over two 'undred tapes?

The lads nod. Debbie absent-mindedly lets wax from the candles drip onto Heinrich's skin. He gasps.

BACON
We make weddin' videos.

DEBBIE
Not the kind of weddin' videos where the underage lesbian bridesmaids kidnap the groom for an orgy in the vicarage?

LEE
Not really.

DEBBIE
All two 'undred tapes?

LADS
Yeah...

DEBBIE
(Shrugging)
Well you owe us six fucking grand, then. Plus compensation
for damage to our reputation.

JAMIE
Tell you what. How 'bout we get yer some more videos?

MOON
For free.

DEBBIE
Oh well that's very fucking kind of you... I tell you what, 'ow
'bout I make a snuff movie starring... four likely lads and a
very pissed off leather-clad mistress.

DEEP THROAT
(Interrupting)
Hold on. Why don't we give the lads a chance.
(False sympathy)
I mean, it was an accident.

Debbie shrugs.

DEEP THROAT (CONT'D)
You got three days to come up with some hardcore nasty shit.
Otherwise, it's fun and games down in the dungeon, alright?

Debbie nods at the trussed-up figure of Heinrich.

DEBBIE
An' they can look after this wanker as well.

Deep Throat looks doubtful.

DEEP THROAT
If Spaghetti's boys find 'im, 'e's as dead as a used 'amster.

DEBBIE
They ain't gonna go lookin' for 'im in some shit-arse pub.

DEEP THROAT
I told 'Amburg we'd keep 'im safe.

DEBBIE
Deep Throat darling, I ain't jokin'. E's safer with them than
with me. I'm gonna do 'im some real damage before long.

Deep Throat turns to the lads.

                    DEEP THROAT
        'E's an arsehole. But we're gunner make a mint out of his
        wares. So keep 'im well hid. Till the deal's done.

END OF ACT ONE

ACT TWO

INT. LAPLAND -- NIGHT

TANYA and the girls are dancing but the place is half-empty. BARBIE is in charge,
looking hassled, getting grief from Candice. Miami watches.

                    CANDICE
        You told me I was doin' the late shift as well.

Barbie looks down at the schedule, puzzled.

                    BARBIE
                    Did I?

                    CANDICE
        Yeah you did. An' you told that Tanya she could 'ave my
                    jaffa cakes.

                    BARBIE
        Listen love, they didn't' 'ave your name writ on 'em did they?

                    CANDICE
        When's Moira comin' back?

                    MIAMI
        Oi, Candice. Give 'er a break, or I'll give you a break.

                    CANDICE
        No disrespect to you Miami. I just don't like me time
                    bein' wasted.

                    MIAMI
        Alright, darlin'. Barbie, straighten 'em out. I want a fuckin'
        top show on tonight. These Chinese geezers 've got a lot
                    of say-so.

Three Feet approaches.

THREE FEET
Word, Guv?

Miami and Three Feet step to one side. Candice wraps her scarf round her neck and storms out. Barbie scrutinises her schedule.

THREE FEET (CONT'D)
You know Bill Bishop.

MIAMI
Remind me.

THREE FEET
We shot 'im in the arse back in the Eighties.

MIAMI
Christ, yeah. Still in the business, is 'e?

THREE FEET
Seems like 'e was. But they just fished 'im out of Lea Valley
Reservoir this morning. Every bone in 'is body busted.

MIAMI
(Smiles)
That'll be Tony the Peacemaker. Spaghetti's boy.

THREE FEET
They're buryin' everyone.

MIAMI
Yeah.

THREE FEET
Think we should 'ave a quiet word with Spaghetti?

MIAMI
No, not yet.

CUT TO:

EXT. STREET -- DAY

Tony stands on the pavement outside another sex shop with a couple of HEAVIES, all cold and bored.

TONY
It's a waste of time. That Kraut could be anywhere. Let's go
an' 'ave a cup of tea.

CUT TO:

INT. LOCK -- DAY

Lads sit round table. Dutchies and Heinrich appear.

                         BACON
          Alright. A quarter of six grand is a grand-an-a-half.

                          LEE
                     I ain't got it.

                         MOON
                     Me neither.

                         JAMIE
                 Thought you was flush?

                         MOON
                        Dogs.

At that moment, in walk Heinrich, Johann and Jaap. Johann and Jaap make
the 'time-out' sign. Jaap looks pretty wired already.

                    JOHANN & JAAP
                 Time out... Time out...

                       HEINRICH
                 Boys. Let's paint the town.

                         JAAP
          We seven go to night club ent pick up seven babes. Heinrich,
                 he has t'ree gram of...

The Dutchies mime snorting and rubbing their gums. Heinrich pats his
chest pocket.

                       HEINRICH
          Let it snow, let it snow, let it snow...

                         JAMIE
              Go ahead lads. We gotta make plans.

                        JOHANN
      You not into za nose candy, you shmoke out, or just get piss on booze.

                       HEINRICH
          I wanna take everyone to Heaven to say thank you.

                          234

JOHANN
Uh? Heffen is club for gay.

HEINRICH
Yeah, but the music's great. And there's babes.

JAAP
Babes?

HEINRICH
Sure. Tell all the guys that you are straight, tell all the girls
you're bi. Works every time.

All three laugh and look to the lads. Their faces show disinterest and impatience.

HEINRICH (CONT'D)
You no coming? OK, cool, no problem.

They exit. Johann practises his new chat-up line as he goes.

JOHANN
Me ent Jaap we are za bisexual guy from za Hook of
Hollant, jah...

It is quiet again.

BACON
Well. We can't pay Deep Throat off. How about, we get
together enough to buy him some tapes, take the place of the
ones we copied over.

JAMIE
What's that, a grand, two grand?

BACON
Grand-and-a-half'll do it, I reckon.

MOON
Piece of piss. Let's get out there.

CUT TO:

INT. LOCK, BACK ROOM -- DAY

Moon takes a brand-new leather jacket off a hanger and lays it in a holdall.
Takes off a gold watch and lays it on top. Then a signet ring. A Playstation.
Takes a Samurai sword down off the wall, kisses it, puts it in the bag. Thinks.

                              MOON
                          Bollocks to that.

Takes the sword out again. Puts it back on the wall. He runs out and comes back
in with a chicken.

                                                                    CUT TO:

EXT. LOCK, YARD -- DAY

Lee is showing a prospective BUYER his Triumph.

                               LEE
              Very reliable. Very. It's gonna break my 'eart to let 'er go...

The buyer doesn't look convinced.

                          LEE (CONT'D)
                        Grand-an'-a-half.

                                                                    CUT TO:

INT. LOCK, BAR -- DAY

Moon's prize chicken and possessions are laid out on a table, in front of a sleazy-
looking SHORT MAN, of about fifty.

                              MOON
                           (Hopefully)
                        Grand-an'-a-half?

                                                                    CUT TO:

INT. LOCK, BACK ROOM -- EVENING

Jamie is shuffling cards, pitching a line to two PUNTERS.

                              JAMIE
              Tell yer what I'm gonna do. Seein' as I'm a gambler at 'eart,
              I'm gonna give you the chance to win back yer stake, alright?
              Course if yer lose, I walk away with a grand-an-a-half but –

Punters shake their heads and walk away from the table.

                          JAMIE (CONT'D)
              'Ang on 'ang on, where yer goin'? I'll give yer a chance!

                                                                    CUT TO:

INT. LOCK -- DAY

Lee joins Moon behind the bar. Moon is filling all the glasses on one tray from a bottle of 'Glensporran Single Malt' whisky.

> LEE
> Can't shift the motor. How's the promotion goin'?

> MOON
> They're fallin' for it. But it's only fifteen quid a bottle.

They look at Bacon on the other side of the pub.

CUT TO:

Bacon with the glasses on his tray arranged into two groups. There are two couples around the table. He is talking to the men.

> BACON
> If you can tell the difference between Scotch and Irish whisky you win yourself a bottle of single malt for only fifteen quid. Retails at thirty. Can you tell the difference between Scotch and Irish? Come on, I want you to win, it's a promotion...

CUT BACK TO:

INT. LOCK -- DAY

The bar. Jamie comes in.

> JAMIE
> What you got?

> LEE
> Nuffin.

> JAMIE
> Didn't you get nothing for them passports?

> LEE
> No-one's buying. Couldn't even flog me dole cards.

> JAMIE
> I've thought of something.

CUT TO:

INT. LOCK -- DAY

237

Jamie outlines his new plan.

> JAMIE
> Look.

He points at the video gear sitting in the corner.

> JAMIE (CONT'D)
> We make... our own.

> LEE
> You're jokin', mate?

> JAMIE
> It's not difficult. That hand-held home video look - it's all the
> rage, it's more real.

> MOON
> Sounds good.

> BACON
> Who we gonna film?

> JAMIE
> I'll give Laura a bell. Moon, what about Tanya?

> MOON
> We'd 'ave to pay her.

> JAMIE
> We'll start with Laura.

> BACON
> With you as the stud?

> JAMIE
> Yeah.

> MOON
> An' we film yer at it?

> JAMIE
> Secretly.

> LEE
> 'Scuse me. I'd rather go and borrow the cash off the Great
> White Loan Shark and offer me balls as security.

JAMIE
Go on then.

CUT TO:

INT. LOCK -- DAY

Bacon, Moon and Lee are setting up the camera. There is a couch, surrounded by lighted candles and a bottle of champagne. Jamie sticks his head round the corner.

JAMIE
She's 'ere. No more noise, alright.

LAURA (O.O.V.)
Jamie...?

JAMIE
No arse shots.

LEE
Whadya mean? We gotta see arses goin' up and down.

MOON
Gotta see that mate.

JAMIE
Just not my bollocks 'angin' down.

MOON
An' push 'er out the way for the money shot.

LAURA (O.O.V.)
Jamie, you there?

Laura appears and the lads duck into hiding.

LAURA
Wha's all this then?

JAMIE
All for you. You're fuckin' worth it.

LAURA
Where's the others?

JAMIE
I let 'em 'ave the day off.

CUT TO:

The lads, hiding, roll their eyes at this.

CUT BACK TO:

> LAURA
> So wha's this job you got for me?

> JAMIE
> Want some bubbly?

> LAURA
> Sure...

Champagne cork pops.

CUT TO LATER:

The champagne is all gone. Laura and Jamie are snuggled up.

CUT TO:

Lads in hiding-place look very bored.

CUT BACK TO:

> LAURA (CONT'D)
> Well you said you 'ad some sorta job.

Jamie goes for the kiss.

> LAURA (CONT'D)
> Bit draughty in 'ere, mate. Where's your bedroom?

> JAMIE
> Bed's too small.

> LAURA
> For what?

> JAMIE
> You mind if I wear a mask?

Jamie pulls out a rubber mask.

CUT TO:

Lads look at each other, mouthing 'Mask?' .

CUT BACK TO:

                    LAURA
        Into the kinky stuff now, are we?

                    JAMIE
                    Yeah...

Jamie pulls the mask on.

                    LAURA
            I'll tie you up then.

                    JAMIE
                    Er...

Too late. Laura produces some hand cuffs and whacks them on Jamie's hands.
Moon clicks record. Everyone freezes. Laura looks around. Does she see the little
red light flashing in the dark? She carries on.

                JAMIE (CONT'D)
            Tha's a bit tight.

                    LAURA
            A bit tight, mistress!

                    JAMIE
                    Uh?

Smack. She whacks him on the arse.

                JAMIE (CONT'D)
                    Ow!

She pulls off his pants.

                JAMIE (CONT'D)
                Aah, no!

                    LAURA
            No, MISTRESS!!

Whack.

CUT TO:

The lads are desperately trying to stifle their laughter. Sound of more and more whacks. Jamie suffers.

CUT BACK TO:

Montage sequence of Jamie and Laura in many different positions and guises until Jamie is in a rather compromising position with Laura pulling his mask off. It's all too much for him and he tries to crawl away.

> JAMIE
> Cut, cut...

Noise as Johann, Jaap and Heinrich come in.

> JOHANN & JAAP
> Woahhh! Crazy!

> HEINRICH
> Hey, you cats rock!

> JOHANN
> We can join in, right?

Heinrich and Johann fumble with their belts. Jaap sees the lads filming.

> JAAP
> You makink home porno? Ah, todally coo-ol!

Laura spins round to face lads, starting to uncuff Jamie.

> LAURA
> Get that? Next time you wanna video me you bleddy
> ask permission...

CUT TO:

INT. PEEPING TOM'S -- EVENING

Deep Throat is on his mobile and Debbie is on the landline.

> DEEP THROAT
> There's been a slight delay, but it's gonna be worth it. All
> spring chickens, mate, you won't be disappointed.

Phone call is finished. Debbie's call, meanwhile, goes on:

> DEBBIE
> Mm... yeah... yeah, but... yeah I know we promised... mmm...

> DEEP THROAT
> 'Ello? It is. Yes... Don't panic. They'll get 'ere. Don't
> threaten me, pal.

Puts the phone down.

> DEBBIE
> We're lookin' like a right bunch of monkeys. Those lads better
> come up with the goods.

CUT TO:

INT. LAPLAND, CORRIDOR AND DRESSING-ROOM -- NIGHT

Moon is sneaking around outside the dressing-room. There is a bottle of mineral water on a tray with some hankies and biscuits. He opens the bottle, pulls a pill out of his pocket, kisses it, and pops it into the water. Someone is coming, he hurries off. Tanya arrives, picks up the tray and walks into the changing-room, where most of the girls are ready. She unscrews the top of the bottle and notices something...

> TANYA
> 'Ere, the seal's broken on this. You know what? I reckon
> they're fillin' it up with tap water. Tight bastards.

Takes a swig.

> CANDICE
> Tha's that stupid secretary.

Takes the bottle from Tanya.

CUT TO:

INT. LAPLAND -- NIGHT

The lads walk into Lapland. Barbie is trying to write something on her clipboard. She's not used to it.

> LEE
> Alright Barb? Moira still away?

> BARBIE
> (Without looking up)
> Yeah, love.

> LEE
> 'Ow you gettin' on?

BARBIE
It's not what I thought. People keep asking me to do things...

LEE
Ah yeah, terrible when that happens.

Moon is hiding a camera in his sports bag. The lens is poking out. Bacon walks in front of Moon to hide it.

BACON
This ain't gonna work.

JAMIE
Course it will. Moon, remember to get those big close-ups.

MOON
'Ow am I gonna do that without stickin' me 'ead in the bag?

JAMIE
Will you lot just stick to the plan?

LEE
I'll get the drinks in.

Lee leaves.

CUT TO:

INT. MIAMI'S OFFICE -- NIGHT

Three Feet enters. Miami is at his desk.

THREE FEET
The Chinese have arrived.

MIAMI
What do they look like?

THREE FEET
Mugs.

MIAMI
Good. Where d'yer leave 'em?

THREE FEET
They're in the Amusements.

MIAMI
We'll take 'em over to the track. Then back to the Ritz.

THREE FEET
You wanna drive 'em past Buckingham Palace an' all that?

MIAMI
Yeah, might as well.

CUT TO:

INT. LAPLAND -- LATER

Tanya is on the stage, so is Candice. Moon and Jamie stand as close as they can.

JAMIE
Your pills are workin'...

Tanya and Candice are giving it far more than normal. It's as if there's a competition between them.

JAMIE (CONT'D)
Make 'er look this way. Say 'ello to 'er.

MOON
She won't say 'ello, she's workin'.

JAMIE
You recordin'?

Moon nods.

JAMIE (CONT'D)
E're y'are girls!

Jamie produces two fivers, one in each hand. Sticks them in Candice and Tanya's G-strings.

TANYA
Steady on... big spender.

CANDICE
D'yer break yer piggy bank?

The girls gyrate in front of the lads for a bit.

JAMIE
Gettin' it?

245

Moon is pushing the bag forward, too far... Jamie tries to stop him giving the game away.

> JAMIE (CONT'D)
> You bloody muppet!

Too late, Candice stops moving.

> CANDICE
> Oi! What you got in there?

(CAMERA'S P.O.V.) – Tanya glaring down the lens. A hand looming across the lens – darkness. The sound of a slap and an 'Ow'.

CUT TO LATER:

Lads are in a quiet corner. Candice and Tanya lap dance in front of them, but this is just concealing the negotiation.

> TANYA
> We want a cut.

> CANDICE
> Fifty-fifty.

> BACON
> Come on girls, that's a bit steep, innit?

> TANYA
> You're right. We'll just tell Miami what you was up to.

> MOON
> Tanya, don't be like that.

> TANYA
> You brought business into it.

> CANDICE
> What's yer best offer?

> JAMIE
> Hundred notes now. A percentage of sales. You can't say fairer–

> CANDICE
> Hundred each now. Plus thirty per cent.

> JAMIE
> Done.

CANDICE
And a copy of the tape.

JAMIE
Whatever. Lee, pay the girls.

Lee's face says it all.

CUT TO:

INT. LOCK, BACK ROOM -- NIGHT

Four lads plus Laura sit watching the video on TV. Piles of tapes around. Laura is skinning up. Jamie is fascinated. The other lads can hardly bear to look.

JAMIE
You know I quite like the end bit. Where you see me face.

LEE
You what?

BACON
Jamie this is bloody awful.

MOON
You think Deep Throat and Debbie are gunner settle for this shit?

He points to the screen. Only Laura looks up, curious.

JAMIE
You lot don't get it. It's great. Look, look it's Lapland now.

LAURA
She's got cellulite, that one.

LEE
Moon, you've got to go and sweet-talk Tanya into doin' a
special show for us... maybe... with Laura.

LAURA
(Unenthusiastic)
Lesbo? Tried it once...

Lads try to tear their minds from this thought.

MOON
Or... we pay a couple of cheap hookers to do some really
mental stuff – with the Dutchies.

Knock on the door. Lee gets up.

                              LEE
          Talk of the Devil. We should give the boys a key...

                             JAMIE
               D'yer really think the tape's shit?

Everyone – even Laura – says, impatiently:

                           EVERYONE
                             Yes!

Lee opens the door to... Tony. He has no idea who Tony is.

                             TONY
              Heard you been filming in Lapland.

                              LEE
                          (Gulping)
          Er... we thought... Miami might... well, what we er... tell 'em,
                        lads... lads?

Lee turns round. Four empty chairs. Laura hasn't moved from hers, cool as
a cucumber.

                             LAURA
                           Alright?

                             TONY
          Evenin' Miss. I'm 'ere to collect a tape. On be'alf of Candice.

                              LEE
              O-oh. Yeah. Tape. Fine. I'll get yer one.

                             TONY
                  Nice little boozer you got.

                              LEE
                           Cheers.

Lee hands over a tape.

                             TONY
                           Cheers.

Exit Tony.

LEE
Oi, come out you chicken-shits.

CUT TO:

INT. LOCK -- DAY

Heinrich brings in a tray with a bottle of Pernod and three glasses for the Dutchies, who are sitting up in their sleeping bags, smoking.

HEINRICH
Hair of za dog.

JOHANN
Cool.

JAAP
Las' night – what time we were comink beck?

The other two shrug. Johann rubs his legs.

JOHANN
My muscle is ache. Maybe I was screwink wiz some sexy babe.

HEINRICH
(Shaking his head)
You were dancing in a funny way.

Heinrich pulls out a revolver, starts checking it. The Dutchies look at each other. Heinrich explains:

HEINRICH (CONT'D)
This guy Spaghetti... Last time I was over here, he tried to make me an offer. Had me in the back of his car. Told me just to take all the business to him, nobody else. I said, Man, that's bullshit.

HEINRICH
You get out of my face right now. I believe in two things – free love, and free trade. Then I got out that car and slammed the door in his fuckin' face. Don't worry, he ain't gonna look for me here. Cheers.

He picks up his drink. Puts the gun down next to him.

CUT TO:

INT. PEEPING TOM'S -- DAY

Lads stand nervously in the shop. Debbie is at the till, chewing gum. Deep Throat appears, through multi-coloured strip curtain, from the back room.

> DEBBIE
> Would you mind stepping this way?

> BACON
> We'd rather stay 'ere.

> JAMIE
> What' d'yer think? We tried to give it that kind ofamateur vibe.

Debbie gets up and wanders over to the shop door.

> LEE
> We wanted something... gritty.

> MOON
> Raw...

Debbie locks the door. Tension rises. Deep Throat clears a space on the counter and points at it.

> DEBBIE
> Six grand.

> JAMIE
> Yer not lookin' for that kind of movie then?

> DEEP THROAT
> I could cream off quicker to 'Aerobics Oz Style'.

> BACON
> We can re-do 'em. Tha's fine.

> MOON
> Put in more... sex.

> JAMIE
> Yeah. We'll try somefin' different.

> DEBBIE
> (Gently)
> Just be good boys and step into the back fucking room.

Deep Throat goes into the back room. Bacon looks at Debbie.

BACON
Be a dear an' unlock the door, eh?

She blows a bubble in her gum, no answer.

JAMIE
Right lads, obviously got a bit of trouble on our 'ands.

Deep Throat appears with a shotgun.

LADS
Shit...

DEEP THROAT
Come on... in you come.

Lads edge towards the back room.

DEBBIE
Snuff movie time...

Bacon stops in his tracks.

BACON
Fuck that.

Bacon grabs the nearest thing, which is a giant triffid of a dildo, and hurls it at Deep Throat's head, knocking him back. The other lads pile in, fling sex toys, rubber gear, mags – anything – at Debbie and Deep Throat. Debbie grabs Lee by the hair. He grabs hers, she screams.

LEE
Not very nice, is it?

Bacon kicks the door hard.

CUT TO:

EXT. PEEPING TOM'S -- DAY

The lads burst out of the door and run for it.

Debbie and Deep Throat emerge from the door but the lads are too far away.

DEBBIE
You little turds...

Moon turns round and gives them the finger.

251

MOON
Tossers!

CUT TO:

EXT. STREET NEAR PEEPING TOM'S -- DAY

The lads are jumping into the car. Jamie driving.

BACON
Go, go, go!

The car screeches off with one door hanging open.

CUT TO:

INT. MOVING CAR -- DAY

Moon is experiencing an adrenaline high.

MOON
What a fuckin' rush.

LEE
(Sarcastic)
Great, yeah, what a buzz.

CUT TO:

INT. LOCK -- DAY

Surrounded by empty Pernod bottles, burgers and fries, the Dutchies and Heinrich
are messing about with the gun, acting out famous scenes from movies, very
badly. Johann points the gun at Jaap. He has a burger in the other hand.

JOHANN
So punk... you got to askink yourself za one question... do I
feelink lucky today... huh?

Heinrich is pissing himself. Jaap picks up the gun and holds out it out in front
 of him.

JAAP
You talkink to me?... You talkink to me?... Huh... Punk?

The other two laugh heartily. Heinrich is tying a sock round his head. Jaap
passes the gun to him. He spins and points it dramatically at his temple like
in *Deer Hunter*.

HEINRICH
Is this what you want? Is this what you want?!

Close up of Dutchies laughing, suddenly BANG. They stop laughing. Heinrich
has shot himself in the head. They are covered in blood. Total and utter silence.
Johann and Jaap are dumbstruck.

CUT TO:

INT. STUDIO SET -- DAY

Spaghetti is having his neck massaged by Candice. They're watching the video
the lads made.

CANDICE
Watch this move... that's an 'ard one. Only me an' Tanya
can do it.

Spaghetti's not listening, he's thinking about someone else.

SPAGHETTI
Who was that bird on before, doing the spanking?

CANDICE
(Irritated)
I dunno.

SPAGHETTI
Candice...

CANDICE
I don't fuckin' know. Tanya's boyfriend's cousin. Lara?
No, Laura.

Spaghetti has suddenly had an idea.

SPAGHETTI
Laura... You know what? I'm gonna hire all you girls from
Lapland. An' I'm gonna put this tape out on Sauce TV tonight.
That'll piss Miami Vice off properly.

CANDICE
We can't all be presenters.

SPAGHETTI
I'll give the girls a slot, fifteen minutes of dancin', in between
Dr Sex and *Man's Best Friend*. And whoever's best can
do presenting.

                          CANDICE
                   Tha's me or Tanya, then.

                         SPAGHETTI
                 Or Laura, whoever's best. OW!

Candice's knuckles dig into his flesh.

                          CANDICE
                          (Coldly)
                 You got a build-up of toxins.

                                                      CUT TO:

INT. LOCK -- DAY

The four lads stare at the scene: Heinrich's body, the gore, the Dutchies, who have
not moved since the last scene.

                           JAMIE
                  What the fuck happened?

                           JAAP
                     Is Heinrich...

                          BACON
                    We can see that.

                         JOHANN
                  Heinrich is dead...

                          BACON
                   No shit, Sherlock.

                           JAAP
                He was best buddy of us, ent...

                          MOON
                 An' yer blew 'is brains out...

                         JOHANN
      No, no, he is blowink out ze own brains wiz gun, was accident.

                           JAAP
            I hate gun... We were makink joke wis gun...

                           LEE
                    Great. Now what?

                            254

JAAP
We give to Heinrich all right ceremony.

JAMIE
We'll stick 'im in the cellar for now.

JOHANN
Zen bury wiz stone or flag, not cross.

BACON
Yeah, yeah, grab 'is arms.

MOON
Well this'll really please Debbie and Deep Throat.

CUT TO:

INT. LAPLAND -- EVENING

A group of CHINESE BANKERS sit at a table in the middle of the room, looking at an empty stage. Miami is looking extremely pissed off. There are no girls. Barbie is checking and re-checking her clipboard.

MIAMI
Flu bug goin' round. You must get the same wiv your staff –
lots of girls sharin' the same teacups an' stuff.

Bankers nod politely. Three Feet appears, bends down to Miami's ear and they have a muttered conversation.

MIAMI (CONT'D)
Found the girls?

THREE FEET
Sort of.

MIAMI
Fuck d'you mean? They dead?

THREE FEET
Better see for yerself.

MIAMI
'Scuse me gentlemen.

CUT TO:

INT. MIAMI'S OFFICE -- EVENING

The channel is Sauce TV (logo in corner of screen). Lapland is on TV. Camera pans clumsily over the lads' faces. Three Feet and Miami look at each other.

> MIAMI
> Right. That lightweight wants to take me on, I'm up for it.

> THREE FEET
> What about the Chinks?

> MIAMI
> You'll 'ave to take 'em somewhere else tonight, really butter
> 'em up good.

> THREE FEET
> Could try the Ten-at-a-time club.

> MIAMI
> Bit rough?

> THREE FEET
> They ain't classy lads, Guv.

CUT TO:

EXT. LOCK BACK YARD -- MORNING

Debbie and Deep Throat walk to the front of the Lock and start to knock on the door.

CUT TO:

EXT. LOCK BACK YARD -- MORNING

Lads behind bar. Lee drinks heavily. Bacon fiddles with gun. There is banging on the door. The lads are ignoring it.

CUT TO:

EXT. LOCK BACK YARD-- MORNING

The door. Into shot races Deep Throat, now taking a run up and wielding an iron bar. But he just bounces off.

CUT TO:

INT. LOCK -- MORNING

The lads are in different positions. Another huge bang.

MOON
Tha's four hours. Don't they ever go to the bog?

JAMIE
I've got an idea.

JAMIE
We blame Spaghetti for Heinrich's little accident.

LEE
What about their six grand?

JAMIE
I ain't worked that out yet.

BACON
Well 'urry up will yer?

CUT TO LATER:

The banging finally stops.

BACON (CONT'D)
Tha's it. They've gone.

LEE
'Ave a look then.

Bacon strides up to the door and opens it wide. Miami and his mob are on the other side.

JAMIE
Miami... gents.

THREE FEET
(Interrupting)
We'd like a quiet word with you boys.

MOON
W-we're all ears.

MIAMI
Like making me look a cunt, do yer?

JAMIE
Eh?

THREE FEET
You must be short of a few rooms upstairs.

JAMIE
Eh?

MIAMI
I 'ad some Far Eastern business partners over last night.
Promised 'em drinks on the house an' a good show. An' all
they saw was dwarves – clothed. Didn't look too clever, a strip
show with no girls.
(To Jamie)
You their agent now?

JAMIE
Us? Ha ha, no.

THREE FEET
Upstairs, I'm watchin' that Sauce TV. Thought it was a bit
funny so I brought the Guvnor up.

MIAMI
An' what do I see? My club on the telly, an' then my little
friends' faces looking back at me, 'avin' a good laugh about it.

THREE FEET
Me an' Mr Vice put two an' two together.

JAMIE
We'll get yer girls back.

Now Miami begins to toy with them.

MIAMI
That's right my son. But that ain't enough. Not for this insult.

Miami signals that Jamie should step closer. Gingerly, he does. He's desperate
to say something to appease Miami.

MIAMI (CONT'D)
I had you down as a bit of a prospect. You let me down badly.
What is it? Did you think Spaghetti Eddy was gonna knock me
off my perch?

JAMIE
We'll make it up to yer.

                    MIAMI
      Yeah? What you gunner do? Go round and take Spaghetti
                    out for me?

                    JAMIE
                  Well... er...

                    MIAMI
      Lost for words eh? I know what you're trying to say. You
      wanna get me something special... something like... a TV
                  station. Yeah... Sauce TV.

                    JAMIE
          Um... yeh... that's what I was gonna say.

                    MIAMI
      Alright. We'll be round there at noon tomorrow. If you're not
      there to open the door for us... I'll cut your bollocks off and
                wear 'em as earrings.

                  THREE FEET
              (To Miami, surprised)
                Tha's very fair.

                    MIAMI
        You know me, Three Feet. I've got a soft spot
                  for entrepreneurs.

Exit Three Feet and Miami. Lads turn to Jamie.

                    JAMIE
            We'll work it out. Trust me.

                     LEE
      Listen, let's all go to Ibiza an' be drug-dealers. It's a better
          idea than what he's just about to say...

                                                    CUT TO:

INT. MIAMI'S ROLLER -- DAY

The heavies, Miami and Three Feet chuckle and shake their heads as they
drive off.

                                                    CUT TO:

END OF ACT TWO

ACT THREE

INT. LOCK -- MORNING

The lads are checking out Sauce TV.

> **LAURA (ON TV)**
> Comin' up is those lovely girls from Lapland. Tell you what... I
> shares a dressing-room with them and they got fit bodies.
> Cor, I 'ad one of 'em on my knee this mornin' an' I nearly –
> what am I sayin'? Tha's just a fantasy!

Someone turns down the sound.

> **MOON**
> They'll never go back to Lapland.

> **JAMIE**
> My plans... never fail.

CUT TO:

INT. STUDIO SET -- DAY

Spaghetti, Candice (face like thunder) and Stuart watch Laura doing a link.
 She's wearing a sexy black dress and extra-high heels. She's good at this, too.

> **LAURA**
> An' I just got an e-mail here from... Matt in Cornwall: 'Dear
> Sauce TV, this is a message for that Laura bird. Hello. Nice to
> see a West Country babe on the box instead of those mingin'
> birds with fake knockers. How 'bout gettin' your tits out for
> all the St Agnes surf crew?' Well, Matt this one's for you... oh,
> I've just been told it's time for a commercial break. Maybe
> after the ads?

She gives the camera a wave. Cut.

> **CANDICE**
> That is the stupidest accent I 'ave ever 'eard. She simple in the 'ead?

> **SPAGHETTI**
> No, no, she's gold dust. Pure, uncut, twenty-four carat talent.
> Spaghetti, you are a genius.

Spaghetti puffs up with pride and cigar smoke.

CUT TO:

INT. SAUCE TV STATION, DRESSING-ROOM -- DAY

The lads are there as the girls change into leopard-skin outfits.

BACON
It's one of them shows where they rescue pets an' birds with
broken wings an' that.

MOON
An' they want a couple of girls to present it. Make it a bit
more sexy.

TANYA
'Ow come they're doin' their auditions in your poxy little pub?

BACON
It's not round our place. It's in the Nine Bars.

MOON
We got connections now we're in the business... we know all
the editors, the producers...

JAMIE
It'll be easy for us to slip your names on the list.

TANYA
An' you wanna do this out the goodness of your heart?

BACON
Nah, if you're good, it makes us look good.

JAMIE
Yeah. They'll say... 'Who are these girls? They got looks,
talent. What genius discovered 'em?'

TANYA
Don't give me compliments, Jamie.

Girls are tempted but still sceptical.

LEE
Free food, as well.

TANYA
Free food?... who d'yer think I am?

Bacon is stealing a leopard-skin outfit.

                    MOON
                 (To the lads)
     See? They're gonna love this lot. So ballsy.

                    JAMIE
     Meet us outside the Nine Bars at eight. Dress to kill.

Lads file out of the door.

                                        CUT TO:

INT. SAUCE TV STATION, CORRIDOR -- DAY

Everyone rounds on Lee.

                    JAMIE
                 Free food?

                    LEE
     They have sandwiches at things like that!

                    JAMIE
             You almost blew it.

                                        CUT TO:

INT. LOCK, CELLAR -- NIGHT

The Dutchies have rigged up a kind of shrine, with candles. They are
seriously stoned.

                   JOHANN
     Life... is game, Heinrich. Crazy, crazy, game.

                    JAAP
     I hope zere is t'ousand angels makink queue for sittink on your face Heinrich...

                                        CUT TO:

EXT. NINE BARS -- NIGHT

Moon and Jamie wait for the girls. A black cab approaches.

                    MOON
             Tanya's gonna do 'er nut.

                    JAMIE
             Say it was my idea.

                     262

                    MOON
                  (Sarcastic)
          Cos' then she'll understand, eh?
                  (Apprehensive)
            This plan jus' better work.

Girls get out of the cab, dolled right up.

                    JAMIE
                    Girls...

                    MOON
                    Ladies...

                    JAMIE
                Don't overdo it.

                                                    CUT TO:

INT. NINE BARS -- NIGHT

They walk into the club. It's empty.

                    TANYA
                 We the first?

                    MOON
          Nah, there's been a few in already.

                    JAMIE
It's lookin' good. The other girls what've been in... they're nice
girls an' everythin' but... they ain't got that special somethin',
                    that spark...

                    TANYA
             Where is everybody?

                    MOON
               Through the back.

                    JAMIE
  They got all this soundproofin' an' that. Technical reasons.

The girls are not stupid. They stop dead in their tracks.

                    TANYA
        Wait a minute... this is bullshit.

                      263

Moon and Jamie look at each other. Then sprint back towards the door, slamming it behind them and locking it.

CUT TO:

EXT. NINE BARS -- NIGHT

>   GIRLS (O.O.V.)
>   Oi! Let us out! You wankers! This ain't funny!

>   JAMIE
>   There's a bottle of spring water in there, and some crisps,
>   salt 'n' vinegar and cheese 'n' onion.

>   MOON
>   We unlocked the toilets.

>   TANYA (O.O.V.)
>   Moon? Open this door.

>   TANYA (O.O.V.)
>   You're in big trouble if you don't let us out, now.

Thunderous hammerings on the door, screams of abuse.

CUT TO:

INT. LOCK -- MORNING

Opening shot of the lads sprawled out across the Lock, blood all over them. Heinrich's body in the middle. A grotesque scene of carnage. Suddenly, Jamie's body sits up.

>   JAMIE
>   Got that?

Cut to Jaap and Johann filming with the video camera. All the lads get up.

>   JAAP
>   OK, now we bury za Heinrich...

>   LEE
>   After you've dropped this tape off at Peepin' Tom's.

>   JOHANN
>   Ent leave him here?

> MOON
> Take care of business first. It's what Heinrich would've
> wanted.

> JOHANN & JAAP
> OK.

CUT TO:

INT. NINE BARS -- MORNING

Girls wrapped in tarpaulin. Empty crisp packets on the floor. Tired and pissed off, some smoking. Tanya looks at her watch: 10.30.

CUT TO:

INT. BLACK MERCEDES -- DAY

Candice and Spaghetti, checking his watch, in the back being chauffeured to the studio.

> CANDICE
> (Casually)
> She's a right slag, y'know, that Laura...

> SPAGHETTI
> (Disinterested)
> Yeah?

> CANDICE
> Y'know that shoot with the masked man on the video, y'know
> what I 'eard?

> SPAGHETTI
> No.

> CANDICE
> These three German blokes turned up, and they all 'ad an orgy,
> so they say...

Spaghetti's eyes light up at the word 'German'.

> SPAGHETTI
> You what?

> CANDICE
> Yeah, all of 'em, a pile-up, it was.

SPAGHETTI
One of these Germans 'ave a mullet?

Candice has no idea, but is glad to finally get a reaction.

CANDICE
Yeah, probably...

Spaghetti is on the mobile right away.

SPAGHETTI
Tony? Get down to the...
(To Candice)
What's that pub?

CANDICE
The Lock...

SPAGHETTI
The Lock. The Kraut with the snout might just be there...

CUT TO:

EXT. PEEPING TOM'S -- DAY

Dutchies place the video on the step, ring the bell, and sprint.

Debbie peers out of the door in her dressing-gown, fag in mouth. Looks around, looks down. Stoops to pick up tape.

CUT TO:

EXT. STREET NEAR PEEPING TOM'S -- DAY

Dutchies stop running, breathless, exhilarated – they quite enjoyed that.
 Jaap looks at Johann.

JAAP
Spirit of Heinrich!

They ring two more doorbells and run off laughing.

CUT TO:

INT. LAPLAND -- MORNING

Miami looks at his watch: 11.00. His Chinese associates are gathered around.

MIAMI
Three Feet, bring the car round.

Miami beams at the Chinese.

CUT TO:

INT. LOCK -- MORNING

The lads are quizzing the Dutchies, who are dragging out Heinrich's corpse.

JAMIE
So you put it through the letterbox and rang the bell?

JOHANN
Zere wasn't letterbox. We put on floor.

LEE
Yer just left it on the step?

JAAP
We ring bell ent run off, owner is find video, I sink.

LEE
You think?!

JOHANN
Listen, me ent Jaap are heffink fuckink big trauma from death
of Heinrich, now we bury, OK?

BACON
Alright lads, go ahead.

The Dutchies haul Heinrich out the back. Jamie checks his watch.

CUT TO:

EXT. LOCK, YARD -- MORNING

Dutchies carry the body out. Tony appears.

TONY
Now where would you be going with that dead Hun?

CUT TO:

INT. PEEPING TOM'S -- MORNING

Debbie and Deep Throat are watching the video of the 'carnage' at the Lock.
A sinister commentary is dubbed on:

> COMMENTARY
> ... The same fate awaits you. Death... to all those who dare...
> to compete with Spaghetti Eddy. We're comin' for you next
> Deep Throat... Debbie... you're next if you don't bring round
> the deeds to your place... by noon.

Deep Throat is already picking out weapons. Debbie is assembling ingredients
for a home-made bomb: rags, string, a bottle of nitroglycerine, and a bottle of
paint-stripper.

> DEBBIE
> Fucking Spaghetti Bollock-knees. Fuck does 'e think 'e is?

> DEEP THROAT
> We're gonna make a day of it, girl.

Deep Throat pulls a bottle of Amyl Nitrate out of the till.

CUT TO:

INT. STUDIO SET -- MORNING

11.35 on the clock. Laura is presenting and the males in the studio ogle her.

> LAURA
> (From autocue)
> Next up is animal lust on *Man's Best Friend*.
> (She adds)
> Do they mean animals 'avin' it away, or humans showing
> their... animal passions? Find out after this little break.
> Cheers.

Laura breezes off, her link finished. Spaghetti is just looking at the clock, getting
very nervous.

> SPAGHETTI
> Where's those girls? Stuart?

A mobile rings on set. Spaghetti is furious.

> SPAGHETTI (CONT'D)
> Whose is that fucking... oh.

It's his. He answers.

SPAGHETTI (CONT'D)
Yeah. Good work, Tony. You bringin' the body 'ere?

A spotty runner, JUSTIN, sidles up with a parcel, marked BY HAND, URGENT.
Spaghetti opens it. He pulls out a leopard-skin top and a note on paper headed
WITH THE COMPLIMENTS OF PEEPING TOM'S – it reads: WE GOT YOUR GIRLS.
AND WE'RE COMING FOR YOUR FUCKING STUDIO. HIGH NOON.

SPAGHETTI (CONT'D)
That fucking Deep Throat...

We can hear Tony's voice, over the phone saying:

TONY (O.O.V.)
Spaghetti? Spaghetti?

SPAGHETTI
Tony, get over 'ere we're expectin' company. No, the
nasty kind.

CUT TO:

EXT. LOCK -- MORNING

11.40. Lads all pacing about. Lee thinks of something.

LEE
What if the girls escape?

JAMIE
Don't matter now. Spaghetti thinks Deep Throat's got 'em.
Deep Throat thinks Spaghetti's after him, it's all gonna
kick off...

Phone rings. They freeze. Moon answers. He seems quite jaunty.

MOON
Yeah... yeah... 2.30, alright. What's the address?... Lovely.
See you there.

Hangs up.

BACON
Well?

MOON
We got a wedding this afternoon. The other firm cancelled
on 'em.

JAMIE
Moon, for Christ's sake...

MOON
If your plan works we should be available.

Phone rings again. Moon picks up.

CUT TO:

INT. VOLVO -- MORNING

The Dutchies lie trussed up in the back of a Volvo estate. Jaap has managed to get the mobile on his belt going. Johann speaks quietly into Jaap's crotch.

JOHANN
Please... zey goink to kill us in horrible way.

CUT TO:

INT. LOCK -- MORNING

Moon nods. Relaxed and reassuring:

MOON
Yeah, don't worry lads, we'll sort you out.

Puts phone down.

MOON (CONT'D)
We need to rescue the Dutchies, if we get time.

CUT TO:

INT. NINE BARS -- MORNING

Cleaner unlocks the door. The Lapland girls steam out.

TANYA
When I get 'old of Moon, I'm gunner nail 'im to the ceiling by 'is ballbag.

CUT TO:

INT. FORD GRANADA -- MORNING

11.55 on car clock. Debbie and Deep Throat sit in the beaten-up old motor, stuck in traffic, sniffing from their bottle. Debbie is rigging up the bomb as Deep Throat drives.

           DEEP THROAT
     Come on, come on, come on...

                                     CUT TO:

EXT. SAUCE TV STATION -- MORNING

Tony meets Spaghetti and two other HENCHMEN in the doorway.

           SPAGHETTI
    Right, get yerselves tooled up, lads.

They enter the building, leaving Dutchies and Heinrich in the back of the car.

                                     CUT TO:

EXT. STREET -- MORNING

Miami's Roller glides through the streets. A Range Rover follows behind carrying Sean and Three Feet.

                                     CUT TO:

INT. MIAMI'S ROLLER -- MORNING

Miami chats to the Chinese.

            MIAMI
 This latest acquisition was a right touch. Got it for next to
             nuffin'.
        (To one of them)
       Go on, translate.

                                     CUT TO:

INT. SAUCE TV STATION -- MORNING

Spaghetti and his boys are clearing the set.

           SPAGHETTI
       Early lunch break.

Everyone is confused. Does he mean it?

         SPAGHETTI (CONT'D)
    Get the fuck out of 'ere NOW!

Everyone scarpers, leaving the mob on their own - 12.00.

CUT TO:

INT. FORD GRANADA -- DAY

Deep Throat's watch: 12.00. He turns into a side-road to get out of traffic.
Grabs a bottle and sniffs hard – almost crashes the car.

> DEEP THROAT
> Aaaah! Fuck me, that's not amyl nitrate!

> DEBBIE
> It's nitroglycerine, love...

Deep Throat looks at what she is doing, freaks:

> DEEP THROAT
> What're you doin'? You'll blow us to fuckin' – AAH!

They're approaching a speed bump in the road. Debbie puts her hand over the
bottle as the car bounces over the bump.

> DEEP THROAT (CONT'D)
> You could of made the bomb back home an' done yer make-
> up in the car...

CUT TO:

EXT. STREET NEAR SAUCE TV -- DAY

The lads walk towards the place of the showdown.

> JAMIE
> They'll take care of each other, I'm tellin' yer. We stand at the
> door, when Miami arrives an' say 'Here you go Mr Vice, your
> TV station, would you like us to go an' get your girls now?'

> LEE
> Wonder if the Dutchies are still alive?

> JAMIE
> Doubt it. Doubt if anyone's left alive.

CUT TO:

INT. VOLVO -- DAY

(Dutchies' P.O.V.) – the lads walk past. The Dutchies struggle to get their
attention. No use.

CUT TO:

INT. SAUCE TV STATION, CORRIDOR -- DAY

The lads walk slowly down the corridor. Eerie silence.

> BACON
> Bit quiet.

Pause.

> LEE
> We shoulda come prepared.

> MOON
> Good job I brought Heinrich's piece.

Pulls out Heinrich's revolver.

> LEE
> I knew this plan wouldn't work. I knew we'd all get shot.

CUT TO:

INT. VOLVO -- DAY

The Dutchies are in an awkward embrace, untying each other. They speak in Dutch, with subtitles.

> JAAP
> Pull it. Not like that, softer.

> JOHANN
> Stop telling me what to do.

> JAAP
> I've got to get out of here. Heinrich is beginning to smell.

> JOHANN
> Don't talk about Heinrich like that.

Jaap pulls his hands free of the ropes.

> JAAP
> I'm free!

He sticks his head up. Sees Debbie and Deep Throat clambering out of the Ford Granada, each carrying a piece. He pulls his head down again.

> JAAP (CONT'D)
> Let's get out of here.

CUT TO:

EXT. SAUCE TV STATION -- DAY

> DEBBIE
> One last dab.

Deep Throat hands her the amyl.

CUT TO:

INT. SAUCE TV STATION, CORRIDOR -- DAY

The end of the corridor. By door to studio.

> JAMIE
> We goin' in?

> BACON
> Come on, le's do it, we ain't got all day.

He pushes the door.

CUT TO:

INT. STUDIO SET -- DAY

The lads see – the back of Spaghetti and his mob on the other side of the room.
Loading up guns. Standing waiting at the other doors.

> SPAGHETTI
> Moment yer see that door move...

Lads stop where they are, frozen to the spot. They close the door as quietly
as possible.

> DEEP THROAT (O.S.)
> Stop waving that thing around...

CUT TO:

INT. SAUCE TV STATION, CORRIDOR -- DAY

Deep Throat and Debbie turning the corner.

DEEP THROAT
... ain't a fucking milk shake.

CUT BACK TO:

Bacon turns back to the others.

BACON
(mouths)
Deep Throat.

They stand stock-still – caught between the two threats as the footsteps of Deep Throat and Debbie are heard coming up towards the doors.

CUT TO:

C.U. – Spaghetti's face. He's heard something. He turns slowly round, followed by his heavies.

The far door is swinging shut. No sign of the lads. No sign of anyone.

Door kicked open. Deep Throat and Debbie boldly stride in, afraid of no-one and nothing. Stand-off with Spaghetti's mob. One second of silence. Then:

CUT TO:

The lads taking cover behind the cookers on set, sound of machine-gun fire, answered with the blast of a shotgun.

The camera stays on the lads as we hear heavy gunfire over their heads. Lads flatten themselves to the floor as bullets fly over them. Gunfire ends.

Moon peers around the edge of the cooker:

Deep Throat and Debbie are shot to shit. Debbie makes a pathetic attempt to throw the home-made bomb.

Half-thrown, half-dropped, the bomb bounces right in front of the cookers... SLOW MOTION... Terry with grenade in hand goes to catch the bomb, dropping the grenade.

Tense silence. No explosion, nothing. The bomb lies there innocuously on the floor. Everyone relaxes.

Spaghetti looks at bomb then looks at grenade – BOOM.

CUT TO:

EXT. SAUCE TV STATION -- DAY

Miami and his entourage get out of his car and react to explosion.

CUT TO:

INT. SAUCE TV STATION, STUDIO -- DAY

Lads stand up, brush themselves down. Look back at the smoke-blackened doorway, and beyond it to the corpses of Spaghetti and his men. Lee looks around in amazement.

> LEE
> We have no right to still be alive.

> BACON
> Let's not 'ang around.

Moon looks at his watch.

> MOON
> We can easily make that wedding.

CUT TO:

INT. SAUCE TV STATION, CORRIDOR -- DAY

Miami and his investors walk down corridor.

> MIAMI
> We'll be making all our own programmes 'ere, won't 'ave to
> buy nothing in.

Miami opens the door to the studio and comes straight up against the lads. He looks them up and down, then nods and turns to his associates.

> MIAMI (CONT'D)
> Three Feet. See if you can find that canteen. It's very popular
> with all the crew.

Three Feet leads the Chinese away. Miami ruffles Moon's hair.

> MIAMI (CONT'D)
> You done well, boys. Girls on their way?

> JAMIE
> We'll go pick 'em up.

276

> MIAMI
> Must get you lot to do more work for me.

Miami strolls off and the lads are left alone.

> MOON
> Reckon the Dutchies made it?

The others shrug.

CUT TO:

INT. VICARAGE -- DAY

A vicar is on the phone, looking out of the window into the churchyard we saw at the beginning.

> VICAR
> I'd like to report two men doing something unspeakable in the churchyard... they're... well, I... it's... they're graverobbers!

CUT TO:

Johann and Jaap are digging a grave for Heinrich, whose corpse is sprawled out by the side of the grave.

CUT TO:

EXT. SAUCE TV STATION -- DAY

Lads sit smoking and drinking coffee out of styrofoam cups.

> JAMIE
> I don't know 'ow I do it.

> BACON
> What?

> JAMIE
> Keep comin' up with brilliant plans.

> BACON
> Jamie, we was supposed to walk in 'ere without any bother.
> We nearly got blown to shit.

> MOON
> We should be dead.

TANYA (O.O.V.)
Don't worry, Moon, you will be.

Lads turn to see the girls from Lapland looking very rough, and very pissed off indeed.

LEE
Fucking... hell...

END

EPISODE 5

LOCK, STOCK... & TWO SIPS

by Bernard Dempsey and Kevin McNally

ACT ONE

EXT. LOCK. GRAND UNION CANAL -- DAY

Birdsong on a crisp early morning. A knot of muffled figures are standing by the side of the lock. They are the current top-table hoods of East London, Greasy John, Rainham Ray, Haggis Moss, Rudolf and top dog, Miami Vice. With them is Terry Gardener, who is being groomed by Miami as a possible enforcer. They are stamping against the cold, impatient. In the background Three Feet and a couple of helpers are wrestling with the workings of an old petrol winch, the arm of which extends over the lock with a cable reaching down into the murky, oily waters below.

> MIAMI
> What is the hold-up, Three Feet?

> THREE FEET
> Nearly there, boss...

The hoods exchange glances between them in anxious anticipation. Suddenly the winch chugs into life and Three Feet gives Miami a delighted thumbs-up.

> MIAMI
> Right. Let's see what we got.

The hawser in the canal strains tight. Slowly a grotesque body emerges from the canal, face contorted in agony, arms outstretched by the lasso of the hawser. There is a calculator shoved in its mouth. It hangs above the canal wrapped in slime.

> MIAMI (CONT'D)
> Well?

> GREASY JOHN
> It's the accountant.

> MIAMI
> 'Scuse me John? I didn't quite 'ear...

> GREASY JOHN
> It's the accountant?

> MIAMI
> The accountant who was doin' your books?

Greasy John nods unhappily. Miami goes over to the winch.

MIAMI (CONT'D)
Well, that's the third accountant in a month.

He turns to face them. They avoid any eye contact.

MIAMI (CONT'D)
Who'd 'ave thought arithmetic could be so dangerous?

Three Feet produces a small axe and cuts the wire of the crane. The body plunges into the canal.

CUT TO:

OPENING TITLES

INT. THE LOCK -- DAY

Lee and Bacon are pulling pints in the bright sunlit bar. Jamie raises a pint and checks its clarity against the bright sunlight.

LEE (V.O.)
...We were having a blindin' year. We sold enough lager to
flood the Thames barrier.

CUT TO:

INT. LOCK. BACK ROOM -- DAY

Moon is pushing large cash bags into the safe. He grins a broad grin at Lee beside him.

LEE (V.O.)
We was in and out of that bank like the tide at Margate...

CUT TO:

INT. LOCK. BAR -- DAY

Moon is sashaying in between tables in the makeshift restaurant ferrying plates among the well-heeled young diners.

LEE (V.O.)
In the kitchen Moon had gone ethnic again but even his
Tongan casseroles was doin' a roarin'...

Moon slaps a dish in front of a punter.

                    LEE (V.O.) (CONT'D)
Life was... What is it when everything's as good as it can get?

                         MOON
                         Sweet...

                       LEE (V.O.)
               That's it. Life was sweet.

                                                    CUT TO:

INT. THE LOCK BACK ROOM -- DAY

                       LEE (V.O.)
And to cap it all we had a very peculiar offer from Moira.

Lee, Jamie, Bacon and Moon sitting at a round walnut table. Across the other
side of the table is Moira, forty-five. Moira is a veteran of the street, now dressed
head to boots in Gucci and current manager of Lapland. The lads are trying to
wrap their heads round an offer Moira has just made them.

                     LEE (CONT'D)
Can we go over this one more time? You are offering us fifty
                  thousand pounds?

                        MOIRA
                         Yes.

                         LEE
       And we don't have to do jack shit to get it?

                        MOIRA
   That's what I like about you boys. Sharp on the uptake.

                        JAMIE
          This may be a stupid question, Moira...

                        MOIRA
   It's not rocket science, Jamie. I would have thought it was
obvious what is goin' down here. I have a party who wishes to
            make an investment in Lapland...

                       LEE (V.O.)
       Ah, Lapland. That palace of dreams...

                                                    CUT TO:

INT. LAPLAND -- NIGHT

Girls dancing among suited businessmen. Tenners and twenties being stuffed into G-strings. Tanya and other lovelies move amongst the tables elegantly gyrating.

At the bar Moira is lifting overflowing takings trays out of the till and bagging up the notes in an echo of the Lock's booming trade. A lap dancer leans forward to a punter only to avert her lips at the last second leaving him filletted with helpless lust.

                                                                    CUT TO:

INT. LOCK. BACK ROOM -- DAY

Back in the meeting.

                          MOIRA (CONT'D)
          But he - or she- does not wish to be identified. Haven't you
                    boys ever heard of Trojan horse trading?

She looks at the lads. They obviously haven't.

                          MOIRA (CONT'D)
          Anonymous investors? Jumping out of the wooden horse
            when the damage is done? You being the Trojan horse?

The boys aren't getting any closer.

                          MOIRA (CONT'D)
                Forget it. I'll find somebody else...

She begins to collect her belongings.

                              MOON
          Hold up, Moira. Can we have a little time to think about it?

                              MOIRA
                               No.

                              MOON
                         OK. We'll do it.

The lads stand and shake Moira's hand, very pleased with themselves.

                              MOIRA
              I'll bring the money round tomorrow.

                           LEE (V.O.)
          She did an' all. And to show her appreciation she even threw
              in the catering contract on the Cabbies' Ball.

CUT TO:

INT. CABBIES' BALL -- DAY

C.U. An ice sculpture of a swan, wings fanning out in frozen flight.

The camera pulls back on a table groaning with exotic foods. Asparagus in aspic, salmon fumee, a suckling pig, pates, Belgian mousses. A tonky jazz band is giving it Georgia Brown in a corner.

> LEE (V.O.)
> Now that was real class...

The clientele is the London demi-monde, suited and booted. Black tie, here and there a debonair tux and cummerbund. Soap actors, TV presenters, page three gals.

> LEE (V.O.) (CONT'D)
> People off the telly, politicians, a radio DJ, even a minor royal
> was spotted 'angin' round the beer tent.

Magnums of champagne stand in silver coolers liberally sprinkled around the tent. Expensive hats perched on the heads of the womenfolk. A high class do. At one table sit Haggis Moss, Greasy John, Rainham Ray and Rudolf the Red Nose with their wives, girlfriends, cousins etc.

> LEE (V.O.) (CONT'D)
> And then there was the real faces. Miami's generals.
> Greasy John.

FREEZE FRAME on Greasy John.

> LEE (V.O.) (CONT'D)
> If you needed a motor he'd sort you out. Import, export, hot,
> cold - he'll have the car of your dreams on your door step
> within the hour.

Then UNFREEZE.

> LEE (V.O.) (CONT'D)
> ... 'Aggis Moss.

FREEZE FRAME on Haggis Moss.

> LEE (V.O.) (CONT'D)
> Now that geezer's got more blags to his name than any other
> face in town. If it was well organised, well tooled and well
> brutal he was the man.

284

Then UNFREEZE.

                    LEE (V.O.) (CONT'D)
                    ... an' Rainham Ray...

FREEZE FRAME on Rainham Ray.

                    LEE (V.O.) (CONT'D)
                 ... is a different kettle of fish.

                         LEE (V.O.)
        He likes getting his fingers dirty. You name it, from Burmese
        girls to celebrity blackmail. He knows every inch of the porn
                       industry - literally.

Then UNFREEZE.

                        LEE (CONT'D)
                        As for Rudolf.

FREEZE FRAME on Rudolf the Red Nose.

                        LEE (CONT'D)
        He does the dodgy booze scam, word is, he runs half of it
                     straight into his gut.

Then UNFREEZE.

                            LEE
     Four of the most vicious bastards as 'ad ever been guests of 'Er Majesty...
       Gold plated genuine 'oods. Not forgettin' the Alpha male 'imself...

Miami signals to a waiter and looks at the food on his tray. FREEZE on Miami.

                    LEE (V.O.) (CONT'D)
                Miami Vice. The top of the food chain.

UNFREEZE.

Jamie, Lee and Bacon are dressed in D.J.s overseeing a posse of young hired staff
in red cutaway jackets, dispensing portions of food and recharging the
champagne glasses.

Lee is eyeing a pretty girl guest with his eyes glued on her cleavage. He clicks his
fingers à la maitre'd. A minion hastens forward filling her glass with a napkin-
wrapped bottle. The girl smiles at Lee, not disinterested. Jamie joins Lee and
signals a waiter to retrieve another cargo of canapés from behind a table. They
watch as notes are stuffed into waiter's pockets.

JAMIE
They're tipping in folding. This is large.

Moira appears from the throng and catches Lee's jacket.

MOIRA
You seen my Tanya?

LEE
Nah.

Bacon heaves up a case of champagne.

BACON
I'm run off my feet here. Where's Moon?

JAMIE
No idea.

CUT TO:

INT. TOILETS. CABBIES' BALL -- DAY

We see a line of toilet doors. One door is closed. There is a rhythmic creaking coming from this cubicle.

TANYA
Oh, fuck me...

MOON
What do you think I'm doing? Sharpenin' a pencil?

CUT TO:

INT. CABBIES' BALL. -- DAY

A stir is created as Terry, in his expensive silk dinner suit, climbs the small makeshift stage and takes the mic. FREEZE FRAME on Terry.

LEE (V.O.)
An' then there was Terry Gardener. Rumour 'ad it that Terry was more than Miami's enforcer, word was, he's next in line to the throne.

UNFREEZE.

TERRY
Ladies and gentlemen, welcome to the annual Charity Ball for

286

Children. Please put your 'ands together for our special guest,
a man who needs no introduction... Mr Miami Vice.

The assembled guests break into a round of applause. Henchmen fan out as
Miami makes his way from the top table to the stage, acknowledging the
greetings of the guests. Applause and cheers. The band, at a signal, give a few
bars of the theme tune of *Hawaii Five-O*. Miami shoots them a brief hostile
glance then generously acknowledges the applause.

Three Feet takes the coat from Miami's shoulders and hands him a glass of
champagne which he does in one draught. The applause subsides.

> MIAMI
> I come every year ya know...And why? Because it's an event,
> as you know dear to my 'eart. Every year these knights of the
> 'ackney carriage trade dip their 'ands in their pockets to send
> the underprivileged youngsters of our great capital out on the
> 'oliday of a lifetime.

Miami gestures to the table of cab drivers as the applause swells for the cabmen.

> MIAMI (CONT'D)
> And this year you generous people 'ave raised a record amount.

Miami and Terry link hands and hold them up in a victory salute. Some
sycophants get to their feet. 'For they are Jolly Good Fellows' breaks out.
Three Feet gets Miami a glass of champagne. Miami speaks out of the corner
of his mouth to Terry.

> MIAMI (CONT'D)
> Where they taking them this year?

> TERRY
> Frinton.

> MIAMI
> Tight bunch of wankers...

He smiles at the crowd. He raises his glass.

> MIAMI (CONT'D)
> To a truly 'umanitarian body of men...

He downs another glass of champagne in one. Back to Terry.

> MIAMI (CONT'D)
> This French lager's murder on the bladder. Let's talk as we
> walk. I'm desperate for an eyelash.

They bid farewell to the adoring crowd. As they go, Moira watches them.

CUT TO:

INT. TOILET. CABBIES' BALL -- DAY

Moon is with Tanya both arranging their dress. Moon opens the door and swiftly ducks behind it as he sees Three Feet coming into the toilets. He presses Tanya against the wall of the cubicle.

Behind Three Feet Miami and Terry come into the cabin. Miami walks to the urinal and takes a leak. Terry behind him leans on a sink. Three Feet kicks open the door of each cubicle. He merely peers into Moon's cubicle and from the angle assumes it empty as well.

>THREE FEET
>Clear, boss.

Miami jerks his head and Three Feet withdraws. In the cubicle Moon and Tanya press back against the wall. Miami finishes his leak, zips up then joins Terry at the sink where he washes his hands.

>MIAMI
>I got a problem with Lapland...

>TERRY
>Reindeer escaped ?

Miami stares at him for a second too long before smiling.

>MIAMI
>That's what I like about you Tel. Always ready wiv' a joke, the
>verbals.

>TERRY
>Sorry, Miami. What's the problem?

>MIAMI
>I bought this gaff for my old man. He used to be acquainted
>with the old boiler that runs the place. What's 'er name?

>TERRY
>Moira.

>MIAMI
>Silly name for a tart. Anyway, the old man used to have a soft
>spot for this Moira when she was on street corners 'awkin' the
>mutton. Used to be a hard spot but age takes its toll.

Terry smiles at the joke.

> MIAMI (CONT'D)
> So last birthday I buys the fucking warren for him but... I let
> the old scrubber keep ten per cent.

> TERRY
> I'm with you.

He leans forward to Terry.

> MIAMI
> I recently made 'er an offer for 'er part in the business.

> TERRY
> And?

> MIAMI
> I find myself involved in a game of ping-pong with a shagged
> out old slapper who's pulling my plonker to the tune of
> twenty grand a time.

He leans closer and confides to Terry.

> MIAMI (CONT'D)
> Some fuckwit has been bidding against me.

In his cubicle Moon closes his eyes in horror.

> TERRY
> And the only fucker who could tell us who it was is now at
> the bottom of the Grand Union Canal.

> MIAMI
> No flies on you, Terry. Tell the lads I want a meeting after this
> chimps' tea-party is over.

Miami and Terry leave the cabin. Back in the cubicle Moon digests the situation.

> TANYA
> Can you believe that guy? He called my mum a scrubber.

She pulls up her knickers.

                                                    CUT TO:

INT. CABBIES' BALL -- DAY

Miami comes back into the main hall with Terry. Moira is talking to Rainham Ray. She looks over at Miami and Terry.

She watches as Terry and Miami make their way over to Haggis's table where Miami greets Haggis like a long-lost friend. She takes a glass of champagne from Lee and goes over to the food table. Moon comes hurrying into the hall where he runs into Bacon.

                    BACON
        And where have you been?

                    MOON
    Never mind, we have got a major fuckin' problem...

                                                    CUT TO:

INT. THE KITCHEN. CABBIES' BALL -- DAY

The kitchen is now empty and practically clean. Lee looks through the window of the door and sees Miami's henchmen.

                    LEE
    It makes sense doesn't it? He wants outright control.

                    MOON
    And we're the little dickie birds who are stopping him getting
            it. We got to dismantle the situation.

                    BACON
        What you talking about you wuss?

                    MOON
        Have you been following any of this?

                    BACON
        We signed the contract legal di'n't we?

                    MOON
    Bacon... Let me make this easy for you... Miami is a murderous
        psycho with a criminal empire. You are a Bermondsey ponce
                    with a penknife...

                    LEE
    The way I see it, Moira's not going to flash that paper to
    Miami till she has to. We take her back her fifty long ones
            and get the contract back. Agreed?

The boys nod agreement.

INT. CABBIES' BALL -- NIGHT.

The guests have all disappeared, except for Miami, Greasy John, Haggis Moss, Rainham Ray, Rudolf and Terry, who sit at a large table with a bottle of whisky and glasses. Behind each of them sit their respective muscle. Haggis is nervously fiddling with a box of matches. Miami leans forward.

> MIAMI
> I tell you what I think - we got a mouse in the pantry...

He lets the accusation hang heavy in the air. Greasy, Haggis and Rainham shift uncomfortably. Haggis still nervously fiddling with the matches. Miami lets them stew then continues in a measured tone.

> MIAMI (CONT'D)
> Another accountant goes for a midnight dip in the Grand
> Union...

> HAGGIS
> Miami...

> MIAMI
> 'Scuse me, 'Aggis, I am not flappin' my gums for dental
> exercise - I am trying to make a point 'ere...

Haggis twirls his matchbox, furious.

> MIAMI (CONT'D)
> And you can stop fiddlin' with them matches...

Haggis tosses the matches on the table and stares at Miami like an insolent teenager.

> MIAMI (CONT'D)
> You're not impressin' me son.

Haggis breaks his stare and holds up his palms in a placatory gesture. Miami holds his look then turns back to his point.

> MIAMI (CONT'D)
> Three accountants go belly-up in as many weeks. It doesn't take
> Miss fuckin' Marple to cop it's something to do with figures. So I
> been lookin' at the books. Or rather yours, yours and yours.

He indicates Greasy, Haggis and Rainham.

> MIAMI (CONT'D)
> And I'm 'ere to tell you that your sums just ain't adding up.

291

Miami summons Three Feet who hands him a ledger. Miami tosses it on the table and looks at Greasy John.

> MIAMI (CONT'D)
> Your remortgage on the car-yard... It's sixty grand light.

Greasy John frowns in disbelief. Miami throws another ledger on the table and turns to Haggis.

> MIAMI (CONT'D)
> The bonded warehouse you done over in May. It's nowhere in the figures...

Haggis blinks incomprehension. Miami turns to Rainham Ray and holds up another ledger.

> MIAMI (CONT'D)
> Page seventeen. Seven grand and seven grand ain't thirteen grand.

He tosses the book before Rainham.

> RAINHAM
> Miami, I swear...

> MIAMI
> Now there are two possibilities - either one or more of you 'as
> been pissin' in the swimmin' pool...

The hoods gesture their denials.

> MIAMI (CONT'D)
> Which is unlikely given you know what I'd do to you. Or,
> some little fuckin' squirrel is nickin' conkers and fiddlin' the
> books to 'ide 'is trail. An' when I find out who it is - 'e'll wish
> 'is dad 'ad 'ad a wank on the night 'e was conceived. Clear?

The various hoods nod compliance. Satisfied Miami turns to Three Feet.

> MIAMI (CONT'D)
> Get the car.

CUT TO:

INT. LAPLAND -- NIGHT

Lee, Bacon, Moon and Jamie are in the club walking towards the office. Lee knocks on the door. The door opens and Three Feet smiles at them, then grabs Bacon and Jamie. Moon and Lee wheel round in their tracks and head for the exit.

As they hurry there, their path is blocked by a bouncer who takes out a vicious-looking Bowie knife and leans on the banisters by the exit, resting the blade on his thigh.

                              MOON
                    I don't feel so well.

                                                          CUT TO:

INT. MIAMI'S OFFICE -- NIGHT

C.U. on the barrel of a shotgun. It is being polished by Three Feet, Miami's chief whip, with exaggerated attention. Miami sits behind his huge desk smoking a pit-prop of a cigar. The lads sit in upright chairs lined up before the desk, each holding a cup of tea in a saucer on their laps. Behind each is a bruiser built on Tyson lines. Miami leans forward confidingly. He glances at Three Feet polishing the gun.

                              MIAMI
          From Purdeys. Lovely piece but I do wish 'e wouldn't polish it in 'ere.

Three Feet holds it up in firing stance looking down the sights. The four heavies behind the lads quickly flinch away from the line of fire.

                          MIAMI (CONT'D)
              Make a right mess of my wallpaper if that goes off...

Three Feet smiles reassuringly and resumes polishing the gun in his lap. The heavies reluctantly take their positions behind the lads, exchanging worried looks between them.

                              LEE
                What.. er... can we do for you, Miami?

Miami gets to his feet and indicates a large framed photograph of
Harry Bellafonte.

                              MIAMI
          See that? Harry Bellafonte at Caesar's Palace, Las Vegas. One of the
          truly great talents of our age. It's signed see? It says 'Knock 'em dead
              tonight Harry, your old pal Frankie.' Any idea who Frankie was?

                             JAMIE
                            Sinatra?

                             MIAMI
          Good boy. Signed not only by Harry Bellafonte himself but by
                        the legendary Frank Sinatra.

> MIAMI
> Know how much I had to pay for that? Go on ask me...

> JAMIE
> How much did you have to pay?

> MIAMI
> None of your fuckin' business, son but I will tell you I
> thought they was the most expensive monikers in the world
> till I found this...

He holds up the lads' agreement with Moira.

> MIAMI (CONT'D)
> ... fifty fuckin' thousand for four names no-one's even 'eard of.

Miami is on his feet and is lowering over the lads in dangerous mood.
The heavies behind them suddenly clamp their hands on the lads' shoulders.

> MIAMI (CONT'D)
> I mean, what is it with you boys? Every time I turn my back
> you're crawling out of the woodwork like some sort of carpet
> beetle. You tired of living or something, 'cos if you are you've
> come to the right place...

Miami snatches hold of the shotgun from Three Feet. Suddenly Lee calmly cuts
through the tirade.

> LEE
> It was only business.

Miami stops short.

> MIAMI
> What?

> LEE
> What were we supposed to do? The lady came round and
> offered us a load of money for doing fuck-all. It would have
> been criminal to turn her down. If you'll forgive the adjective.
> If it was an adjective.

Miami reflects. Despite his anger he is impressed by Lee's bottle and logic. He
gives the gun back to Three Feet and returns to his desk. He surveys the boys
thoughtfully and says, as if he were the softest touch in the world:

> MIAMI
> All right, let's do business. I want twenty grand by tomorrow.

INT. THE LOCK -- DAY

Lee grabs bottle which is full of coins, from shelf. He smashes it and takes out a bunch of notes.

INT. LOCK. BACK ROOM -- DAY

Bacon puts his hands through a floorboard. Pulls out a teddy, throws it away. Pulls out porn mag and throws it away. Grabs a bundle of notes.

INT. THE LOCK. BAR -- DAY

Moon at bar, fishing money out from behind fridge.

INT. THE LOCK. KITCHEN -- DAY

Jamie fishes round under the sink; water pours out and he pulls out a bundle of notes caked in shit.

CUT TO:

INT. LOCK. BACK ROOM -- DAY

Three wads of money are put on the table then a hand covered in shit adds a few old pieces of shitty money. Camera pulls back to see Jamie looking worried.

> JAMIE
> Cash-flow ? Well, let's say there's a major blockage in the system, alright ?

> BACON
> You wanna give Miami two-ton-fifty, covered in shit ?

> MOON
> That'll show 'im who's boss.

> JAMIE
> It's what I got left. Listen, I need...

Jamie searches for the right word.

> BACON
> A smack in the mouth ?

> JAMIE
> A loan is what it comes down to.

> MOON
> We're all cleaned out. Look...

                              LEE
                    What about your Uncle ?

                             JAMIE
                         Uncle John?

A series of still 1980s photographs of Jamie's Uncle John...

Uncle John in Santa outfit handing out presents to four little five-year-olds...

Uncle John juggling balls, much to the boys' delight...

Uncle John handing out candy floss to the boys at a funfair...

Uncle John hoisting little Jamie in warm Uncle arms.

Back on Jamie and Lee.

                              LEE
            Jamie, 'e's in Australia, ain't 'e ? I mean Uncle Keith...

A similar series of Uncle Keith from their boyhood...

Uncle Keith scowling at the camera...

Uncle Keith with orange-peel Dracula fangs scaring the life out of the four little
boys...

Uncle Keith bearing down on little Jamie brandishing a belt...

Uncle Keith pulling up little Jamie by the tie as the other lads look on in horror...

Back to Jamie, with nauseous expression.

                             JAMIE
                    OK... I'm desperate, right ?

Three nodding heads look back at him.

                                                              CUT TO:

INT. THE LOCK. BAR -- NIGHT

Uncle Keith is sitting in a booth in the bar ladling Tongan noodles into his mouth
from an outsize bowl on the table before him. Jamie sits opposite him full of
childhood fears and revulsion. As Uncle Keith speaks he liberally covers the table
with spittle and noodles.

                              UNCLE KEITH
        I hear you've landed yourself in the shit again. You always did
             have 'ars'ole' written through you like a stick of rock.

Uncle Keith laughs richly, genuinely enjoying Jamie's plight.

                                 JAMIE
               But we have to see the family alright don't we?

                              UNCLE KEITH
                                Do what?

                                 JAMIE
                               Forget it...

Uncle Keith shovels another load of food into his mouth and gurgles a half litre
of Kronenburg to wash it down.

                              UNCLE KEITH
            I also know who you owe this money to, an' all. Miami
                              fuckin' Vice.

Uncle Keith suddenly gives vent to a prolonged bay of laughter interspersed with
coughing on his noodles, spraying the booth with more food. The laughter gives
way to choking – he seems about to burst a blood vessel.

Jamie watches him stony-faced until the laughter subsides enough for him to get
a word in.

                                 JAMIE
            Uncle Keith... I've always hated you worse than death. I
           wouldn't piss on you if you was on fire. You're a cunt. Either
                             help me out, or fuck off.

Jamie gets to his feet. Uncle Keith suddenly grabs him by the lapel and pulls him
to his face. Uncle Keith looks dangerous for a second then releases his grip,
smiles and waggles his finger.

                              UNCLE KEITH
              Don't piss off the pier 'til you know which way the wind's
                        blowin'. I'm going to lend you some money...

He drags over another bowl of sweetmeats and spoons them into his mouth.
Jamie sits stunned.

                         UNCLE KEITH (CONT'D)
             Course, there's something you have to do for me. Which if
                you fuck it up will mean your life won't be worth living.

He smiles from ear to ear.

                    UNCLE KEITH (CONT'D)
                    Still interested?

                                                    CUT TO:

INT. THE LOCK. BACK ROOM -- DAY

Three Feet sets up a money counter. The cash is batched up with rubber bands
waiting to be counted. Lee and Moon stand by the table.

                    LEE
                    'Ere 'e comes.

In comes Jamie with his wad, looking hassled. Slaps it down.

                    THREE FEET
        You want me to count 'em separate, so you know who to
                    blame if it's short ?

                    JAMIE
                    It's all there.

Puts the first wad into the counter. The notes whizz through. Stinker comes
tramping in.

                    STINKER
            You know what you got down there...

                    LEE
                    What?

                    STINKER
        Dogget and Clark imperial lead feed pipe. Brummie firm...

                    LEE
                    Can you fix it?

                    STINKER
            I never expected to see it this far south.

                    LEE
                    Can you fix it?

                    STINKER
        Trouble is, someone's joined it to a copper modern metric...

LEE
Does that mean yer can't fix it ?

STINKER
That's like painting a tash on the Mona Lisa. Bloody disgrace.

Moon explains to Three Feet.

MOON
'E's 'ere to fix the drains.

THREE FEET
(Sniffing)
Glad someone is...

Three Feet has finished counting. Starts packing up.

THREE FEET (CONT'D)
'Til the next time, eh?

Three Feet leaves through one door...

STINKER
Bad news is... I'll have to have your water off for at least
an hour.

MOON
Just do it!

Stinker screws up the empty packet. They turn to Jamie:

LEE
(Expectantly)
Jamie ?

JAMIE
(Casual)
Morning.

LEE
Well?

JAMIE
Uncle Keith ? He did make me a proposition.

MOON
What we gotta do for 'im ?

Lee shoots a look at Stinker, then sees that Bacon is listening, having come in from the bar.

> JAMIE
> We have to put someone up for a few days. In the back room.

> BACON
> What's the story?

> JAMIE
> An ex-pat mate of Uncle Keith's from the Costa. Goes by the name of Two Sips.

> LEE
> And?

> JAMIE
> An old face. A face Miami will not want to see again. Uncle Keith wants him watched like an hawk for a few days. Make sure 'e don't wander into anywhere 'e ain't welcome.

> BACON
> What's 'e back 'ere for anyway ?

> JAMIE
> That I do not know.

> LEE
> Let's be honest, if he's a friend of Uncle Keith's he's as welcome as a dose of the clap.

> MOON
> When does 'e get in ?

> JAMIE
> Tonight.

> LEE
> City or Stansted?

> JAMIE
> Not that simple, Lee...

CUT TO:

EXT. CABIN CRUISER. THE THAMES. TILBURY -- NIGHT

The cabin cruiser at anchor on the Thames as the dinghy approaches. The captain looks from the stern deck and calls to the lads.

>   CAPTAIN
>   Bring her in on the slack...

>   BACON
>   What's he say?

>   CAPTAIN
>   Ride her up on the ebbtide and bring her alongside on the
>   slack.

>   MOON
>   Don't give us that bollocks - just chuck us a rope!

                                                    CUT TO:

EXT. CABIN CRUISER DECK.-- NIGHT

Jamie, Bacon and Lee are hanging grimly to the rail of the cabin cruiser as they haul Moon from the dinghy. The Captain smiles as they accustom themselves to the yawing boat.

>   CAPTAIN
>   Can't find your sea-legs, lads?

>   MOON
>   Listen Pugwash, I'm cold, wet and I've just ruined a pair of
>   Kenzos worth more than this boat. I don't need salty sea-dog
>   banter so if you know what's good for you, you'll button it.

>   JAMIE
>   Where is he?

The Captain gestures to the back of the boat.

>   JAMIE (CONT'D)
>   Two Sips?

A figure appears from the shadow. It is Two Sips. His face is ashen - in a rictus.

Two Sips suddenly pitches his head over the side of the boat; there is the sound of a prolonged chunder.

>   CAPTAIN
>   Been like that since Bilbao.

END OF ACT ONE

ACT TWO

CUT TO:

INT. THE LOCK. BAR -- NIGHT

Bacon, Moon and Lee are in the bar chugging beers. Jamie comes into the bar from the back.

                         BACON
        How long we gotta play nursemaid to that Status Quo drummer?

Jamie goes behind the bar and tops an ice-cold Dos Equis from which he drinks deep.

                         JAMIE
            'Til Uncle Keith says it's home-time.

                         BACON
        I ain't keen on 'angin' out with anyone who's in Miami's bad
                    books, know what I mean ?

                         JAMIE
            Relax, we just stay in a lot.

The lads swing round to see Two Sips palming back his long (now gelled) hair. He looks dapper in his pressed jeans and a suit jacket. A man fully recovered who looks like a drummer from Status Quo.

                     JAMIE (CONT'D)
                        Sure.

                       TWO SIPS
                  I'll have a Guinness.

He sits on a bar stool and watches in anticipation as Jamie draws the pint. While the pint is being poured the lads unselfconsciously stare at Two Sips with curiosity. Jamie serves the Guinness onto the bar. Two Sips picks up the pint, addresses it.

                         BACON
              So why they call you Two...

Two Sips drinks half a pint in one. He relishes the coolness in his throat for a second then sculls back the remaining half.

                       TWO SIPS
                         Eh?

302

BACON
Nuffin...

CUT TO:

MONTAGE; DAYS OF CARDS AND BOOZE

Two Sips holds court, coming in and out of various different stories.

TWO SIPS
So there I was, with two Alsatians coming towards me... but
like I said, it's amazing how fast reactions and a couple of
elastic bands can get you out of trouble.

CUT TO:

TWO SIPS (CONT'D)
It wasn't until I pulled his last tooth out that he told me
where old Two Faced Dave was hiding.

CUT TO:

TWO SIPS (CONT'D)
We found him dead, stapled to a life-size cut-out of Keith Richards.

CUT TO:

TWO SIPS (CONT'D)
Reggie was a great pal of me Dad's, like an uncle to me, never
forgot me birthday.

CUT TO:

TWO SIPS (CONT'D)
What you lads don't understand is that the Royal Family are great
ambassadors that bring a fuck of a lot of tourism to this country.

CUT TO:

TWO SIPS (CONT'D)
Me Dad was never the same after theGreat Train Robbery.

CUT TO:

TWO SIPS (CONT'D)
The magic bullet theory is bollocks. Lee Harvey Oswald was
innocent. There were three people firing and one was
definitely on the grassy knoll.

CUT TO:

TWO SIPS (CONT'D)
Kids nower days have got no idea. They don't think. Guns
should only be used as the last possible choice.

CUT TO:

TWO SIPS (CONT'D)
I blame Third World Debt on the greed of the large banks.

CUT TO:

TWO SIPS (CONT'D)
It's good for focusing the mind, keeps you in tip-top shape.
There you go... look, a cockerel.

Two Sips produces a piece of origami.

CUT TO:

TWO SIPS (CONT'D)
You see, I always wanted to work with children.

We come out of the montage to see the lads with very sympathetic faces...

TWO SIPS (CONT'D)
It's 'somethin' you 'ave to come to terms with... but, what can
you do? I 'ad to feel my feet on English soil, y'know? Ain't
sure 'ow long I got. Six months, doctor said. It's in me chest.
Y'know I ain't never even been to Madame Tussaud's ?

Two Sips sparks up a cheroot. Taunts it.

TWO SIPS (CONT'D)
You can't 'urt me now !

MOON
Tha's the spirit, mate.

TWO SIPS
Gotta say my farewells. 'Specially 'Aggis Moss - me an' 'im
done time together. 'Is old sort used to smuggle in the baccy
for us, in her bra. 'Ere, does 'e still go to the boxing?

JAMIE
Haggis ? Regular as clockwork.

> TWO SIPS
> I'd like to see him one last time.

> BACON
> Well...

> TWO SIPS
> Not if it's a risk. I'm gonna die soon enough as it is !

> LEE
> A mate's a mate, innit ?

> JAMIE
> No problem Two Sips, whatever you want.

CUT TO:

EXT. BOXING VENUE -- NIGHT.

The lads, looking worried, are with Two Sips at the boxing.

CUT TO:

INT. BOXING VENUE. HOSPITALITY SUITE -- NIGHT.

Miami and Three Feet, Terry, Greasy John, Rainham Ray, Rudolf and a posse of minders in 'monkey suits'. A white-jacketed waiter stands by the side of a table laden with an expensive feast of finger foods.

Miami wanders over to the table and examines the spread.

> MIAMI
> Champagne, oysters, caviar... No cockles?

He points to Three Feet who starts to walk over to the waiter.

CUT TO:

EXT. THE SAME THROUGH BINOCULARS -- NIGHT.

Three Feet has words with the waiter.

CUT TO:

INT. BOXING VENUE -- NIGHT.

Two Sips lowers his binoculars. He is wearing a disguise of sorts. Hat, dark glasses and up turned collar. Jamie and Two Sips stand side by side watching the parade of boxers. Jamie hands him a drink.

Two Sips puts the binoculars back to his eyes. From his P.O.V. we see first Terry, then Miami come out onto the balcony. Jamie looking at Boxer programme.

> JAMIE
> Which one do you fancy in the middleweights?

> TWO SIPS
> I'm still thinking about the heavyweights Jamie.

CUT TO:

EXT. SUITE. BALCONY OVERLOOKING THE RING -- NIGHT.

Miami and Terry are talking quietly away from the others.

> MIAMI
> Just to warn you that things might kick off tonight. I thought
> you should know.

Terry looks concerned.

> TERRY
> Why's that, Miami?

> MIAMI
> Old Haggis is on his way over from a bunch of number-
> crunchers in the city. With some crystal-clear results, my boy.

Pats Terry on cheek. Terry has recovered well, nods firmly.

CUT TO:

INT. BOXING VENUE -- NIGHT.

Two Sips now looking at the boxers.

> TWO SIPS
> You know, I wasn't much older than you when I had to get out
> of the country.

> JAMIE
> At least you've got the weather over there...

> TWO SIPS
> Don't matter a shit. It's not just the usual bollocks you miss:
> beer, rain, West Ham, phoneboxes... what you really miss is the

Great English Pub Fight... Eleven o'clock ? Ding-ding, down
yer pint, steam outside, bottle in yer hand - Come on !! Let's
'ave some !!

CUT TO:

INT. HOSPITALITY SUITE -- NIGHT

Three Feet has pinned the waiter to the wall, speaking quietly but threateningly.

> THREE FEET
> I'm not arguin', son. He wants some cockles..

> MIAMI (O.O.V.)
> Plenty of vinegar.

> THREE FEET
> With plenty of vinegar.

The waiter scoots out of the suite. Three Feet and a couple of his posse follow
him out. Terry collars one of Greasy John's minders and speaks in his ear. At a
nod from Terry a couple of his guys also leave the room. We see Miami catch
the exchange.

CUT TO:

INT. BOXING VENUE. CORRIDOR -- NIGHT

Haggis Moss enters the boxing ring. Seen through Two Sips' binoculars.

CUT TO:

INT. BOXING RING --NIGHT

The crowd's roar starts to build as the fight builds.

CUT TO:

INT. BOXING VENUE --NIGHT

Lads watching fight.

> MOON
> (shouting)
> Tha's it mate, yeah, jab 'im, jab'im, no, don't stand off for Christ's sake.

> JAMIE
> Two Sips your man in the red ain't...

307

Jamie stops. Two Sips' chair is empty apart from a pair of binoculars.

> JAMIE (CONT'D)
> Oh no. E's gone walkabout.

> BACON
> Shit.

CUT TO:

EXT. BALCONY. BOXING VENUE -- NIGHT

Miami with Terry. Miami is staring down at the ring.

> MIAMI
> I've seen it all before. They start with two bob, two quid, two
> grand. Then two 'undred grand but you've got four 'undred
> and they get the 'ump. Envy. Envy of the other man.

Three Feet appears with a jar of cockles on a tray. Miami digs in with a wooden
fork and takes a large mouthful.

> MIAMI (CONT'D)
> Cockle, Terry?

Three Feet puts the jar in front of Terry.

> MIAMI (CONT'D)
> Bottle job, I'm afraid.

CUT TO:

INT. BOXING VENUE -- NIGHT

The fight continues. The lads run around looking for Two Sips.

CUT TO:

INT. BOXING VENUE. CORRIDORS -- NIGHT

Two Sips walks towards Haggis Moss. They come face to face. Haggis looks
scared and starts to run. Two Sips follows.

CUT TO:

EXT. BOXING VENUE. -- NIGHT

The lads still looking for Two Sips. Boxer in red trunks hits the floor.

CUT TO:

INT. BOXING VENUE. CORRIDOR -- NIGHT

Haggis trying to get out but the exit doors won't budge. He charges down the corridor and almost runs into Two Sips. Turns around. Runs off trying every door. Toilet door is the one that opens. Two Sips follows.

CUT TO:

EXT. BOXING RING -- NIGHT

Audience applaud boxer who has won. Lads looking for Two Sips.

CUT TO:

INT. BOXING VENUE. GENTS -- NIGHT

Two Sips walks in, pulls out gun. Haggis is trying to get out of the window but the basin he's standing on breaks. He falls to the floor.

> HAGGIS
> No... No... I've just 'ad a... nephew. 'E's my son, 'e's...

The gun goes off. Blood splatters the tiled wall. Two Sips pours out his measure of wine. Lads steam in.

> JAMIE
> Oh for fuck's sake. I thought 'e was your mate.

> TWO SIPS
> Times change.

> LEE
> I can see that...

> TWO SIPS
> How 'bout a trip to Lapland ? See 'ow Moira's gettin' on.
> She still doin' that thing with the python?

As the lads and Two Sips go to exit the toilet, No Hope Harry pushes through them. He turns with a surprised look on his face and watches them all leave the toilet.

> NO HOPE
> Well I'll be fucked...

CUT TO:

INT. BOXING VENUE. HOSPITALITY SUITE -- NIGHT.

Miami is alone on the balcony. The lights are up; people are clearing up after the boxing match. Three Feet appears from behind him and whispers some news in his ear.

                                                              CUT TO:

INT. LAPLAND -- NIGHT

The lads walk into Lapland followed by Two Sips with gun in pocket. Tanya is on stage giving it some.

                          BACON
                       (Whispering)
                  This is not good Jamie.

                          JAMIE
                      (Sarcastically)
        The man has got a gun in 'is pocket that 'e likes to make a
                     noise with - 'capice'?

                          MOON
              This mullarkey gives me the horn.

Others give him pitying looks.

                          BACON
              You got somethin' wrong with you.

                        TWO SIPS
              Nice touch, those dwarves, yeah.

Two Sips walks on ahead.

                           LEE
        This is madness. 'E ain't supposed to be in the same country as
                    Miami let alone in 'is club.

Two Sips turns round again. Lads freeze.

                        TWO SIPS
              I've gotta say 'ello to Moira.

Lads nod uncertainly. Two Sips wanders towards Moira. Lads wait with bated breath. SLO-MO: Two Sips' hand slides into inside pocket. Moira looks up. Half-recognition. Then she smiles. Lads grimace. Two Sips stops when he reaches point-blank range, one hand in pocket...

>   MOON
>   Nooo !

Two Sips pulls out... a single red rose. Plastic binding. Huge sigh of relief. Two Sips hands it over.

>   MOIRA
>   (Affectionate)
>   Two Sips.

They snog.

>   LEE
>   Right, that's it. I'm off.

Jamie and Bacon follow.

>   MOON
>   I'm gonna hang around for a bit.

The others give him questioning looks.

>   MOON (CONT'D)
>   Tanya's just finished 'er shift.

He moves in on Tanya as she leaves the stage.

>   BACON
>   'E'll be alright.

They scarper.

INT. LAPLAND --NIGHT

Tanya and Moon snogging

>   MOON
>   You're well up for it aren't yer ?

>   TANYA
>   Shut up, and get your head down there.

Pushes his head down.

>   CUT TO:

INT. THE LOCK. BAR -- MORNING

Jamie, Moon and Lee are having a quiet meeting. We can guess that Jamie's been taking some flak over all this.

> JAMIE
> Look, I'll be the first to admit, there are better ways of raising twenty grand than babysittin' a maniac, but we gotta work out how to stop 'im takin' out any more of 'is old enemies.

> MOON
> Keep 'im indoors. Maybe we could... rent some videos for 'im. Comedies, nothing violent.

> LEE
> He might go for that. Bein' on 'is last legs.

> JAMIE
> (Exasperated)
> Lee...

> MOON
> Lee, 'e was not entirely truthful about the cancer...

> LEE
> (Realising)
> Fuckin' bastard...

Bacon arrives.

> BACON
> Right Jamie, what's your plan ?

> JAMIE
> Keep the fucker inside these four walls.

Everyone nods. Stinker appears from behind a table crowded with empties. Gropes around for a glass not quite finished.

> BACON
> What is the plumber doing in the bar, drinking a pint an hour before we open?

> MOON
> Drinking his wages. We paid him in pints. He's got fifty in the bin.

Moon takes a book from the side of the till.

> MOON (CONT'D)
> That's his thirty-fourth.

Bacon opens the till. Empty.

Sound of toilet flushing. Enter Two Sips, bright and breezy.

> TWO SIPS
> Right. We're goin' out.

> JAMIE
> We thought we'd stay 'ere.

> BACON
> Keep our heads down.

Two Sips flicks back his lapel, checks his gun is loaded.

> TWO SIPS
> Who's drivin' ?

On lads' reaction.

CUT TO:

EXT. THE LOCK. BACK YARD -- DAY

Jamie is nervous. Can't start the car. Two Sips is trying to reach someone on the mobile. Lads speak quietly next to car.

> MOON
> Y'know I'm missin' out on a shag 'ere ?

> LEE
> Gutted for yer.

> MOON
> Tanya's goin' through one of 'er creative periods.

> BACON
> Moon. E's gonna do someone again.

Jamie accidentally toots the horn. Everyone glares at him.

> BACON (CONT'D)
> We'll 'ave to bag 'im up, or something.

> LEE
> Don't be dense, 'e's a pro.

TWO SIPS
(Into phone)
Rainy...

Lads react to this news as Jamie's car starts. They all climb in.

TWO SIPS (O.O.V.) (CONT'D)
(Into phone)
I wanted to have a little word with you... Something I saw at
the boxing last night. Something that happened in the bog...
What say I pop round and we get down to cases?

Jamie manages to bunny hop the car out the drive.

EXT. RAINHAM RAY'S HOUSE - FRONT DOOR -- DAY.

The house has all the accoutrements of the Essex villain.

Lads and Two Sips stand by front door. All the lads are a bit wary about what
Two Sips is about to do.

JAMIE
So, er, you an' Rainham get on do yer, Two Sips ?

TWO SIPS
Peas in a pod.

Lee clocks something:

LEE
Look at that pool, this place must be worth a fortune.

BACON
Peas in a pod get on, then ?

TWO SIPS
Ray and me ? Brothers in all but name.

Two Sips rings the doorbell again. Starts to hum 'Imagine'. No sound or
movement from inside. Lads look nervous. Then without warning, the Georgian
door swings open and Rainham Ray appears on the doorstep. Pause as the two
men stare at each other.

RAINHAM
Two Sips, me old mucker.

TWO SIPS
Rainham Ray, gorgeous as ever.

314

They embrace manfully. Lads breathe another sigh of relief, smile at each other sheepishly.

EXT. RAINHAM RAY'S HOUSE - NEAR POOL --DAY

They stand near the pool. The mood is friendly and relaxed.

                              LEE
          Lovely house, mate. Did ya put that pool in yourself?

                            RAINHAM
      Yeah, I did as a matter of fact. Almost done me back in, liftin'
              that crazy pavin' off the missis' rockery!

                             MOON
                Bet she weren't too happy about that!

                            RAINHAM
       Fuckin' paid for it boys, shagging was out for a month!

More laughter.

                              LEE
          So where d'yer get that marble from? Pretty rare that type
                            isn't it?

                            RAINHAM
                       (Looking out to pond)
                Well, no son, you can actually...

BANG. Two Sips has blown Ray's head off. Blood everywhere.
Stunned silence, at first. (As lads speak, Two Sips goes through
  his routine of pouring wine from a miniature bottle into a
  glass. He takes a sip, crosses himself, takes another sip and
  crosses himself again.) Lee's got blood on him - freaks out.

                              LEE
          AAH ! You fucking mental case ! Will you stop
                       shootin' people !

                            BACON
             You're meant to be keepin' a low profile.

                              LEE
          Poor bastard never got to answer the question.

Two Sips wipes the glass and places it by the dead body.

TWO SIPS

You can buy marble anywhere these days. Better give us the
car keys, eh lad?

Jamie hands over car keys.

END OF ACT TWO

ACT THREE

INT. THE LOCK. KITCHEN -- DAY

Bacon and Lee are standing by the kitchen range. Jamie sits at the table nursing
an outsize tumbler of Scotch.

BACON

So where is he now?

LEE

He's having a lie down. Said he was tired.

BACON

Well, 'e's had a busy day, 'asn't 'e?

MOON

I'll give you this, James, life around you is never boring.

MOON

If anyone else 'ad a friend of their uncle's over for a few days,
you'd know what to expect. Tower of London, Nelson's
Column, bit of the zoo. But not Jamie's mate. His idea of a
good time is to pop round to an old chum and blow his brains
all over the Formica.

JAMIE

It was a bit of an eyebrow-raiser for me an' all.

LEE

What do we do now?

JAMIE

Get in touch with Uncle Keith and sort 'is escape route out.

CUT TO:

INT. LOCK-UP GARAGE -- NIGHT

Terry, Greasy John, Rudolph and Three Feet. They are dressed in dark suits and black ties and are plainly tooled up. The atmosphere is tense. From out of the shadows Miami appears, speaking.

> MIAMI
> Rainham Ray is no more. An old and trusted friend, he 'as left a big 'ole where once 'e stood. 'E was a man you could rely on, one of the old school.

> MIAMI (CONT'D)
> We all know these untimely departures can leave a bit of a vacuum. So I've asked you 'ere in a spirit of free and frank discussion to iron out any problems. Greasy John. You want to ask Rudolph a question?

Miami nods from Greasy John to Rudolph. Greasy John steels himself.

> GREASY JOHN
> Did you top Rainham ?

> RUDOLPH
> No.

> MIAMI
> Do you believe him ?

Greasy John shrugs.

> MIAMI (CONT'D)
> Do you fucking believe him?

> GREASY JOHN
> Yes.

> MIAMI
> Ask Terry.

Greasy is uncomfortable, feeling picked on. Terry is giving out that he is at ease with this, right in with Miami.

> TERRY
> Come on, ask me. What's the problem?

> MIAMI
> Let him ask you.

> GREASY JOHN
> Did you top Ray?

317

> TERRY
> No way, John.

Terry turns and smiles at Miami smugly.

> MIAMI
> Now ask me.

> GREASY JOHN
> Leave it out, Miami.

> MIAMI
> Ask me!

Greasy John wavers. This is Miami at his most dangerous and he knows it. Terry is grinning.

> GREASY JOHN
> Was it you?

Miami goes right up to his face.

> MIAMI
> How fuckin' dare you? Ray was my friend. Of course I had
> nothing to do with it. It was an outsider. I haven't told any
> of you this yet but they found a bottle of communion wine on
> the kitchen table.

The hoods are shocked.

> GREASY JOHN
> Two Sips? My God, I thought he was dead.

> MIAMI
> No, he was in Spain...

> TERRY
> ...which comes to much the same thing.

Miami shoots a really irritated look to Terry.

> GREASY JOHN
> So what we gonna do about it?

> MIAMI
> (To Rudolph and John)
> You two... are going to offer a little reward.

Terry looks cocky.

CUT TO:

INT. THE LOCK. BAR --NIGHT

Jamie is on the phone in the corner making notes on a pad. Bacon is behind the jump anxiously looking at his watch. The bar is closed, deserted except for Stinker who is draining yet another of his free pints. Bacon pulls a sloppy pint and slaps it on the bar in front of Stinker.

BACON

That's your last one, it's way past last orders. So finish it and get out.

Jamie puts down the phone.

JAMIE

It's all sorted. Two Sips is on his way home - tonight.

Lee comes into the bar. He locks and bolts the door behind him.

BACON
How?

He goes over to Jamie as Two Sips enters, a little ruffled from his forty winks. He goes to the other side of the bar and watches TV from about two feet away.

JAMIE

There's a boat waiting at Tilbury. We slap him on it and we go Alzheimers on the whole business...

LEE

We're not going anywhere. There is now a price on our Mr Two Sips' head put up by Greasy John and Rudolph. Where is Moon?

He whips out his mobile and dials.

CUT TO:

INT. TANYA'S BEDROOM -- NIGHT

Close-up Moon's mobile phone. It rings and rings as we pan up to see Moon, gagged and stark naked save for a black leather posing pouch, his wrists and ankles handcuffed and roped to a brass bed. Tanya comes into shot. Back view. She is dressed skimpy dominatrix. She drags a cat o' nine tails gently across his crotch.

319

                              TANYA
                 Now I'm using this as me new act.

                                                              CUT TO:

INT. THE LOCK -- NIGHT.

Lee on the phone. He closes it up.

                               LEE
                 Christ, I hope he's not in trouble.

                              BACON
                How much they offering for Two Sips?

                               LEE
            Five hundred thousand. Every psycho with a knuckleduster
                will be out on the streets trying to get lucky.

                              BACON
           You'd 'ave to 'ave a deathwish to step out the door next to
                             that geezer.

                              JAMIE
                  We can't 'ang around 'ere.

                               LEE
                    OK, we're fucked.

                                                              CUT TO:

INT. CAR AUCTION OFFICE -- NIGHT

The Spartan bare-bulbed shack which serves as the office for the yard. Behind
piles of grubby snide MOTs stacked on the desk sits No Hope Harry flanked by
two heavies.

Greasy John goes to a shabby cabinet, takes out a Scotch bottle and pours a fist
of whisky into a tumbler and turns to No Hope Harry.

                             NO HOPE
                 I couldn't 'ave a shot of that, could I?

                           GREASY JOHN
                             Correct.

He drains his glass.

GREASY JOHN (CONT'D)
What 'ave you got to tell me?

NO HOPE
There's a little matter of money first, isn't there?

Wearily Greasy John nods to his lieutenant and No Hope Harry is lifted from his chair, the table swept of its MOTs and No Hope is slam dunked onto the table.

NO HOPE (CONT'D)
No, wait, hold on...!

Greasy John's lieutenant produces a pair of rusty long-handled pruning shears.

LIEUTENANT
Which one first, boss, left or right?

NO HOPE
Oh, Christ, no, please...!

GREASY JOHN
Where is Two Sips?

NO HOPE
I don't know!

The lieutenant pulls No Hope's trousers down to his knees.

NO HOPE (CONT'D)
But I know who he's with!!!

CUT TO:

INT. THE LOCK -- NIGHT

The lads are in the bar with Stinker and Two Sips.

BACON
So, 'ow we gonna get you to Tilbury? Order a minicab?

STINKER
I could get you there...

They turn to see Stinker gripping onto his stool boggle-eyed.

STINKER (CONT'D)
... and not a single soul'd see ya...

He waves his glass for another pint.

CUT TO:

EXT. THE LOCK -- NIGHT

Moon and Tanya come down the street. All is quiet.

> TANYA
> So what do you reckon?

> MOON
> I reckon black suits you. Brings out the colour of your eyes.

> TANYA
> I didn't notice you lookin' at my eyes...

They halt as a screech of tyres announces the arrival of Greasy John's mob outside the lock. Moon pulls out his phone and starts to dial All the while John's heavies start blocking the exits of the street and preparing a military style raid on the club. The phone is answered.

> MOON
> Lee, you don't want to be there. Something wicked your
> way comes.

CUT TO:

INT. THE LOCK -- NIGHT

Lee is on the phone with the rest in background.

> LEE
> Meet us in the yard.

As he puts down the phone, they hear an axe coming through the front door. They make off through the back of the club. Stinker picks up a yellow hard hat with lamp attached.

CUT TO:

EXT. THE LOCK -- NIGHT

The heavies and Greasy John are piling in through the destroyed door of the Lock.

CUT TO:

EXT. THE LOCK. BACK YARD -- NIGHT

Lee, Bacon, Jamie, Stinker and Two Sips are barring the back door as Moon and Tanya come round the corner.

> MOON
> I leave you for five minutes and all hell breaks loose.

Stinker is halfway down the sewer.

CUT TO:

EXT. THE LOCK. BACK YARD -- NIGHT

The heavies and Greasy John have kicked the lads, back door down. Greasy John walks into yard and notices the manhole cover.

> GREASY JOHN
> Get a torch.

CUT TO:

INT. SEWER -- NIGHT

Lee, Bacon, Jamie, Moon, Tanya and Two Sips follow Stinker.

> TWO SIPS
> Very *Third Man.*

> BACON
> So the plan is that I have to walk, knee deep in shit, in a sewer, with a drunken sheep-shagger in charge. Is that it?

> LEE
> You got a better one?

> MOON
> I've got a good one. Public Enemy Number One stops going round toppin' people.

> TANYA
> This is not my idea of a good time, Moon.

STINKER draws down a deep lungful of air, a happy man in his element.

> STINKER
> The Lee Valley spur. I've always wondered what this would look like...

> TANYA
> I don't know who you are but you've got to try and get out more.

323

Stinker starts to head down. The others follow.

INT. SEWER. -- NIGHT

The heavies are following Greasy John, who drops his torch, which smashes. The noise echoes.

> GREASY JOHN
> Balls.

CUT TO:

INT. STORM DRAIN -- NIGHT.

Stinker, Lee, Bacon, Jamie, Moon, Tanya and Two Sips are making their way through the tunnel, when they hear the noise.

> JAMIE
> What was that?

> TWO SIPS
> We're being followed.

> MOON
> Fuck, come on.

They all start to run.

INT. SEWER -- NIGHT

The lads etc. run through the sewer being chased by the heavies. Montage sequence.

CUT TO:

INT. SEWER -- NIGHT.

The lads etc. turn a corner and stop for a breath. Two Sips is not with them.

> JAMIE
> Fuck, where's Two Sips? We'll have to go back.

> BACON
> You go back. I'm out of here.

They all run off. Jamie left for a moment follows on.

INT. SEWER -- NIGHT.

The heavies are still stumbling through the tunnel. Suddenly the driver's face is lit by a powerful torch.

GREASY JOHN
Where'd you get that?

There is a loud gunshot. Greasy John arches in the air and we hear a loud thud. The other heavy runs away. Pull back to see Two Sips.

CUT TO:

INT. STORM TUNNEL -- NIGHT.

The group are still running.

TANYA
What's that smell?

They all put hands over nose etc.

MOON
Come on.

Stinker stops and looks at the sluice gate, which has a plate on it; he rubs away the grime and reads the plate.

STINKER
I don't believe it. This is a Farrington and Maplin double-gated sluice. Miracles of engineering these things. A hundred and fifty years old.

He wanders off down another tunnel.

INT. SEWER -- NIGHT.

Lads and Tanya running, holding noses.

INT. SEWER -- NIGHT.

Dark sewer – the voice of henchmen can be heard.

DRIVER
I can't see a thing.

LIEUTENANT
Where are you? Hold my hand.

DRIVER
I am holding your hand.

> ### LIEUTENANT
> No you're not. Hang on, I've got a lighter somewhere.

Sound of Zippo being opened.

> ### STINKER
> I wouldn't do that my dear. We're in a pocket of
> hydrogenated sulphate - choke damp to you.

Driver raises gun. More urgency in Stinker's voice.

> ### STINKER (CONT'D)
> In layman's terms - the spark from your gun will ignite all this
> gas and blow the three of us - to shit...
> (Resigned to death)
> You don't believe me do you?

There is a huge explosion.

INT. SEWER -- NIGHT

Explosion rips down sewer.

CUT TO:

EXT. CREEKMOUTH. THAMES -- DAWN

The lads and Tanya jump out of the sewer.

CUT TO:

EXT. CREEKMOUTH. THAMES -- DAWN.

The lads and Tanya are lying in mud. Tanya has two tear-tracks through the mud on her cheeks.

> ### TANYA
> Cost me sixty quid to 'ave my 'air done...

> ### MOON
> Good for yer complexion though.

> ### JAMIE
> Everyone 'ere ? Where's Stinker ?

There is a yellow hard hat on the ground, burnt.

MOON
Oh no, I'll have to tell his Mum.

JAMIE
Two Sips?

They stagger to their feet.

TWO SIPS
I don't mean to criticise, lads. But wouldn't the Docklands
Railway have been easier?

They wheel round to see Two Sips looking immaculate.

CUT TO:

EXT. THAMES -- DAY.

Bacon, Moon, Jamie, Tanya, Two Sips and Lee are in a dinghy, still sodden and
soiled, they row as best they can towards the cabin cruiser which is moored to a
buoy in the middle of the river. As they near the boat they see the Captain who
imported Two Sips.

BACON
Chuck us a line.

The Captain doesn't move as the dinghy bumps against the side of the boat.

BACON (CONT'D)
What's his problem?

MOON
You. Rope. Now.

Terry Gardener's head appears behind the Captain's.

TERRY
I thought you'd never get 'ere.

He throws down a rope then aims down a shotgun into the dinghy.

CUT TO:

EXT. DECK OF CABIN CRUISER -- DAY

Jamie, Lee, Bacon, Moon and Tanya are huddled in the aft deck of the boat with
Terry training the gun on them from above. Beside him is Two Sips looking down
on them impassively. Terry milks the moment.

TERRY
Lads, lads, you are impressin' me so much. I thought you'd all
be goin' mouldy in the cellar by now - but you pulled through.
Terrific.

TERRY
I said to Two Sips, you'll prob'ly 'ave to take 'em out at some
point - but he's a... clean worker.

Jamie looks up at the shotgun trained on them. He whispers from the side of
his mouth.

JAMIE
We could jump, scatter in different directions...

BACON
No.

JAMIE
He can't get us all...

TERRY
I particularly feel sorry for you darlin'.

He winks at Tanya.

TERRY (CONT'D)
I mean what a waste...

He hands the pump-action shotgun to Two Sips. Two Sips stares at the gun then
raises it into the firing position.

TWO SIPS
It's nothing personal, lads. Purely business.

C.U. on the lads and Tanya. They close their eyes and wince as they await the
blast. There is a loud blast from the shotgun. Silence as they wait the next shot.
There isn't one, just the noise of a splash.

MIAMI (O.O.V.)
I see we got shot of the fucker then?

They open their eyes to see Miami standing on the deck above with Two Sips -
Three Feet hovers behind. Terry is nowhere to be seen, a scarlet gash on the deck
where he was standing.

328

                          MIAMI
    I knew it was only a matter of time with Terry. Too careless,
                   too flash, too fuckin' stupid.

Fixes his stare on Two Sips.

                       MIAMI (CONT'D)
    What a world we live in Two Sips. You never know who's your
    mate. Everyone, runnning around double-crossing everyone
                   else. I tell you, it's fucked up...

BANG.

                       MIAMI (CONT'D)
                      ... It really is.

Two Sips is stretched out on the deck, dead. Miami turns back to the lads.

                       MIAMI (CONT'D)
    And you lot - keep out of my face. And get off my fuckin'
                        boat... NOW.

The lads have no choice but to jump overboard. Freeze frame on
their expressions.

                          END

EPISODE 6

LOCK, STOCK... & ONE BIG BULLOCK

by Chris Baker and Andrew Day

ACT ONE

EXT. DISUSED ROAD -- DAY

A remote disused road under a railway bridge. Rubbish everywhere. In the middle of this crap is a huge articulated lorry with its ramp down at the back.

                                                        CUT TO:

INT. ARTICULATED LORRY -- DAY

C.U. – TWO GUNS blazing away. The faces of BUNNY and MACCA. They are smiling.

                                                        CUT TO:

EXT. DISUSED ROAD -- DAY

A ROLLS ROYCE drives up to the articulated lorry and stops. MIAMI and THREE FEET get out. They walk up the ramp into the container.

                                                        CUT TO:

INT. ARTICULATED LORRY -- DAY

MIAMI and THREE FEET stand next to BUNNY and MACCA, who are a bit uneasy. They all look down at a group of blood-spattered corpses.

> MIAMI
> Bunny... What 'appened?

                                                        CUT TO:

OPENING SEQUENCE

                                                        CUT TO:

EXT/INT. ABATTOIR -- DAY

C.U. – large hunks of meat. Through the meat we see JAMIE, LEE, MOON and BACON who are handballing chunks of meat off the back of a van to the inside of the abattoir. KOUROS oversees. There's a mixture of carcasses, in different shapes and sizes.

> KOUROS
> Whassis?

In one hand is a stringy, skinned animal. In the other hand he has a little collar with a tinkly bell on it.

                    LEE
Moon, what's in that box?

                    MOON
Rabbit. Everyfin' in that box is rabbit.

                    KOUROS
It's just Nefarius don't want no 'amster or nuffink 'idden underneaf.

                    BACON
Well Nefarius ain't payin' fussy prices, Kouros.

                    JAMIE
He still owes us a monkey from the last run.

                    KOUROS
I know. It's jus' a question of transfer the money, inni?

                    MOON
It's a question of payin' my cousins, mate. We'll just 'ave to tell 'em YOU ain't paid us. An' they'll be up 'ere after their cider money.

                    CUT TO:

EXT. CRUSTY CAMP, CENTRE -- DAY

UNCLE BRIAN, leader of the CRUSTIES, and TERRY JIFFER, head of the JIFFER family, a man of considerable bulk, are arm-wrestling across a table. The VIOLENT FACES of the JIFFER and CRUSTY families. The air is full of tension and hate.

EXT./INT. ABATTOIR -- DAY

The lads are still un-loading the meat.

                    KOUROS
Oh, money, money, money. Tha's de only fing anybody want inni? I pay yer 'alf.

Pulls out a roll and counts out £250. JAMIE counts the money.

                    KOUROS (CONT'D)
Next week all of it. Nefarius gotta big payout comin' through.

                        JAMIE
                Next week you settle up.

                        KOUROS
        Yeah, yeah, next week Nefarius pay you inni? Listen – he'll
        give yer a bit extra... it's 'is nephew's weddin' comin' up, 'e
        need a load of lamb, tha' soft an' tender kind, y'know?

Hands over another couple of fifties.

                        LEE
        You mean lamb from actual lambs. When d'yer need it for?

                        KOUROS
                Next Saturday. But fresh, yeah?

                        JAMIE
                Just 'ave the rest of the money.

                                                        CUT TO:

INT. ARTICULATED LORRY -- DAY

BUNNY stands next to MIAMI.

                        BUNNY
                Dem fucker didn't 'ave no gear on 'em man.

                        MIAMI
                So... where is the gear?

Pause. MACCA is trying to roll a cigarette, a bit fidgety.

                        BUNNY
                Dey started givin' it large...

                        MIAMI
                So you took 'em out, I can fuckin' SEE that.

                        MACCA
                They was gettin' all lippy like...

                        BUNNY
        Dey was bad-mouthin' us. Dey was bad-mouthin' you...

                        MIAMI
                        (Calmly)
                Give me the fuckin' drugs.

                        334

THREE FEET
I don't fink they got the drugs.

MIAMI
Give me the fuckin' money back.

BUNNY
You shoulda seen 'em – dey was on the edge, it was gonna be
us or dem – I felt it – I...

As BUNNY hands over a duffle bag, MIAMI looks into his eyes.

MIAMI
(Interrupting)
You wired son?

BUNNY
Nah... we 'ad a little toot jus' before, like we always do... keeps
you dancin' on your toes...

MIAMI
We don't want you doin' the fucking waltz, we want you doin'
the business. But you don't. Every time I ask you to do a
simple job... you land me with a bill from the undertakers.

BUNNY
I tell ya, dey was kickin' off, man.

MIAMI
You all think you're Al Pacino. I can't think of a single job
where you 'aven't shot somebody.

MACCA
What about Golders Green?

MIAMI
Weren't through want of tryin', was it? By the time you
muppets had shot twenty rounds at the bulletproof glass
they'd all buggered off out the back...

BUNNY
Das not true an' you –

MIAMI
Bunny, I don't wanna fuckin' argue. Your record speaks for
itself. You're a bunch of fuckin' cowboys.

MIAMI and THREE FEET turn to go.

                              BUNNY
            Wait, wait, we got the Russian job comin' up, inni?

                              MIAMI
            No, WE got the Russian job comin' up. You're parting
                          company with us.

                              BUNNY
                          Come on man...

                           THREE FEET
            Just be thankful you ain't partin' company with yer 'eads.

                              MIAMI
            Better clear up this little mess. Otherwise you'll leave red
                   footprints all the way to your door.

            MIAMI and THREE FEET are walking back down the ramp.
            BUNNY turns to MACCA, frustrated, as the car doors slam.

                              BUNNY
            Shit, shit, dat next deal gunner make I a rich man.

MACCA is hurriedly cutting up lines.

                              MACCA
                   How we gonna clean this up, Bun?

                              BUNNY
            We no cleanin' nuttin' up... we no cleanin' woman, right?

                              MACCA
            Yeah, fockin' right. Fockin' Miami. Le's fockin' do'im.

                              BUNNY
            Ah, white boy, ya got no style. We goin' take de Russian deal.

Does a line of Charles.

                          BUNNY (CONT'D)
                       From under Miami nose.

                                                              CUT TO:

EXT. DISUSED ROAD -- DAY

Miami's Roller is driving away.

                               336

CUT TO:

INT. MIAMI'S ROLLER -- DAY

> THREE FEET
> What does the future 'old for those two then, Guv ?

> MIAMI
> Get Mr Skin and Mr Bone in. I want those two fuckers sliced
> up thin and packed into bubble bags.

CUT TO:

INT. SKIN AND BONE'S WAREHOUSE -- DAY

Close up of SKIN and BONE putting large sharp objects into a bag.

CUT TO:

EXT. CRUSTY CAMP, CENTRE -- DAY

UNCLE DEREK and TERRY JIFFER continue their struggle. The families urge
them on.

The PRINCE OF WALES, a prize bull, is locked in a pen.

Two hands locked together across a table. Two faces, strained, sweaty and red.

UNCLE BRIAN, DEREK's brother, leans forward and bellows:

> BRIAN
> Get on, Derek! Fuckin' nut the bastard! Nut im!

> DEREK
> That there bull is mine, an' you knows it...

> TERRY
> Over my dead body.

> DEREK
> Tha' may be Terry, tha' may be...

They both re-double their efforts. The crowd goad them on.

CUT TO:

EXT./INT. RUSSIAN LORRY -- DAY

The RUSSIAN LORRY is travelling through a tunnel. ATTILA, SERGEI and YURI, (shaven-headed Ruskies). ATTILA is driving. They pass round a bottle of vodka. ATTILA takes a huge swig. They are having some kind of heated argument.

> YURI
> Of course Chekhov was political.

> ATTILA
> Typical Russian.

YURI snorts dismissively.

> ATTILA (CONT'D)
> You don't know the difference... between ethics and politics.

> YURI
> You don't know Chekhov.

> ATTILA
> I've read *The Seagull* fifty times.

> YURI
> The Seagull is the soul of Russia... shot down by a landowner...

> ATTILA
> Soil of Russia?

> YURI
> No, SOUL... Cherry Orchard is the soil of Russia.

SERGEI is cleaning his AK-47.

> SERGEI
> Guys... you've argued about Chekhov since Bilbao.

> ATTILA
> So ?

> SERGEI
> There are other issues we can discuss.

> YURI
> Like the siege of Stalingrad, again?

> ATTILA
> When your Grandfather held back a whole Panzer division...
> with a broomstick?

SERGEI
My Grandfather fought two world wars... while your ancestors
were picking potatoes in Latvia.

SERGEI points his gun at them. Tense moment eyes blaze.

ATTILA
Sergei... there's no need for such silliness.

Serious pause as they all look at each other then tension breaks and they all roar
with laughter.

YURI
Look at us!

SERGEI
Cabin fever...

ATTILA
Sergei? It's a long time since you and I... played chess...

CUT TO:

EXT. TUNNEL ENTRANCE -- DAY

The Russian lorry comes out of the tunnel.

EXT. CRUSTY CAMP, CENTRE -- DAY

Camera pans along BULL and then moves to the arm-wrestlers. However, most of
the audience have wandered off or dozed off. DEREK leans right forward. TERRY
does the same.

DEREK
You dozy bastard, I can finish you off any time I wants.

TERRY
You'm all piss an wind, boy...

DEREK glances at BRIAN, who nods and winks. No-one else is watching. Derek's
teeth clamp down on Terry's knuckle.

TERRY (CONT'D)
Ah you...

DEREK slams TERRY's hand down onto the table.

DEREK
Right. Bull's mine. I'm the winner.

Heads turn, people hurry over to see DEREK standing triumphantly. Both men rise and face each other.

TERRY
You cheatin' bloody bastard. He bit me 'and!

BRIAN
Now come on, Terry, everybeddy saw you lose...

TERRY
You bunch of bleddy liars!

BRIAN and DEREK both change mood at the same – go cold. The CRUSTY CLAN swarm together, ready for a fight.

DEREK
You got somethin' to say about my family?

Tension, then:

TERRY
You ain't 'eard the last of this you gypos...

LITTLE MICHAEL winks at TERRY as he leaves. TERRY kicks the table over.
His family console him.

CUT TO:

INT. LOCK BAR -- DAY

MIAMI and THREE FEET are waiting. The LADS come in.

THREE FEET
'Allo boys.

JAMIE
Mr Vice. Three Feet. Everythin' alright?

MIAMI
How's your little meat business going?

JAMIE
Quite well, thanks, yeah.

MIAMI
That's good.

Sips his tea. LADS still wondering why he's here.

MIAMI (CONT'D)
Now I recently moved into the meat industry, y'know?

MOON
Meat industry?

LEE
No, no, we didn't know that, we 'ad no idea at all.

MIAMI
Don't worry, it's not a problem. I was hoping we could...
co-operate.

LEE
Oh...

THREE FEET
We'd like to start straight away.

MIAMI
We've got a container of beef comin' in, down where you go
to see your suppliers. Two birds, one stone.

MOON
Fine, we're goin' down there tomorrow.

MIAMI
My container comes in today. You got time for a cup of tea
before you go. Three Feet's made you a map.

BACON
Er, probably a stupid question... What was in it for us again?

THREE FEET
Peace of mind.

THREE FEET passes over the map and a duffle bag.

MIAMI
There's a lot of money in there so don't leave it in the bogs.
You hand that over to three Russian geezers, they give you the
beef. They're not very pleasant, but who is in this day and
age? Watch yourselves, alright?

341

LADS nod. MIAMI stands.

>   MIAMI (CONT'D)
>   Lads. This is very good of you.

>   LADS
>   No problem... Fine...

MIAMI and THREE FEET exit.

>   BACON
>   I don't like it.

MOON is sniffing.

>   MOON
>   I 'ave GOT to 'ave a bath before we go.

He disappears.

>   LEE
>   I s'pose if we're workin' for Miami Vice, we're protected...
>   ain't we?

>   CUT TO:

EXT. BUNNY'S YARD -- DAY

BUNNY comes out of his office with an armful of guns. He locks the door with a padlock.

MACCA is sitting in the passenger seat of Bunny's van, chopping a line on a mirror on the dashboard. BUNNY gets into the van.

>   BUNNY
>   Right... le's see where this bamb'clat place is den. Get in da
>   van muppet-man.

He snatches the map off MACCA. The van drives off.

EXT. URBAN ROAD -- DAY

The Russian lorry drives past.

>   CUT TO:

INT. RUSSIAN LORRY -- DAY

The RUSSIANS are still driving along. They are smoking filterless fags and swigging vodka. They play chess without a board, remembering the board.

> SERGEI
> D4.

> ATTILA
> D4? D5.

> SERGEI
> (Dramatically)
> C4...

> YURI
> C4 ? Queen's Gambit?... At least this game will be
> over quickly...

CUT TO:

EXT. CRUSTY CAMP, CENTRE -- DAY

The PRINCE OF WALES is in his pen being treated like royalty. LITTLE MICHAEL is holding up a saucepan of milk for the Prince. DEREK and BRIAN wander up.

> LITTLE MICHAEL
> 'E ain't drinkin' much.

> DEREK
> What you givin' 'im, there? Milk? Course 'e ain't drinkin', 'e
> wants cream, don't 'e?

DEREK grabs MICHAEL'S collar and gives him a cuff, and LITTLE MICHAEL scuttles off. BRIAN shouts after him:

> BRIAN
> Take that milk back to yer ma, make sure she boils it !

The two men contemplate the animal.

CUT TO:

INT. BUNNY'S VAN -- DAY

Some old ska track playing. MACCA, talc bottle in hand, passes a mirror to BUNNY. It has three huge lines on it. BUNNY snorts with an emptied-out biro, then passes the mirror back to MACCA as he drives.

BUNNY

Macca you shithead. Why you cuttin' up with talc when we's
da ones who's doin' it ?

MACCA

Added that in for you, mate.

BUNNY turns and glares at MACCA. Then grins.

BUNNY

We're gonna be RICH!

Slaps MACCA so hard on the back that powder drops out of MACCA's nose.

MACCA

Fockin' 'ell, man.

Laughter.

CUT TO:

EXT. CRUSTY CAMP, ENTRANCE ROAD -- DAY

The lads' van comes down the entrance road.

INT. LADS' VAN -- DAY

MOON and BACON are sleeping in the back. JAMIE drives, LEE next to him.

JAMIE

Alright, lads. We're 'ere.

MOON and BACON stir.

MOON

I ain't feelin' too good.

LEE

Shouldn't've eaten two breakfasts, yer greedy bastard.

BACON

What 'appened to that 'ealthy diet you was on ?

MOON

Caused havoc with me plumbing system.

EXT. CRUSTY CAMP, ENTRANCE ROAD/CENTRE -- DAY

The lads' van pulls up and the LADS get out. LEE throws the duffle bag over his shoulder.

> JAMIE
> Where you going with that?

> LEE
> Ain't leavin' it in 'ere. Place is crawlin' with tea-leaves.

> JAMIE
> Just don't like all the cash in that bag. Can't we put it in somethin' else?

> BACON
> Don't fuck about with it, mate.

> MOON
> He's right. Don't touch it, don't look at it, it's Miami's business.

> LEE
> Slung over me shoulder it don't look nuffin'. No-one'd guess.

BRIAN and DEREK arrive with a couple of other CRUSTIES. LEE keeps the bag close.

> BRIAN
> We weren't expectin' you 'til tomorrow.

> JAMIE
> We was collectin' somethin' else in the area, thought we'd pick up your stuff today.

> MOON
> One day fresher...

They walk towards the centre of the camp.

> DEREK
> What else you down 'ere for then?

> LEE
> We're doin' someone a favour – 'e don't want us to shout it round.

> DEREK
> Aah, top secret is it?

LEE
Well no, but blabbin' would be unprofessional.

DEREK points at the duffle bag.

DEREK
What yer got in yer handbag, the fuckin' crown jewels?

Everyone laughs at LEE, who looks uneasy.

BRIAN
(To Jamie)
Seen much of ol' Laura up London?

JAMIE
Time to time.

BRIAN
(Winking)
See 'er on the telly did yer? 'E there's got it on the video!

Points to one of his nephews. BACON sees the PRINCE OF WALES.

BACON
'Ello, that for us?

DEREK
Jesus Christ, don't even joke about it. Tha' there's the Elvis
Presley of bulls. 'E's a fuckin' superstar.

BACON
So where's our fresh meat, then?

CUT TO:

EXT. CRUSTY CAMP, CENTRE -- DAY

The faces of the four LADS, plus DEREK and BRIAN, looking at meat which we
don't see.

JAMIE
It ain't fresh.

DEREK
It's meat.

LEE
Only just.

                    MOON
              Uncle Brian...

                    BRIAN
        You ain't the ones eatin' it are yer?

                    MOON
                    No...

                    BRIAN
              Then it's fine.

                                        CUT TO:

EXT. CRUSTY CAMP, ENTRANCE ROAD/INT. LADS' VAN -- DAY

The meat has been loaded into the freezers in the back of the van. LEE is holding
his nose.

                    JAMIE
    We can't accept this. It's not even completely dead any more.

                    LEE
                 (To Jamie)
              Go tell 'em, then.

                    MOON
     We'll tell Nefarius 'is meat comes with free mushrooms.

MOON shuts the van doors.

                                        CUT TO:

EXT. SCRAP YARD -- DAY

The Russian lorry is parked in the middle of the scrapyard. Scrap cars are piled
high all round. The THREE RUSSIANS outside the lorry. YURI sits. ATTILA and
SERGEI stand, pacing occasionally, like pieces on a chess board.

                    ATTILA
              Pawn takes E5.

                    SERGEI
            Pawn, not knight?

                    ATTILA
            You've got no chance.
                 (To Yuri)

                    347

Korchnoi played this whole variation... against Karpov back
in '81...

YURI
Is that supposed to make it more interesting?

SERGEI
(Ignoring Yuri)
I'll wipe that smile off your pompous face... bishop takes –

Mobile phone rings. ATTILA and SERGEI look at YURI.

ATTILA
You better answer.

SERGEI
You speak the best English.

YURI answers, the other two listen. He can barely speak English at all.

YURI
Err... you come... OK, OK, we is wait... OK. I sorry for English.

CUT TO:

EXT. CRUSTY CAMP, ENTRANCE ROAD -- DAY

In the van, JAMIE is on the mobile. Speaks slowly and clearly for the
dim-witted foreigner.

JAMIE
We're a couple of miles away. Not far. Near. Yeah. Half-an-
hour. Half... That's right, we come. Four-thirty. Dumpton
Cross. Just stay there, yeah?

Puts down phone.

JAMIE (CONT'D)
(To lads)
Don't think he understood a word I said.

LITTLE MICHAEL is hiding nearby. Runs off to BRIAN and DEREK.

CUT TO:

EXT. CRUSTY CAMP, CENTRE -- DAY

DEREK, BRIAN and a couple of others are gathered.

                    DEREK
   Dumpton Cross? Us'll find the lorry easy enough...
                (To LITTLE MICHAEL)
           You nobblin' their wagon?

LITTLE MICHAEL smiles proudly.

                    BRIAN
                 Good lad.

                    DEREK
        Well let's get scroungin' then.

                                                CUT TO:

EXT. BUNNY'S YARD -- DAY

THREE FEET, MR SKIN and MR BONE come through the main gates of Bunny's
yard. They walk towards the office door. It is padlocked.

                                                CUT TO:

INT. MIAMI'S OFFICE -- DAY

MIAMI practises his golf swing with Nick Faldo's clubs. THREE FEET enters.

                    MIAMI
                  Done?

                 THREE FEET
              Not really Guv.

The nine-iron freezes in the air.

              THREE FEET (CONT'D)
   Went down there with the boys, but Bunny's done a runner.

                    MIAMI
               Any ideas?

                 THREE FEET
     We, er, interviewed 'is bird. Looks like 'e's gone out to
                the countryside.

The nine-iron is returned to the bag. MIAMI removes his golf gloves with a sigh.

                                                CUT TO:

EXT. CRUSTY CAMP, ENTRANCE ROAD -- DAY

LADS in van. JAMIE tries ignition. Nothing.

> BACON
> You're floggin' a dead 'orse, mate.

> MOON
> You must've left the lights on.

JAMIE looks out at LITTLE MICHAEL in the distance – he is grinning and watching.

> LEE
> That kid's up to something.

BACON jumps out.

> BACON
> Oi! You!

MICHAEL scarpers. JAMIE tries to fire the engine again. BACON picks up something off the ground.

> BACON (CONT'D)
> We got a job on our 'ands.

BACON shows them the empty sugar bag.

> JAMIE
> Little bastard.

CUT TO:

EXT. SCRAP YARD -- DAY

The CRUSTIES shamble across the scrapyard to meet the RUSKIES.

> DEREK
> Alright mate?

YURI holds a Russian-English dictionary.

> YURI
> Dis your cow. Meat. Extra somesing in.

DEREK looks at the cover of the dictionary.

DEREK
Russian? Where y' from?

YURI
Yes. From is... Russia.

SERGEI brandishes his gun.

SERGEI
Too many you! More forty guy!

SERGEI holds up four fingers.

SERGEI (CONT'D)
(In Russian)
Have they got the money or not ?

YURI
Please you is pay.

BRIAN looks very obliging, makes the money sign.

DEREK
Now where is that money?

DEREK pats his pockets. Meanwhile, BRIAN and the rest of the CRUSTIES
are swarming around the lorry, acting like dumb yokels. One kicks the tyres.
One opens the door to the cabin.

CRUSTIES
Nice... yeah... ooh...

RUSKIES confused. Start jabbering In Russian:

ATTILA
Don't let them in the lorry!

YURI
We're not. Is that one getting the money out?

ATTILA
I don't know. Keep an eye on them!

BRIAN starts fiddling with the container.

BRIAN
Can't seem to open it.

YURI warns him:

> YURI
> Hey!! No!!

> ATTILA
> (To Derek)
> No. You pay pound-sterlink.

> DEREK
> Hark at you! No bleddy manners.

Puts his hand into his chest-pocket again, then – spins round and knocks YURI out with a wrench.

CUT TO:

INT. MIAMI'S OFFICE -- DAY

MIAMI with the phone to his ear. THREE FEET is leaning against the door.

> MIAMI
> They ain't answering.

He puts the phone down.

> MIAMI (CONT'D)
> Three Feet, get yer passport an' a map. We're crossing
> the river.

> THREE FEET
> It's a jungle over there. No proper firms...

CUT TO:

EXT. CRUSTY CAMP, ENTRANCE ROAD -- DAY

The LADS are smeared with oil and grease. MOON and BACON finish draining the petrol tank. LEE is cleaning the cylinders with paraffin. JAMIE is looking at his phone.

MOON pours clean petrol in.

> MOON
> Pure as the driven snow...

> BACON
> That was Miami, wasn't it?

JAMIE nods.

                          LEE
        And you don't answer the phone to Miami Vice, these days?

                          JAMIE
        And say what? I ain't speakin' to 'im 'til we got his beef.

The LADS drive off.

END OF ACT ONE

ACT TWO

EXT. SCRAPYARD -- DAY

The CRUSTIES are loading the Ruskie meat into their truck. BUNNY and MACCA
are lurking amongst the scrap vehicles – watching the events unfold.

                         MACCA
                    Fancy another line?

                         BUNNY
                    Ya just 'ave one.

                         MACCA
              Well come on, let's do 'em then.

BUNNY grabs MACCA and holds him back.

                         BUNNY
        Sit yer white arse down, boy, an' chill. We's gonna follow de
                beef, an' move in when de time is right.

The CRUSTIES finish loading. Slam the doors shut. Start the engine and
drive off.

                                                              CUT TO:

EXT. DERELICT BUILDING -- DAY

A group of about six rough country men (THE JIFFERS) stand around listening.
Murderous mood.

                                    TERRY
        You all seen they gypos tryin' to cheat me outter the Prince of
        Wales. I got two hundred and thirty cows needs impregnatin'
                              by that ole bastard.

Looks for reaction. The other JIFFERS nod.

                                TERRY (CONT'D)
        You remember back along they boys dug that skeleton up? Been down
            there two 'undred years. Man was tied up an drowned in a ditch.
            What for? We knows don't we? For rustlin'. Only way now is
            Natural Justice. Morris, you checked the shotguns?

A white-haired man nods.

                                                                CUT TO:

INT. RUSSIAN LORRY -- DAY

SERGEI regains consciousness. YURI is sitting on the floor staring into the
distance with a bottle of vodka. ATTILA is still KO'd.

                                    SERGEI
                        We must escape and kill them.

                                    YURI
            Once again, we are shat on... The great Russian people bend
                        over... and take it from behind –

SERGEI pulls out a pistol from his trousers.

                                    SERGEI
                    This isn't the time... for tears of self-pity.

ATTILA wakes up to see SERGEI aiming his gun at the door.

                                    ATTILA
                                  No Sergei.

                                                                CUT TO:

EXT. SCRAPYARD -- DAY

The noise of SERGEI firing at the iron door. Bullets ricochet. The door shudders.
Sub-title over scene.

                                ATTILA (V.O.)
                You stupid fucking Cossack... you shot my ear off.

                                    354

CUT TO:

INT. MIAMI'S ROLLER -- DAY

THREE FEET drives. MIAMI on mobile, listening to recorded voice-mail message
from BUNNY.

> MIAMI
> Bunny, answer your fucking phone. If you're where I think
> you are... you are going to suffer for the sins of man, my son.

Lowers the phone.

> THREE FEET
> Thinks he's gunner muscle in, don't 'e ? Reckon he knows
> what's in them cows?

> MIAMI
> Even Bunny can work that out. What worries me is... he won't
> even wait to sell it. He'll be packin' it up 'is nose like putty.

> THREE FEET
> He don't know the value of good Charles, that lad.

Silence. THREE FEET tries to cheer MIAMI up. Points at the radio.

> THREE FEET (CONT'D)
> How 'bout some music then, Guv?

MIAMI gives THREE FEET a withering look.

CUT TO:

EXT. SCRAPYARD -- DAY

LADS stand outside the RUSSIAN LORRY.

> BACON
> I think there's someone in there.

> LEE
> Have a look then.

> BACON
> You 'ave a look.

> JAMIE
> Who's there?

355

SERGEI (O.O.V.)
We... promise... no kill.

JAMIE
He promises not to kill us, that's good.

A shouted conversation begins.

BACON
You Russians?

SERGEI (O.O.V.)
Yes.

BACON
We're 'ere from Miami Vice, understand?

SERGEI (O.O.V.)
Yes.

BACON
Where's our beef?

SERGEI (O.O.V.)
No.

JAMIE
Where... is... the... beef?

SERGEI (O.O.V.)
You hev beef. We forgive. No kill.

JAMIE
What are you on about? We just got 'ere!

SERGEI (O.O.V.)
(In Russian)
Attila, speak to this guy. My English is crap...

ATTILA
(In Russian)
Eat shit, you son of a bitch, I'm maimed!!

YURI (O.O.V.)
(In Russian)
Attila get a grip, you want to die in here?
(In English)

He-elp. Please, let go. One man is maybe to die. One man is
go to crazy.

LADS look at each other.

> BACON
> No. Not 'til you tell us where that beef is.

Pause.

> SERGEI (O.O.V.)
> Beef is in here.

> MOON
> Tha's a problem.

> LEE
> Hold up, a minute ago you said we 'ad the beef.

Pause.

> SERGEI (O.O.V.)
> My English is very small.

> JAMIE
> We'll let you out. But no money, 'til we see that beef. Right?

> SERGEI (O.O.V.)
> All right.

JAMIE unlocks the door. Immediately there is a gun under his chin. An enraged
and confused Russian is on the other end of it:

> SERGEI
> Who fuck you?

> LEE
> We're from Miami ain't we?

The other two RUSSIANS appear behind SERGEI. ATTILA holds his bleeding ear.

> YURI
> Miami guys come, take beef, no pay money.

LADS look at each other.

> JAMIE
> Were they... odd-looking?

SERGEI
Uh?

JAMIE
Horrible faces, horrible clothes, horrible everything.

The RUSKIES nod, SERGEI'S gun droops to his side.

JAMIE (CONT'D)
Well there ain't no big fucking mystery there, then.

They all look at each other. They've all been done.

CUT TO:

EXT. CRUSTY CAMP, ENTRANCE ROAD -- DAY

The JIFFERS march along carrying their weapons.

CUT TO:

EXT. CRUSTY CAMP, RUSSIANS' HIDING-PLACE -- DAY

The three RUSSIANS crouch, watching the lads walk down to the centre of the CRUSTY camp.

YURI is getting drunker and sulkier.

YURI
And what if these boys just... disappear with the beef and the
money, uh ?

SERGEI
We follow them and kill them... My move is... E6 takes E7.
Bye, bye, rook.

ATTILA
What rook?

SERGEI
The rook that WAS on E7.

ATTILA
No, no, I moved it from E7 to A7.

SERGEI
When?

358

ATTILA
Ages ago.
(Closes his eyes)
I can see it, now. On A7.

SERGEI
My board has a rook on E7.

ATTILA
It's not on my board. Yuri?

YURI has no idea, just wants to fuck up the game.

YURI
I see a rook on E7.

SERGEI'S AK-47 is raised again.

SERGEI
You filthy lying bastard... you haven't even been watching!

YURI
(Highly patronising)
Sergei, it's just a game.

SERGEI
A game I must win.

CUT TO:

EXT. CRUSTY CAMP, CENTRE -- DAY

The LADS and the CRUSTIES stand in a ring in the centre of the camp.

DEREK
Sugar? Tha's a bastard to get out.

MOON
I can see the beef from 'ere.

Everyone looks at the beef on the back of the Crusty truck.

BRIAN
Beef... Derek, is that beef in that there truck?

Before DEREK can answer, JAMIE steps in.

JAMIE
Listen. There's gotter be a way we can work this out. 'Ow
about... a game of cards?

DEREK and BRIAN look at each other, then smile at the lads.

DEREK
Alright me lover.

CUT TO:

EXT. CRUSTY CAMP, RUSSIANS' HIDING-PLACE -- DAY

BUNNY and MACCA are clumsily stumbling through the gloom near the
RUSSIANS' hiding-place.

MACCA
This is fockin' ridiculous.

BUNNY
Behave.

MACCA
Can't see a fockin' – ow, shit.

Trips over a loose brick.

MACCA (CONT'D)
'Old up. We already been this fockin' way... I remember that
rusty old cooker.

CUT TO:

YURI is asleep. SERGEI wakes him, Vietnam-style, with a hand over his mouth.
The three RUSKIES listen to the sound of stumbling round in the dark.

SERGEI
Over there...

He pulls out a real hardcore blade.

SERGEI (CONT'D)
Time for the cutting of throats.

ATTILA
Wait, they are moving away...

The voices of BUNNY and MACCA move away.

360

BUNNY (O.S.)
I's t'rough 'ere somewhere. I's dis way for sure.

MACCA (O.S.)
Just admit we're lost.

The RUSSIANS relax. BUNNY and MACCA head off into the gloom.

CUT TO:

EXT. CRUSTY CAMP, CENTRE -- DAY

A table is being set up by a fire.

LEE
Reckon you can win?

JAMIE
I'll win if they don't cheat.

BACON
They will cheat.

JAMIE
Yeah. S'pose I better cheat as well then, eh ?

TIME JUMP:

EXT. CRUSTY CAMP, CENTRE -- DAY

Card game is in full flow. BRIAN against JAMIE. JAMIE is winning. As BRIAN is about to deal again.

BRIAN
Wait a minute, wait a minute.

He inspects the cards.

BRIAN (CONT'D)
We got the right cards, 'ere? No, look these ain't the lucky ones.

JAMIE
Eh?

BRIAN
God, I was wonderin' why I was gettin' such an 'ammerin' there.

DEREK scoops them up and removes them from the table.

> BRIAN (CONT'D)
> Get the other set you dozy bugger.

> BACON
> Hold on, what you on about?

BRIAN and DEREK play dumb again.

> DEREK
> Us travelling folk is a bit superstitious, y'see?

> BRIAN
> This other pack's kind o' charmed.

> DEREK
> Just 'elps 'is confidence really.

> JAMIE
> No, no, no.

> DEREK
> (Fierce again)
> You callin' my brother a cheat?

CUT TO:

EXT. CRUSTY CAMP, CENTRE/ARCHES -- DAY

The JIFFERS sneak through the gloom with their weapons. MOON is sneaking about round the back, working out how to nick the beef when a double-barrelled shotgun appears in his face. MOON looks up. TERRY JIFFERS is looking down at him, surrounded by other JIFFERS.

> TERRY
> On yer feet boy.

MOON stands up. Arms raised.

> TERRY (CONT'D)
> Where's my bull?

MOON looks deeply puzzled. LITTLE MICHAEL crawling about nearby. He pulls out a catapult and loads a stone. Aims at TERRY.

> MOON
> Saw some cows earlier.

TERRY
So?

MOON
If I was a bull, that's where I'd be.

TERRY
Funny fucker, eh?

TERRY cocks the shotgun. Stone flies through the air and whacks TERRY out. MOON scarpers. LITTLE MICHAEL runs towards the card game.

CUT TO:

EXT. CRUSTY CAMP, CENTRE -- DAY

The card game is in progress. LITTLE MICHAEL arrives.

LITTLE MICHAEL
The Jiffers is 'ere.

The CRUSTIES leap up.

DEREK
Jiffers? We'll 'ave 'em!

BRIAN
Where is 'em, boy?!

The JIFFERS come charging through the camp. JAMIE dives back and the LADS peg it off to the arches where they find MOON, almost catatonic after his near-death experience.

MOON
Alright, lads?

LEE
Yeah, you?

Blood-curdling roars of vengeance, gunshots. Sounds of destruction.

MOON
Can't complain... considerin'.

CUT TO:

EXT. CRUSTY CAMP, RUSSIANS' HIDING-PLACE -- DAY

View from the arches. All hell breaking loose below. RUSSIANS open-mouthed.

CUT TO:

EXT. CRUSTY CAMP, BUNNY AND MACCA'S HIDING-PLACE -- DAY

BUNNY and MACCA stare down at the same spectacle, open-mouthed.

CUT TO:

EXT. CRUSTY CAMP, CENTRE -- DAY

Chaos. More like a medieval battle than anything else. Pitchforks and shovels are wielded. LITTLE MICHAEL throws hay on the camp fire. Thick smoke belches out. One CRUSTY comes charging out of the smoke like a demon.

CUT TO:

EXT. CRUSTY CAMP, CENTRE/ARCHES -- DAY

JAMIE
Lee, go get the van.

LEE looks round at the mêlée. Shakes his head.

JAMIE (CONT'D)
Drive it round to the beef, we nab it and scarper, go on!

LEE
You're comin' with me, mate.

JAMIE
Alright, alright, let's go.

Those two peg it off.

BACON
S'pose we just stay 'ere, eh Moon?

MOON
Whatever.

MOON is still contemplating the brevity of our mortal existence.

CUT TO:

EXT. CRUSTY CAMP, CENTRE -- DAY

The JIFFERS lead the PRINCE OF WALES out of his pen, dragging him towards the BULL TRUCK.

CUT TO:

EXT. CRUSTY CAMP, TUNNEL ROAD -- DAY

The lads' van comes racing down the Tunnel road.

EXT. CRUSTY CAMP, SIDE ROAD/CENTRE -- DAY

The lads' van screams round the corner and screeches to a halt next to the Crusties' truck. JAMIE and LEE jump out and call to MOON and BACON. MOON and BACON rush over and they start to load their van with the meat from the Crusties' truck.

JAMIE
Hurry up!

LEE
Well, give us a hand, then!

CUT TO:

EXT. CRUSTY CAMP, ENTRANCE ROAD -- DAY

The JIFFERS arrive at the bull truck with the PRINCE OF WALES. They struggle to get him in.

CUT TO:

EXT. CRUSTY CAMP, CENTRE -- DAY

The battle rages on as the LADS' VAN drives off.

CUT TO:

EXT. CRUSTY CAMP, BUNNY AND MACCA'S HIDING-PLACE -- DAY

BUNNY
Nah! Dem boys is nickin' mah beef.

MACCA
Bastards.

BUNNY
Le's get da fuckin' van...

365

They run off.

CUT TO:

EXT. CRUSTY CAMP, ENTRANCE ROAD -- DAY

The JIFFERS get into the bull truck and start the engine. SERGEI, ATTILA and YURI appear out of the dark in front of the windscreen, Arnie-like:

SERGEI
Hello.

JIFFERS can't believe their eyes as Sergei raises his gun.

SERGEI (CONT'D)
Goodbye.

He points it though the open window and shoots the driver. BLOOD splats on the windscreen.

CUT TO:

EXT. CRUSTY CAMP, SIDE ROAD/TUNNEL ROAD -- DAY

The lads' van is escaping fast. At the end of the side-road it turns left into the Tunnel road. Bunny's van is lying in wait as the lads' van disappears down the Tunnel road. Bunny's van follows.

CUT TO:

EXT./INT. LADS' VAN -- DAY

LADS in van. MOON is driving.

LEE
Old Miami's gunner be well-pleased with us. We got 'is beef
an' is dosh.

BACON
Why not just... keep his money?

The others look at each other, shake their heads.

MOON
Some fucker's right up my arse.

EXT. CRUSTY'S CAMP TUNNEL ROAD -- DAY

Bunny's van overtakes the lads' van. Swerving in front and bringing it to a halt.
BUNNY leaps out – heavily armed.

CUT TO:

EXT./INT. LADS' VAN -- DAY

BUNNY approaching, heavily armed.

> BACON
> Oh my god...

> JAMIE
> That's... wha's 'is name?

> LEE
> Bunny, wha's 'e doin' 'ere?!

BUNNY comes to the driver's door window.

> MOON
> You're a long way from Lewisham, Bun.

> BUNNY
> Get out or we kill ya.

> JAMIE
> What's 'e say?

> BACON
> Says he's gunner kill us if we don't get out.

> LEE
> We'll get out then.

> MOON
> What d'yer want with us, Bun?

> BUNNY
> I want mah fuckin' beef, sweetmeat not no conversation, now
> get the fuck out!

> MOON
> Now yer see, it ain't your beef, is it?

> LEE
> Moon, just give it to 'em. Ain't worth dyin' over a few
> T-bones, eh lads?

                         JAMIE
                  Yeah, just give it to him.

                         BACON
                       Whatever.

                         MOON
                    Bollocks to that.

MOON opens the door and smashes it into BUNNY. He slams the van into gear
and reverses fast down the Tunnel road.

                         BUNNY
                    You fuckin'....

BUNNY is left behind as MOON accelerates away.

                         JAMIE
                  Jesus Christ, Moon.

                         BACON
                       I like it.

BACON slaps MOON on the back. BUNNY rolls over on the ground and watches
the lads' van drive away.

END OF ACT TWO

ACT THREE

EXT. SCRAPYARD -- DAY

RUSKIES pull up in the bull truck and climb out. They speak in Russian,
with subtitles

                         ATTILA
                  That was some battle.

                         SERGEI
          Battle, yeah. Like... from the days when men were really men.

                         YURI
          And what did we risk our lives for, uh? What's in this thing ?

                         ATTILA
                    Well, let's see...

ATTILA opens the bull truck to see the huge head of the PRINCE OF WALES staring back at them, not happy.

>   ATTILA (CONT'D)
>   Shit.

Slams the door again. Boom. The PRINCE OF WALES wants out.

>   SERGEI
>   That animal is angry.

>   ATTILA
>   (To Yuri)
>   Give it some vodka.

>   YURI
>   I'm almost out.

ATTILA grabs the half-empty bottle from YURI. YURI quivers.

>   YURI (CONT'D)
>   You think because I am a pacifist... I have no breaking point ?

ATTILA and SERGEI look at him scornfully. The PRINCE OF WALES is still very fidgety in there.

>   SERGEI
>   Go ahead... show us your breaking point.

>   ATTILA
>   Do something interesting Yuri!

>   YURI
>   (Unconvincing)
>   I will not waste my anger... on insignificant people.

YURI stomps off back to the RUSSIAN LORRY. ATTILA hands the bottle to SERGEI.

>   ATTILA
>   Pour the vodka into his water bowl.

>   SERGEI
>   Who made you leader, all of a sudden?

>   ATTILA
>   I am stuck in England... with a paranoid alcoholic... and a
>   trigger-happy macho-man... who can't take a joke... That's
>   what makes me the leader!

369

Before SERGEI can answer this they hear YURI piping up.

> YURI (O.O.V.)
> Guys? You better come here...

CUT TO:

EXT. SCRAPYARD -- DAY

ATTILA and SERGEI walking towards the Russian lorry. Waiting for them are MIAMI and THREE FEET, guns in hands, and YURI with his hands up.

> SERGEI
> Who fuck you, uh ?!

> THREE FEET
> This is Mr Miami Vice. He's come a long way. You remember
> your manners, sunshine.

RUSSIANS don't really understand him.

> MIAMI
> My lads been to see you?

> ATTILA
> No understand.

> YURI
> You pay!

MIAMI looks at the bull truck.

> MIAMI
> That my beef?

SERGEI thinks.

> SERGEI
> Yes, is beef in.

> MIAMI
> Where's... the lads? What have you done to the four lads?

> ATTILA
> Er, lads is not come.

> SERGEI
> Nothing lads.

The RUSKIES make shrugging gestures. MIAMI scrutinises them.

> MIAMI
> Don't piss me about.

> SERGEI
> We is wait, wait, nobody come.

> YURI
> You pay!

> THREE FEET
> You give me the keys to that fuckin' truck, then we'll dish out the dosh.

> SERGEI
> OK.

The RUSKIES scurry off to do his bidding.

> MIAMI
> (To Three Feet)
> Understood that alright, didn't they?

                                                            CUT TO:

EXT. CRUSTY CAMP, SIDE/TUNNEL ROAD -- DAY

The LADS' VAN driving fast (several shots).

                                                            CUT TO:

INT. LADS' VAN -- DAY

MOON is driving fast. The lads are triumphant

> BACON
> We are... the bollocks.

LEE is talking up MOON's moment of glory.

> LEE
> Excellent, weren't it ? 'Get out,' he goes. 'Fuck you mate',
> smashes the door into him – way to go, Moon.

MOON puts on his best modest look.

> MOON
> Way to get yerself respected, that is.

JAMIE is not so impressed. Probably just jealous.

> JAMIE
> Get yerself killed...

                                                           CUT TO:

EXT. SCRAPYARD -- DAY

The bull truck is next to the Rolls Royce.

The THREE RUSSIANS are tied to three scrap vehicles. MIAMI and THREE FEET look down at them.

> THREE FEET
> Could try out me new gizmo. Jaws of Death.

> MIAMI
> You brought that with yer ?

> THREE FEET
> In the boot.

> MIAMI
> Ain't really the time for experiments.

THREE FEET really wants to do this. MIAMI pulls out a big cigar.

> MIAMI (CONT'D)
> You've got until I finish this. Then I wanna be on my way.

THREE FEET's face lights up.

                                                        TIME JUMP:

EXT. SCRAPYARD -- DAY

The RUSSIANS are tied to the scrap cars. THREE FEET has a car battery with two leads coming out of it with crocodile clips on the end. He opens the jaws of the clip and clamps it to SERGEI'S ear. SERGEI is defiant.

> SERGEI
> You English... is all drug addict, homosexual, lick arse of
> America...

> THREE FEET
> Tell me if this 'urts.

Closes the jaws of the other clip on SERGEI'S other ear.

> SERGEI
> (Licking noises)
> Yum, yum, Mr Presid- aaaaah !

CUT TO:

EXT./INT. SCRAPYARD/ROLLS ROYCE -- DAY

MIAMI is finishing his cigar. Another scream from the other side of the yard.
MIAMI shakes his head.

> MIAMI
> (Calling)
> Three Feet? Wind it up!

Throws cigar butt out of the window.

CUT TO:

EXT. SCRAPYARD -- DAY

THREE FEET crouches in front of SERGEI with his contraption, gets ready to go.
Has to ask:

> THREE FEET
> On a scale of one to ten. One bein' uncomfortable, ten bein'
> unbearable... how painful is what you've –

ATTILA, YURI and SERGEI struggle like mad. Desperate to escape the torture.

> MIAMI (O.S.)
> Three Feet...

THREE FEET turns to see MIAMI above him. No arguments. THREE FEET turns
back to the RUSKIES.

> THREE FEET
> Somebody up there's well keen on you. Now get back
> to Moscow.

CUT TO:

EXT. SCRAPYARD -- DAY

THREE FEET is putting the jaws of death into the boot of the Rolls Royce.

MIAMI
Workin' is it ?

THREE FEET
Needs fine-tuning.

MIAMI smiles. THREE FEET turns and gets into the BULL TRUCK and starts
the engine.

EXT. LADS' VAN -- DAY

Lads' van driving fast down the Tunnel road. (several shots).

CUT TO:

INT. LADS' VAN, TUNNEL ROAD -- DAY

BACON looks out of the window.

BACON
I recognise this...

LEE is not listening, still rejoicing in their new, harder, image.

LEE
Moon, you got the right idea, mate.

MOON
Gotter stick up to some of these arse-wipes, ain't we?

JAMIE is listening to BACON.

JAMIE
I recognise it, too.

LEE
Right. Most of these wankers are more scared of us than we
are of them.

MOON swings the lads' van round the corner and sees BUNNY ahead of him –
fully armed. He screeches to a halt

MOON
Oh fuck.

Slams the van into gear – looks round, about to reverse when the headlights of
Bunny's van (driven by MACCA) come round the corner.

LEE
What's 'e doin' 'ere ?!

MOON
We've gone round in a fuckin' circle.

The LADS jump out of the VAN. BACON grabs the duffle bag and flings the door open.

CUT TO:

EXT. CRUSTY CAMP, TUNNEL ROAD -- DAY

The lads pile out, sprint off between the arches. BUNNY raises the gun. BANG. The lads are pegging it. BANG. Bravado roars:

EXT. CRUSTY CAMP, TUNNEL ROAD/ARCHES -- DAY

LADS
Waaargh!

The firing thins out, becomes sporadic. BANG. LEE cries out in a different way.

LEE
Aah! Shit!

MOON stops, horrified.

MOON
Lee? Lee?

LEE comes tearing past him.

LEE
Stepped in fucking shit...

BANG. Another shot.

EXT. CRUSTY CAMP, TUNNEL ROAD -- DAY

BUNNY and MACCA jump into the lads' van.

MACCA
Le's get the bastard started.

They drive off in the lads' van.

CUT TO:

EXT. SCRAP YARD -- DAY

The RUSSIANS are freeing themselves and smashing the scrap vehicles.

> SERGEI (O.O.V.)
> RRRR-Arrr-GH!!

> YURI
> I can't feel my legs.

> SERGEI
> That's because you're drunk.

They clamber free. They talk in Russian, with subtitles.

> YURI
> Look at us, humiliated.

> ATTILA
> I won't go back to Moscow with nothing.

> SERGEI
> Brothers, we will go back to Moscow... carrying the heads of
> those twisted, sadistic... maniacs under our arms!!

> ATTILA
> KGB would have loved them.

> YURI
> Let's get some sleep and...

> SERGEI
> Sleep?! I will not rest... until I have revenge... until I have eaten their hearts!

CUT TO:

EXT. CRUSTY CAMP, ARCHES -- DAY

Four LADS wander around the labrynthine tunnels.

> LEE
> You still reckon you know where yer going do yer?

> MOON
> I've got a mental map in my head.

> BACON
> It's mental alright.

> JAMIE
> No, no, we been this way...

They walk off into the dark.

> BACON
> We are in deeper shit than I thought.

CUT TO:

INT. Russian Lorry -- DAY

The three RUSSIANS sit inside, all swigging from the bottle. ATTILA drives.

An arsenal of weapons is visible in the back. They sing a rollicking, military song, swaying from side to side in a comradely fashion.

The Russian lorry roars along the road.

CUT TO:

EXT. CRUSTY CAMP, CENTRE -- DAY

The aftermath of the battle. CRUSTIES sit. Some wounded, many shell-shocked, an expensive victory.

Uncle BRIAN spits, then lifts a 4-pint plastic bottle of scrumpy to his mouth and swigs. LITTLE MICHAEL drags a DEAD JIFFER past.

CUT TO:

EXT. URBAN ROAD -- DAY

Miami's Rolls Royce and THREE FEET in the bull truck are in convoy.

INT. MIAMI'S ROLLER/BULL TRUCK -- DAY

MIAMI and THREE FEET are speaking to each other on their mobiles – (inter-cut).

> MIAMI
> I s'pose those lads and Bunny cancelled each other out, then?

> THREE FEET
> Seems like it.

> MIAMI
> The problem with those lads, they was always tryin' to do
> things too clever.

THREE FEET
Pity about the money though, innit?

MIAMI
Well... it wasn't a hundred grand sterling.

THREE FEET
Alright, but even in dollars it's still a lot.

MIAMI
It was in Russian roubles, mate. Not worth the pot yer piss in.

The two of them chuckle away.

JUMP CUT:

EXT. CRUSTY CAMP, CENTRE -- DAY

LADS walk in. The CRUSTY mob look them up and down.

MOON
What's the damage, 'ere then?

DEREK looks up.

DEREK
Some fucker's nicked the Prince of Wales.

JAMIE
Prince of Wales ?

DEREK
Our bull.

MOON
Weren't that mob over there then?

MOON points to the fresh graves.

BRIAN
Us was wonderin' if it might be you...

MOON
Uncle Derek. Would we do that?

DEREK
You got the same blood as us, bey.

378

BACON
If we'd nicked your bull, we wouldn't be comin' back 'ere.

BRIAN
I reckon not. Not unless you got shit for brains.

DEREK
That bull was gunner make us money.

BRIAN
Cor, fuck, yeah...

JAMIE
(Casual)
I think I know who's got yer bull.

CUT TO:

EXT. CRUSTY CAMP, CENTRE -- DAY

CRUSTIES pile into the Crusties' truck, bringing anything they can lay their hands on that can conceivably be used as a weapon. The LADS watch.

LEE
Hope this don't backfire.

JAMIE
Nah, we'll come up smelling like roses.

MOON
I hate usin' my family.

JAMIE
Christ's sake, Moon. They ripped us right off. For a change.

BACON
If nothin' else we get a lift back to London.

CUT TO:

EXT. MIAMI'S WAREHOUSE -- DAY

Miami's Rolls Royce and bull truck drive up in convoy. The doors open to MIAMI'S warehouse and the vehicles drive in.

CUT TO:

INT. MIAMI'S WAREHOUSE -- DAY

Miami's Roller and the bull truck pull in. Waiting for them are MR BONE and MR SKIN. Out steps MIAMI.

> MIAMI
> Morning lads. Get the kettle on then.

A snorting noise is heard.

> MIAMI (CONT'D)
> Three Feet? You wanna blow your nose?

THREE FEET looks puzzled. But MIAMI has gone.

CUT TO:

EXT. EAST END -- DAY

The Crusties' Truck makes its way through the streets. It's packed with CRUSTIES and the LADS.

CUT TO:

INT. BUNNY'S YARD, LADS' VAN -- DAY

Lads' van with the beef in has its doors open. Ramp down to floor level. Tons of beef. MACCA has opened up one of the hanging carcasses and is holding a huge bag of cocaine.

> BUNNY
> Macca you playin' stupid.

> MACCA
> What? ... It's once in a lifetime.

He has a line, snaking its way across the floor like the Mississippi.

CUT TO:

INT. MIAMI'S OFFICE -- DAY

The RUSSIANS are trying to intimidate BARBIE. She is wrapped up in telephone cable with the phone in her mouth.

SERGEI holds scissors in his hands, cuts a lump out of her hair. YURI is looking for threatening words in the dictionary. ATTILA pulls the phone out.

> ATTILA
> Where Miami?

> BARBIE
> I told you already, love.

> ATTILA
> My English is small, you answer to me slow. WHERE MIAMI
> HOUSE?

> BARBIE
> He's in his WAREHOUSE!

> ATTILA
> Yes, WHERE HOUSE?!

SERGEI hacks off another lump of hair and flings it down on the desk.

> BARBIE
> Stop it, will yer?

> YURI
> Sergei was barber. To Moscow.

> ATTILA
> He very bad barber. He give cut to customer. Sometime
> cut head.

> SERGEI
> Head is off! Sergei is off head!

CUT TO:

INT. MIAMI'S WAREHOUSE -- DAY

MR SKIN and MR BONE are watching as MIAMI and THREE FEET are about to
open the bull truck.

> MIAMI
> Let's see what we got, then.

The phone rings just as his hands touch the handles of the door. He stops.

CUT TO:

INT. MIAMI'S OFFICE -- DAY

BARBIE is on the phone, fuming. Her hair is hacked to pieces and she has
streaks of mascara running down her cheeks. The phone cable still wrapped
round her neck.

                              BARBIE
          Mr Vice. I 'ad three men here. I think they was German. They
                        was very angry, anyway.

                                                              CUT TO:

INT. MIAMI'S WAREHOUSE -- DAY

MIAMI puts the phone down.

                               MIAMI
                    Looks like the Red Army's on its way.

                                                              CUT TO:

EXT. BUNNY'S YARD -- DAY

CRUSTIES' truck pulls up. DEREK sticks his head out of the driver's window.

                               DEREK
                              This it?

JAMIE nods. DEREK looks at the tyre shop and mutters:

                          DEREK (CONT'D)
          Think y'can just drive off with our prize bull eh? Well, get a
                          fucking load of this.

                                                              CUT TO:

EXT. MIAMI'S WAREHOUSE -- DAY

RUSSIAN LORRY pulls up. Russians step out and open up the back of the vehicle
Full of hardcore weaponry. SERGEI pulls out two machine-guns. YURI opens
another bottle of vodka.

                               YURI
                            Nostrovya.

Swigs, and tosses the bottle to ATTILA.

                                                              CUT TO:

INT. LADS' VAN -- DAY

BUNNY and MACCA have decided to do a Mississippi line each. MACCA is
smashing his head against a piece of hanging beef.

                                382

MACCA
This would normally, 'urt like. Can't feel a fuckin' thing.

BUNNY is laughing.

CUT TO:

EXT. BUNNY'S YARD -- DAY

CRUSTIES slam the doors of the Crusty truck.

BRIAN
Le's get our Prince back.

LADS stand aside. JAMIE takes a deep breath.

CUT TO:

EXT. MIAMI'S WAREHOUSE -- DAY

RUSSIANS walk up to the doors of the warehouse, weapons ready.

CUT TO:

INT. BUNNY'S YARD, LADS' VAN -- DAY

Doors open. BUNNY and MACCA look up. Jaws open wide. CRUSTIES stand
before them.

BUNNY
Babylon...

CUT TO:

INT. MIAMI'S WAREHOUSE -- DAY

RUSSIANS come in and creep cautiously through the warehouse.

CUT TO:

INT. LADS' VAN -- DAY

DEREK
(Roars)
Where's my fuckin' bull?

SLOW MOTION. BUNNY and MACCA look up from their trough of cocaine, snouts
dusted white. Totally fucked. They get to their feet, hardly sensing danger.

BUNNY tears the rib-cage out of the split cocaine carcass, swings it at DEREK.

Huge fight erupts. BUNNY and MACCA try to defend themselves with hunks of meat. CRUSTIES steam in with their machine parts and agricultural tools.

Close-up of an axe connecting with a side of beef.

MACCA swipes out with an entire leg of beef, the flesh tearing off and the white bone bare.

                                                            CUT TO:

EXT. BUNNY'S YARD -- DAY

Sounds of yelling from the lads' van. Awe-struck looks on the lads' faces. It's serious in there.

                          BACON
                Looks like Bunny was in, then.

                                                            CUT TO:

INT. MIAMI'S WAREHOUSE -- DAY

RUSSIANS stand in a line. Machine-guns poised.

                       MR SKIN (O.O.V.)
                Mr Vice'll be back in a m –

                                                            CUT TO:

BAM-BAM-BAM... Pie and Mash take serious lead.

Shot after shot sinks into the writhing bodies. Unnecessary violence.

                                                            CUT TO:

The Russians again. Barrels smoking. Satisfied faces.

A whistle. They turn. THREE FEET and MIAMI have appeared from a back door.

                          MIAMI
                You looking for something?

                          SERGEI
                We look at YOU fucker.

384

> MIAMI
> (Calmly)
> Well come on then, let's have it.

CLICK, CLUNK. Nothing. The Russians have expended all their ammo.

> MIAMI (CONT'D)
> Looks like you'll 'ave another chance to put your new
> contraption through its paces, Three Feet.

CUT TO:

INT. BUNNY'S YARD, LADS' VAN -- DAY

The meat fight continues.

CUT TO:

EXT. BUNNY'S YARD, LADS' VAN -- DAY

The LADS arm themselves with lumps of timber in case someone comes out.
Stand by the ramp leading down from the van.

CUT TO:

INT. MIAMI'S WAREHOUSE -- DAY

C.U. – THE JAWS OF DEATH

We move along the lead to the clip at the end. In THREE FEET's hands. THREE
FEET smiles at YURI. The clip looms large in SERGEI'S eyes as it moves closer to
his face. The THREE RUSSIANS are strung up on a metal warehouse frame.

Anticipation on THREE FEET's face. The jaws of the clip snap shut on YURI'S nose.

> YURI
> Ow !

The teeth of the clip are digging into his nose. That's all. THREE FEET's face falls.
He fiddles with the battery. MIAMI makes an embarassed cough.

> MIAMI
> Three Feet. I think that's what we call an anticlimax.

> THREE FEET
> Must be dirty terminals. Or something.

                              MIAMI
        Time to fall back on more traditional methods, I reckon.

                            THREE FEET
                          (Unhappy grunt)
                              Yeah...

                              ATTILA
         Hey, we go back to Russia, never give you any –

MIAMI is suddenly vicious.

                              MIAMI
        You fuckers 'ad your chance to get down from the table.
                     You stuck around for seconds.

MIAMI nods. Enough mucking around. THREE FEET has prised open the battery,
flings the acid in the direction of YURI'S face.

                                                            CUT TO:

YURI'S lower body. We see it shudder and lock with agony. The hands tremble
and curl up. Agonised gurgle.

                                                            CUT TO:

EXT. BUNNY'S YARD -- DAY

The lads look at the inside of the lads' van. Meat all over the place. MACCA and
BUNNY hanging up.

                              BRIAN
                        Fuckin' animals...

                              DEREK
                            (To Brian)
                 Animals is better 'n' this scum.
                            (To lads)
          They skinned 'im. They skinned the Prince of fuckin' Wales.

BRIAN grabs one of the carcasses and pulls it close.

                              BRIAN
                 Which one was 'e', d'yer reckin?

                              DEREK
                     Don't think about it, Bri.

                               386

The LADS are looking deeply sympathetic.

                    JAMIE
              Yeah, let it go.

DEREK pulls BRIAN away and the depressed CRUSTIES file out.

The faces of the LADS change as soon as the CRUSTIES are gone.

               JAMIE (CONT'D)
    Fuckin' brilliant. Let's get this over to Miami's, eh?

They slam the back doors and then jump into the front.

                     LEE
    Can't understand all this bother over a grand's worth of beef...

                    BACON
              Sign of the times, I s'pose.

The LADS' VAN drives off.

                                                    CUT TO:

INT. MIAMI'S WAREHOUSE -- DAY

MIAMI is about to open the container, When his mobile rings. THREE FEET is
wrapping a bandage around his arm.

                    MIAMI
    Hallo Jamie? You're alive? That is funny. Yeah, don't worry, I
      got the beef. You know what, I'm feelin' extra generous today.
              You just keep the money, eh?

MIAMI shuts off the phone. We've never seen him so satisfied.

               MIAMI (CONT'D)
    Three Feet, remind me to get Barbie a big bunch of flowers.

                                                    CUT TO:

INT. LADS' VAN -- DAY

JAMIE is staring at his phone as if it's been taken over by aliens.

                    JAMIE
    Miami says... he's got his beef and we can keep the dosh.
              That's what he said.

387

BACON
How's that then?

JAMIE
Dunno, mate. But we are fucking sorted.

CUT TO:

INT. MIAMI'S WAREHOUSE -- DAY

MIAMI is trying to open the damaged doors of the bull truck. Grabs a crowbar starts wrenching the handle off. Loud snort.

MIAMI
You hear that, Three Feet?

THREE FEET
I think I did, Guv, yeah...

MIAMI snaps the doors open. The crowbar bounces and clangs on the floor. MIAMI steps back. Jaw drops.

MIAMI
Fuckin' 'ell.

The PRINCE OF WALES is snorting at him. vodka bottles lie all over the floor of the container. MIAMI tugs his mobile out of his pocket again.

CUT TO:

EXT. ABATTOIR -- DAY

LADS' VAN is empty. Sound of mobile ringing.

CUT TO:

EXT./INT. ABATTOIR -- DAY

Everyone looks happy, unaware of the phone ringing. KOUROS stares at all the meat.

KOUROS
Dis is great lads. The weddin's gunner 'ave a real feast now.
I's gonna be a 'uge fuckin' success. I'll set the mincer up.

He hands JAMIE a roll of notes. LADS look pleased with themselves.

CUT TO:

INT. MIAMI'S WAREHOUSE -- DAY

MIAMI drops the phone to the floor. BULL looks furious. Turns head-on to MIAMI. Takes a step. Scuffs his hoof. Snorts again. MIAMI realises what is about to happen. Too late.

C.U. of bull's eyes. C.U. of MIAMI's eyes and FREEZE on MIAMI's face.

END

EPISODE 7

LOCK, STOCK... & A GOOD SLOPPING OUT

by Chris Baker and Andrew Day

ACT ONE

INT. THE LOCK/ BAR -- DAY

Music playing. JAMIE and LEE flick through holiday brochures. MOON is reading the local paper. BACON is counting coins into bags. Tea cups around.

> JAMIE
> Look at this. Las Vegas has got everything.

> BACON
> We can't afford those hotels.

> JAMIE
> We can go to a motel, like in the films.

> MOON
> Someone always dies in them kind of films.
> (In the paper)
> Someone's sellin' a wardrobe 'ere. Twenty-five quid. As new.
> (To JAMIE)
> For all your jackets, Jamie.

MOON is ignored. LEE shows them a picture of a beautiful beach.

> LEE
> Check that out.

> BACON
> See? That's where we wanna be goin'. Where is it?

> LEE
> Thailand.

> MOON
> Don't trust myself in Thailand. We should just go to Ibiza.

> JAMIE
> Again?

> BACON
> We gotter go somewhere cheap. Cos I don't wanna share a
> room with any of you animals. Not after last time.

MOON notices something in the paper.

> MOON
> Eh, eh. The Saint's just gone down. He got five years.

                    LEE
        Saint Micky of Farrel? What for?

                    MOON
    Aggravated burglary. Broke into St Paul's Cathedral, tried to
        knock the vicar out with some crucifix.

                    BACON
    Thank fuck we won't be seein' that nutter for a while.

                                                    CUT TO:

INT. LOCK/BAR -- NIGHT (FLASHBACK)

MICKY FARREL sits in the pub. Round his neck is a guitar with only three strings.
He has a harmonica round his neck. He plays neither, singing manically, out of
tune and banging the table with such force that he is out of time:

                    MICK
        Gunner lay down my sword and shield
                (BANG-BANG)
            Down by the riverside
                (BANG-BANG)
            Down by the riverside...
                (BANG-BANG)

He has driven virtually all the punters out. All four LADS glare at him.
The jukebox is drowned out in the background.

                MICK (CONT'D)
        Ain't gunner study war no more.

He reaches the end of his verse and starts thumping the guitar strings and
blowing into the harmonica. An excruciating racket.

                                              CUT BACK TO:

INT. LOCK/BAR -- DAY

                    MOON
    Yeah, we should stick to Spain – we understand the money, I
                know a bit of Spanish...

BACON and JAMIE glance at each other, sceptical.

                MOON (CONT'D)
            We know what to expect.

                                    BACON
                    Spain? Fine. Just not Ibiza again.

                                     LEE
                 Says 'ere you can go surfing in Tenerife.

                                    BACON
                         Only if you can surf.

                                    JAMIE
                          Can't be that hard.

                                    BACON
                          Alright. Tenerife?

Everyone agrees. LEE and JAMIE clink teacups.

                                    MOON
                 Bugger me. Old Jimmy Silver's dead.

                                                            CUT TO:

EXT. GRAVEYARD -- DAY

A queue of MOURNERS by the graveside. Most of them look like ex-boxers.
MIAMI VICE and THREE FEET are looking into the grave. We see the inscription on
the coffin

A BLOW-UP PICTURE on an easel by the grave. The face of an old gangster called
JIMMY SILVER. JIMMY has an ironic grin on his face.

Next to the picture a PRETTY BOY stands, head bowed. His face is out of keeping
with the rest of the crowd.

                                    MIAMI
           Christ it took a long time for that old fuck to croak.

                                 THREE FEET
                             That it did, Guv.

                                    MIAMI
          You did a good job with that solicitor. You have to pay him much?

THREE FEET thinks.

                                                            CUT TO:

INT. BASEMENT -- DAY (FLASHBACK) -- DAY

C.U. – Woman screaming.

Reveal – A suited man, face seen through the water in a septic tank.

CUT TO:

EXT. GRAVEYARD -- DAY

THREE FEET shifts uncomfortably.

>   THREE FEET
>   No... it weren't... too expensive.

MIAMI has turned his attention to the pretty boy.

>   MIAMI
>   What I can't make out... is why Jimmy Silver would leave his
>   whole pile to that little whippet. What's that all about ?

>   THREE FEET
>   (Knows full well)
>   Dunno, Guv.

>   MIAMI
>   Well, he was a fool to leave it all in cash. That's an invitation
>   for me to go and take what's mine.

>   THREE FEET
>   Fuckin' right. Whole of London knows he owes yer for the
>   Black Monday scam.

This is too explicit for MIAMI – the words are painful.

>   MIAMI
>   Yeah alright. From this day on, the whole of London is
>   gunner know ... I made Jimmy Silver cough up – from beyond
>   the grave.

MIAMI turns casually to a GRAVEDIGGER, holding a shovel.

>   MIAMI (CONT'D)
>   Leave 'im room to turn.

MIAMI smiles at the thought of what is happening right now:

CUT TO:

INT. BANK VAULT -- DAY

Two MEN IN STOCKING MASKS (TOOTHLESS and FRANKIE) stand in the vault with shotguns. A GUARD lies on the floor. Another lies holding his bleeding shoulder, breathing heavily as if in shock.

TOOTHLESS fumbles with keys, trying to locate a particular safety deposit box.

                                                          CUT TO:

EXT. GRAVEYARD -- DAY

MIAMI and THREE FEET walk away from the grave. MIAMI nods recognition to GANGSTERS in the queue.

MIAMI notices TWO WOMEN in their fifties standing by the grave sobbing.

                    THREE FEET
                (Changing the subject)
        Weren't they at the Kosher brothers funeral?

He nods at the two WEEPING WOMEN.

                    MIAMI
        Yeah. I believe they charge two hundred quid a send-off.

                    THREE FEET
        What they use, then? Onions?

MIAMI nods.

                    THREE FEET (CONT'D)
                They do a good job.

                    MIAMI
        I'll book 'em for you then. When the time comes.

MIAMI looks at his watch.

                    MIAMI (CONT'D)
            Our boys ready to move, then?

                    THREE FEET
        They should be in there right now.

                                                          CUT TO:

INT. BANK VAULT -- DAY

TOOTHLESS rips open a safety deposit box. Looks inside.

C.U. – A pink key.

> TOOTHLESS
> Well, bugger me.

They take off their stocking masks.

> FRANKIE
> What? That it? A fuckin' poxy key?

Chucks box across the room. About to hurl the pink key.

> TOOTHLESS
> Oi. 'Old onto that.

TOOTHLESS takes the key from FRANKIE. Looks at it. Pockets it.

> TOOTHLESS (CONT'D)
> Might come in 'andy.

Pause. TOOTHLESS grins a golden grin. His front two teeth are solid gold.

CUT TO:

EXT. GRAVEYARD -- DAY

MIAMI and THREE FEET have left the gathering behind.

> MIAMI
> TOOTHLESS should be on his way out by now. With Jimmy
> Silver's piggy bank under his arm.

Moment of doubt from MIAMI:

> MIAMI (CONT'D)
> He'll be alright, won't he ?

> THREE FEET
> Oh yeah, long as he don't get greedy.

CUT TO:

INT. BANK VAULT -- DAY

> TOOTHLESS
> Now let's do the whole gaff.

FRANKIE grins back.

MONTAGE:

With CROWBARS and SHOTGUN butts they smash open safety deposit boxes. Chucking contents into duffle bags – diamonds, letters, a teddy bear – everything goes.

MONTAGE END.

> FRANKIE
> Right that'll do. Let's go.

TOOTHLESS is looking at the big circular safe at the end of the vault.

> TOOTHLESS
> Not yet...

Grabs a GUARD by the scruff of the neck.

> TOOTHLESS (CONT'D)
> Open it.

Pushes gun barrel into GUARD'S mouth. GUARD faints.

> TOOTHLESS (CONT'D)
> Oi, wake up.

Shakes the GUARD.

> FRANKIE
> Forget it, Toothless.

TOOTHLESS turns towards FRANKIE.

> TOOTHLESS
> What did you...

Sees a row of ARMED POLICE behind FRANKIE, aiming assault rifles.

> TOOTHLESS (CONT'D)
> Shit.

Drops the GUARD.

FREEZE

OPENING TITLES.

CUT TO:

EXT. HMP NICKHAM -- DAY

Miami's Rolls Royce draws up. MIAMI and THREE FEET get out and walk towards the prison.

                                                                    CUT TO:

INT. H.M.P. NICKHAM/LANDINGS -- DAY

TOOTHLESS is escorted from his cell.

                                                                    CUT TO:

EXT./INT. HMP NICKHAM RECEPTION -- DAY

MIAMI and THREE FEET go into the prison.

                                                                    CUT TO:

INT. HMP NICKHAM/LANDINGS -- DAY

TOOTHLESS is escorted towards the visitors' area.

                                                                    CUT TO:

INT. HMP NICKHAM/CHECK-IN AREA -- DAY

MIAMI is patted down. None too pleased. Metal detector locates his antique hip flask.

THREE FEET patted down. METAL DETECTOR goes berserk.

                            MIAMI
                    He's all nuts and bolts.

                                                                    CUT TO:

INT. HMP NICKHAM/VISITORS' ROOM -- DAY

THREE FEET and MIAMI sitting in the centre of the visitors room. They look and feel out of place among all the wives and kids and Mums and Dads.

P.O.V. - TOOTHLESS APPROACHING

MIAMI and THREE FEET staring up.

TOOTHLESS sits down opposite them. Grimaces as he lowers himself carefully into his chair.

Stony silence.

> TOOTHLESS
> What can I do for yer?

> THREE FEET
> Hand that key over.

> TOOTHLESS
> Bit special is it?

> THREE FEET
> Toothless, there ain't no need for us to 'use methods', is there?

> TOOTHLESS
> Half of what this key's worth an' you can walk away with it.

MIAMI'S hackles rise.

> MIAMI
> That key is mine.

> TOOTHLESS
> Jimmy Silver was a wealthy man.

> MIAMI
> What else you plannin' to sell me? My house? My car? You
> want me to make you an offer for these shoes?

MIAMI points down to the SHOES on his feet.

> TOOTHLESS
> I want what I'm owed.

> MIAMI
> Oh, you'll get that, my son.

THREE FEET steps in, trying to control his anger.

> THREE FEET
> Toothless. We done a deal.

TOOTHLESS grins his golden grin.

> TOOTHLESS
> It's all different now. I'm lookin' at ten years...

THREE FEET
That's yer own fault.

TOOTHLESS
I ain't 'ad nothing out that job.

THREE FEET
Because yer fucked it up.

TOOTHLESS
Seems to me old Jimmy Silver 'ad an ace up 'is sleeve... seems
like he was one step ahead of you Miami, just like he
always was.

This is the worst thing anyone could say to MIAMI Vice. MIAMI's face darkens.

TOOTHLESS (CONT'D)
An' I'm gunner keep good 'old of this key 'til I find out exac'ly
what it's worth.

MIAMI
You can use that key – right now – to buy back the rest of
your natural life. Or I'll 'ave you ripped apart... before the end
of the week.

TOOTHLESS
You're avin' a laugh. You ain't got no weight in 'ere.

TOOTHLESS stands up. He walks off, a little awkwardly.

THREE FEET
Fucker's right. All our boys are in Parkhurst and Long Larten.

MIAMI
Well, we'd better get someone in 'ere then, 'adn't we ?

CUT TO:

INT. MIAMI'S OFFICE -- DAY

MIAMI sits at his desk. THREE FEET stands to his side. The four LADS stand in
front of him. Two HENCHMEN by the door.

MIAMI
Fifty grand. Fancy that?

Uneasy feeling spreads through the LADS.

                         BACON
            Course. You know us, it's just...

                         JAMIE
            Don't know if we'll be available.

                         MOON
            We was just off to the airport, see?

                         JAMIE
                       Tenerife.

The LADS point to their luggage (sports bags and suitcases) and
shrug apologetically.

                         MIAMI
            I've already booked you an 'oliday.

                          LEE
                Sweet. Anywhere nice?

                      THREE FEET
         Package. Her Majesty's Prison Service.

                          LEE
                     Not so sweet.

                         MIAMI
              You've 'eard of Toothless.

                          LEE
              Yeah. Top blag merchant.

                         MIAMI
      Blag merchant. Dunno if I would go so far as to say 'top'.

                      LEE shrugs.

                    MIAMI (CONT'D)
      TOOTHLESS 'as a key... about 'is person... that is very... very...
      important to me. Trouble is, 'e's got a ten-year stretch ahead
                 of 'im. And I ain't known for my patience.

LADS look slightly disturbed. THREE FEET talks like the deal is done.

                      THREE FEET
       We organise the fit-up. You get nabbed. Soon as you're on
                 the in, we feed you all the orders.

                          402

                              MIAMI
         When yer got the key, we get the charges dropped an' you
                           walk. With the fifty.

                              JAMIE
                    I dunno if this is really what –

                              MIAMI
                          (Interrupting)
          I didn't tell you to think it over, did I ? You're the only
                   muppets I know who don't 'ave a record.

                              MOON
           Er... Miami, I'm on probation at the moment. Still got six
               months left. I can't get sent down again.

MIAMI very slowly and deliberately turns his attention to MOON.

                              MIAMI
             I'll leave you out of that arrangement for the time being.

Consternation on MOON's face.

                                                              CUT TO:

INT. MIAMI'S OFFICE, RECEPTION -- DAY

Plain clothes POLICE OFFICERS take a statement from BARBIE. She holds a hankie
to her nose, sniffing.

                              BARBIE
             It was 'orrible. They just, like, leapt on me, like animals.

POLICE OFFICER nods sympathetically.

                         BARBIE (CONT'D)
            They was pullin' me 'air. An' they grabbed me bag with
            everyfin' in it. One of 'em grabbed my arse. I'll 'ave mental
            scars, right up 'til me pension... And you know what?... I can
                         tell you where those bastards live.

                                                              CUT TO:

INT. LOCK/BAR -- DAY

BACON is tucking into a fry-up. Seemingly relaxed.

JAMIE is holding a tequila bottle, deep in thought.

                                403

MOON is farting about, making some special breakfast, whistling.

LEE's looking out of the window. Walks away from it. Walks back. Trying to prepare himself for the ordeal. He is gabbling:

> LEE
> All you gotter do, if you wanna survive, is keep yer 'ead down. An' stick up for yerself. Obviously. Bit of both.

> JAMIE
> Keep yer nose clean...

> LEE
> Yeah, keep yer nose clean, that's right. But not too clean. You don't wanna come on like a Mummy's boy.

> BACON
> Will you relax ?

> LEE
> You lot seem to think this is gunner be a doddle. But we are in shit.

> MOON
> Just get the key an' you'll be straight out... Simple.

> BACON
> Moon... You can shut up. Fuckin' lightweight.
> (Imitating MOON)
> 'Got another six months on me probation, Mr Vice Sir.'

> MOON
> Well it's true innit?

BLUE LIGHTS flashing outside.

> BACON
> Eh, eh. Looks like rain and I ain't even finished me breakfast.

Trying to wolf it down.

CUT TO:

EXT. HMP NICKHAM -- DAY

The security van draws up and goes through the main gates of the prison.

CUT TO:

EXT. HMP NICKHAM -- DAY

The security van backs up to the inner gates. The LADS are led out of a security van in civilian clothes by TWO GUARDS. They go into the prison.

CUT TO:

INT. HMP NICKHAM RECEPTION AREA -- DAY

LADS do their fingerprints.

CUT TO:

LADS stripping down, dumping their clothes and possessions in plastic boxes.

CUT TO:

LADS collect remand prisoners' uniforms.

CUT TO:

LADS having their photos taken... glum.

CUT TO:

INT. HMP NICKHAM/LANDINGS -- DAY

Association. PRISONERS are all over the place. Loads of noise. A lot of deals going down. Hands furtively exchange unseen goods. Prisoners gawp at the new fish.

The LADS are being led by FOLEY to the second floor. As they reach the first floor landing, they turn...

>   JAMIE
>   Oh shit...

MICK stands up ahead of them. He turns and mutters to Jesus, who is standing next to him but not visible to the rest of us.

>   MICK
>   They dared to mock you Jesus, but now you've delivered them
>   into my castle... eh me Lord?

FOLEY leads the LADS onto the next staircase. Leaving MICKY behind. He shouts up to them.

405

MICK (CONT'D)
You spat in the face of the Lord's glad tidings. And the Lord
speakef to me clear on this matter... dincha?... Yeah.

MICK is pulled away by a GUARD. MICK shouts after them.

MICK (CONT'D)
Lord said, MICKY FUCKIN' DO 'EM!!

MICK is silenced by a huge shove from the GUARD.

BACON
Oh no that's all we need. I mean what's his fuckin' problem -
we only threw him out the pub.

LEE
Great. That nutter's been certified. Wha's he doing in here?

BACON
He's got more than certificates. He must've got medals for
bein' mad.

LEE
Right anyone clocked Toothless yet?

LADS look around.

JAMIE
Up on the threes.

LEE
Let's do it then... let's get that fucking key and get the fuck
out of 'ere...

LEE is all psyched up to do TOOTHLESS straightaway. Pushes
forward. The other two pull him back.

JAMIE
Wait a minute...

BACON
Can't just do it in front of everyone.

JAMIE
We just got 'ere.

LEE
I don't wanna be here another day, I've 'ad enough.

Two MEN peer down at the LADS. One of them is TOOTHLESS. Next to him, FRANKIE.

> TOOTHLESS
> Reckon it's one o' them?

FRANKIE is rolling a cigarette.

> FRANKIE
> Seen 'em round at MIAMI's.

> TOOTHLESS
> It's them then.

> FRANKIE
> (Shakes his head)
> Hitmen work alone.

TOOTHLESS takes FRANKIE's rollie from him and lights it.

> TOOTHLESS
> Can't be that headbanger, can it?

He is looking at MICKY now.

> FRANKIE
> Too mad.

LADS now on second floor.

FOLEY shoves JAMIE into a cell.

> FOLEY
> Special Brew? Yer new cell-mate.

FOLEY turns to LEE and BACON.

> FOLEY (CONT'D)
> You're in there.

It's the cell next to JAMIE's.

CUT TO:

INT. HMP NICKHAM/JAMIE'S CELL -- DAY

A tiny cell with two bunks and a slop out tin. Lying on one of the beds, back to us, is SPECIAL BREW - a huge Glaswegian with a pathological hatred of the English.

A knackered old CELTIC POSTER is his only addition to the wall.

JAMIE
Alright?

SPECIAL BREW turns over, pissed off.

SPECIAL BREW
You fockin' English?

JAMIE thinks 'Oh shit...'

CUT TO:

INT. HMP NICKHAM/LEE AND BACON'S CELL -- DAY

Four-man cell. Just BACON and LEE in there for now. Ridiculously cramped. LEE sits on a bed. Cell next to them is blaring out hip-hop music.

LEE
Home sweet home.

BACON
Wonder who we got in with us...

LEE
Yeah, right. Fuckin' 'ell, could be anyone.

BACON
Did yer plug anything up?

LEE
Nah. You?

BACON
Thought about it. Couldn't quite bring meself.

They both sit on beds. There is a long, empty silence. LEE is getting very nervous.

LEE
Shit...

BACON
What?

LEE fidgeting. Stir crazy already.

408

                          LEE
                  I hate small places.

                         BACON
        LEE... let's just chill out a bit shall we? I mean we've only been
                      'ere half an hour.

                          LEE
        Christ I'm bored already. We're supposed to be in Tene-
              fuckin'-rife. Let's get that key. Now.

                                                            CUT TO:

INT. HMP NICKHAM/JAMIE'S CELL -- DAY

SPECIAL BREW is blocking the doorway.

                         JAMIE
                       I'm Jamie.

                      SPECIAL BREW
                        So what?

JAMIE sighs. This isn't going to be easy.

                         JAMIE
              Well I'm a bit Scottish actually.

SPECIAL BREW looks at him with total contempt.

                      SPECIAL BREW
                     Are yae fock.

                         JAMIE
              Me Mum was called Campbell.

                                                            CUT TO:

INT. HMP NICKHAM/LEE AND BACON'S CELL -- DAY

LEE and BACON look out of their cell.

                         BACON
                       (Pointing)
              He came out of that cell there.

                          LEE
              We walk past, slip in, search it.

                          409

They move out.

CUT TO:

INT. HMP NICKHAM/LANDINGS -- DAY

As LEE and BACON walk to TOOTHLESS'S cell they see that JAMIE is hemmed in by SPECIAL BREW.

> SPECIAL BREW
> Campbell?! Yae better tae be an Englishman than one of that
> fockin' scum that got intae bed with the redcoats.

JAMIE sees them walk past the door. They see SPECIAL BREW blocking the way and just keep walking.

They keep going until they are just about to get to TOOTHLESS'S cell. They mutter to each other:

> LEE
> Still clear ?

> BACON
> Yeah. Don't bottle it.

BRUMMIE and IRONBAR come across and intercept LEE and BACON.

> IRONBAR
> That's our cell.

The LADS stop dead in their tracks. Then BRUMMIE nods down to their cell.

> BRUMMIE
> Looks like you're our new cell-mates... Alright, lads?

> BACON
> Yeah.

> IRONBAR
> (Sinister)
> Settlin' in?

> BRUMMIE
> Ain't easy, bein' the new fish in the tank. But you just need to
> learn the rules.

They walk them away from TOOTHLESS'S cell.

> LEE
> What's the rules then?

BRUMMIE takes his time.

> BRUMMIE
> First of all. If yer gotter 'ave a dump in the night you do
> a flyin' pasty.

> BACON
> A flyin' what?

> IRONBAR
> Flyin' pasty. Shit on a piece of paper, wrap it up, bung it out
> the window. You'll stink the whole drum out else.

LEE and BACON grimace.

> BRUMMIE
> If you're into smack, don't cook up then leave your shit about
> cos we ain't going down the block on your account, alright?

> BACON
> Right.

> BRUMMIE
> If yer need a toss you wait 'til association. We take it in turns,
> the rest of us go out. Don't wanna hear you bumping the
> blanket in the middle of the night.

> LEE
> Fair enough.

> BRUMMIE
> Sort you out with anything? Bit of puff.

LEE and BACON look dubious.

> LEE
> We don't 'ave too much ready cash right now.

> BRUMMIE
> We ain't askin' you to pay now. 'Ere y'are.

Sticks his hands down his pants and pulls out a SIXTEENTH. Pushes it into
LEE's hand.

                              LEE
                         Listen mate...

                            BRUMMIE
        Eh, I know what it's like first time inside. Bit of a head fuck.

LEE looks at the HASH. Fancies it.

                              LEE
                         I'm not sure.

                            BRUMMIE
             Whenever you 'ave the cash. No worries.

                              LEE
                      What's the damage?

                            IRONBAR
                         Thirty quid.

                             BACON
             Bollocks to that, that's tourist prices.

                              LEE
             Thirty quid? You can take it back, mate.

                            IRONBAR
        He ain't the fuckin' Avon lady. You got it. You keep it. An
                          you pay us.

                            BRUMMIE
                    When yer got the cash...

BRUMMIE and IRONBAR walk away.

                             BACON
              Well, we could've handled that better.

                              LEE
               At least we got something to do...

Sniffing the hash.

                             BACON
        What? Get stoned, get in debt and get our legs broken, yeah
                   great... Nice one, Lee.

                                                        CUT TO:

INT. HMP NICKHAM/JAMIE'S CELL -- DAY

SPECIAL BREW slams cell door shut. Pushes a chair in front of the door.

> SPECIAL BREW
> Right.

JAMIE looks concerned.

SPECIAL unscrews a bed leg from his bed. Looks like a handy weapon. JAMIE prepares to fight for his life.

SPECIAL BREW lifts the bed leg to his mouth and gulps. JAMIE's eyes widen. What the fuck is going on?

> JAMIE
> What's that?

> SPECIAL BREW
> Two fockin' basic rules for yae pal. Keep yer nose oot and shut yer mouth.

SPECIAL BREW slurps from the bed post again.

> SPECIAL BREW (CONT'D)
> Piece of Cockney shit.

> JAMIE
> What's your problem? You ain't never laid eyes on me before. What reason you got to call me a piece of shit?

SPECIAL BREW sits up and faces JAMIE down.

> SPECIAL BREW
> What reason? Does the word 'Glencoe' nae mean anythin' t'yer?

JAMIE thinks.

> JAMIE
> Did I sell yer some dodgy Scotch?

> SPECIAL BREW
> Yae English make me sick. Yae shite all o'er the other coontries yer whole fockin' history! End yer don't even fockin' REMEMBER!!

> JAMIE
> I weren't there mate.

413

SPECIAL BREW

Well let me tell yer somethin'. Yae bastards can tek our land,
yae kin tek our oil, yae kin beat os at the fitbae once ev'ry ten
years but ye'll never tek our pride...

JAMIE

Don't want yer fuckin' pride. Fuckin' nutcase.

CUT TO:

INT. HMP NICKHAM/FOOD SERVING AREA -- DAY

BACON, LEE and JAMIE queuing up for food. Nearing the front.

C.U. – FOOD

LADS' reactions to the food slopped onto their trays.

JAMIE arrives.

JAMIE

I couldn't get out. Fucking Celtic fan wants to talk to me.

BACON

Yeah well our cell-mates are a bit fucking keen, as well.

LEE

We was tryin' to get into Toothless's cell, but –

BACON

Eh, ee. He's on 'is way down.

TOOTHLESS and FRANKIE are coming down the stairs.

BACON (CONT'D)

What about Micky?

LEE

Micky? Up there.

JAMIE

Wha's 'e doin'?

LEE

'E's, er... got himself a book.

MICKY holding a book open and chewing. He lifts the book to his face and takes
another mouthful of pages. Chews again then spits out the paper. A CON stands

414

next to him mouth open wide. MICKY glares at the lads. Mouthful of paper.

LADS shake their heads in disbelief.

> LEE (CONT'D)
> I wish he'd stop staring at us.

> BACON
> Right... anyway, we got two minutes to get that key out of
> Toothless's cell.

> LEE
> Yeah right. Forget this shit.

They leave their trays and set off towards the cells.

> CRAWLEY (O.S.)
> Alright, Jamie?

JAMIE turns round to recognise CRAWLEY, a lad his own age, grinning at him.

> JAMIE
> Crawley? What you doin' –

SMACK. CRAWLEY smacks JAMIE in the mouth. Looks round to check no
screws saw.

> CRAWLEY
> That's for pokin' my bird, you cunt.

> JAMIE
> You prick. That was eight years ago. She already dumped yer.

JAMIE puts his hand to his lip. BACON grabs his arm.

> BACON
> Come on, we ain't got time for that.

CUT TO:

INT. PRISON -- DAY

LEE and BACON head off to their cells. TOOTHLESS is looking at CRAWLEY now.

> TOOTHLESS
> Maybe he's the one. Looks well nasty. Like he'd do a geezer
> for a few quid.

415

FRANKIE
Nah. It's always the quiet ones. The one's yer don't expect.

TOOTHLESS
What if it's all three of 'em?

FRANKIE
Maybe. They get younger every day. Most of 'em don't do the
job proper. Just hack you up a bit or shoot yer in the gut.
Might be hours before yer cop it.

TOOTHLESS
Yeah, alright Frankie.

CUT TO:

INT. HMP NICKHAM TOOTHLESS'S CELL -- DAY

JAMIE wipes blood off his lip and keeps watch. The other two search frantically
through TOOTHLESS and FRANKIE'S stuff.

JAMIE
Dunno wha' his problem is.

BACON
Crawley? Forget it. Give us an 'and will yer?

LEE
No. Look out for Toothless. An' Micky.

JAMIE stands by the doorway, still pre-occupied. The other
two go over the room double-quick.

JAMIE
I'm gunner clatter 'im.

BACON
Jamie shut it.

JAMIE
You remember 'er. She had a body like a bag of soup. Made a
noise like Donald Duck.

LEE
Did she?

JAMIE
When yer shagged 'er... eh, eh, TOOTHLESS is on 'is way.

416

BACON and LEE speed up their search.

> JAMIE (CONT'D)
> Get outta there!

BACON and LEE throw everything back to its proper place. They step onto the landing next to JAMIE just as TOOTHLESS approaches.

> BACON
> The fuckin' key ain't 'ere.

> LEE
> We'll never get out of here.

> JAMIE
> Well... now it'll 'ave to get nasty.

END OF ACT ONE

ACT TWO

INT. LOCK/BAR -- DAY

Soft music in the background. MOON lays a black satin sheet over the bar. He wears his dressing gown and shorts.

> MOON
> Tanya? There's some honey in the cupboard. Behind the
> Weetabix. Bring that too?

Deep sigh of satisfaction and anticipation. He jumps onto the bar and lets his dressing gown fall away.

MOON hears the door open and close. Footsteps.

> MOON (CONT'D)
> Alright, sweetheart. Do me.

He opens his eyes to see MIAMI and THREE FEET hovering over him. He sits bolt upright and pulls his dressing gown round him.

> MOON (CONT'D)
> Fuck-ing shit... God. Thought you was er, Tanya, I...

> MIAMI
> (Calmly)

417

What the fuck's goin' on ?

MOON
Well... me an' Tanya were jus'...

THREE FEET
He's talkin' about the key.

MOON
Oh right, well...

TANYA walks in with a tray of honey, cream, chocolate spread, ice cubes and ice cream. Sees the back of MIAMI and THREE FEET, turns round and walks straight out.

MOON (CONT'D)
Er, still waitin' really for...

THREE FEET
Ain't you 'ad no news ?

MOON shakes his head.

MIAMI
My mind... is on that key. All the time.

MOON
Yeah, yeah...

MIAMI
Maybe your mates need your help. Maybe you should be on the inside too.

MOON
I'd love to be there with 'em, but I still got...

MIAMI
(Interrupting)
We've heard your story... Y'know, TOOTHLESS ain't such a bad bloke. When yer get to know 'im. That's what I want you to do.

MOON doesn't really understand.

MIAMI (CONT'D)
He's just signed up for the Food Preparation course. An' I found out something very interesting about you. You... are a qualified chef.

CUT TO:

EXT. HMP NICKHAM/PRISON GATES -- DAY

Little old MRS EVANS walks out of the prison, tying her headscarf round her head. She holds two cookery books under one arm.

THREE FEET's head appears from MIAMI's Roller.

                    THREE FEET
          Mrs Evans? Can we 'ave a word?

CUT TO:

INT. MIAMI'S ROLLER -- DAY

MRS EVANS looks frightened. THREE FEET on one side of her. MIAMI on the other, arm across the seat behind her shoulders, but he's looking straight ahead.

                    MIAMI
               (Matter-of-fact)
      So it's best if you forget all about boiled sprouts and suet pud,
        sweetheart. You call in sick, with somethin' nasty. An' you
        don't never go back. Alright? Or instead of them weekend
          trips to Southend, you'll be doin' weekend trips to Epping
               Forest to visit old Bert's unmarked grave.

THREE FEET looks out at the houses.

                    THREE FEET
             This your house?

MRS EVANS nods. The driver gets out to open the door for her. We stay on THREE FEET. He doesn't like having to intimidate old ladies.

                    THREE FEET (CONT'D)
        Shouldn't be allowed anyway, decent women going into places
                    like that.

CUT TO:

INT. HMP NICKHAM/KITCHEN -- MORNING

MOON walks in with an officer – FOLEY. FOLEY has a clipboard. Waiting for their new cooking teacher is a line of about eight convicts – including TOOTHLESS and SPECIAL BREW.

MOON looks round. There are signs on the wall: A Good Chef Always Washes His Hands, A Good Chef Never Loses His Temper. The knives are on a rack, with their outlines traced onto the wall so you can see if there's one missing.

>   FOLEY
> Right, gentlemen. This is our new chef. While Mrs Evans is
>   convalescing. His name's...

Looks down at the sheet on his clipboard. Shows it to MOON. MOON nods.

>   FOLEY (CONT'D)
>   Er, Moon. That it son, 'Moon'?

>   MOON
>   Yeah.

>   FOLEY
>   Right well, I'll leave yer to it then.

Exit FOLEY.

>   MOON
>   Alright lads?

>   SPECIAL BREW
>   (Menacing)
>   Mrs Evans lets us do wha' we want, pal.

>   MOON
>   Right.

SPECIAL BREW goes to a drum of oil, opens it. Pulls out another container. More Hooch.

>   SPECIAL BREW
>   I'm makin' a Bovril sandwich. In a minute.

>   MOON
>   Great, great... I just thought we could all... make something
>   together.

The whole kitchen freezes. Everyone looks at him like he's mad.

>   MOON (CONT'D)
>   Steak and chips?

Everyone grins. Apart from Toothless.

TOOTHLESS
I'm making an omelette.

MOON
I've got a great recipe for a Spanish one.

TOOTHLESS
Fuck off.

CUT TO:

INT. HMP NICKHAM/FOOD SERVING AREA -- DAY

The LADS are queuing up for food. MOON supervises the cons serving them.

MOON
Alright?

BACON
Moon?

MOON
You alright Lee?

LEE is looking out of it.

LEE
Eh? Yeah... yeah... you?

Looking over his shoulder then back to MOON.

LEE (CONT'D)
You got any chocolate?

MOON shakes his head.

BACON
Fuck you doing 'ere?

MOON
Miami's got us a job, innit?

JAMIE
You what?

MOON
Part of 'is plan.

JAMIE
What's the rest of the plan?

Pause.

MOON
You ain't gunner like it.

BACON
Can't get much worse...
(Doubt)
Can it Moon... ?

The three LADS listen intently to MOON, as they wait for the plan.

MOON
Miami says, the plan is... you kill Toothless, and gimme the key
to smuggle out.

BACON
What? That it?

LEE
That ain't much of a plan y'know?

MOON
An'... if you don't do it, Barbie don't drop them charges.

CUT TO:

EXT. HMP NICKHAM/EXERCISE YARD -- DAY

LEE, BACON and JAMIE watch a load of PRISONERS walking round in a circle.
TOOTHLESS stands on the opposite side of the yard with FRANKIE.

JAMIE
We do Toothless an' we'll be in 'ere a long time.

BACON
If we don't we'll be dead when we get out.

LEE
We've got to get out of 'ere. I owe Brummie a lot of
dope money.

JAMIE
This is fucked. Really fucked.

LEE surreptitiously pulls out a roach, lights it up. Takes a quick drag, passes it to BACON. Who refuses.

> BACON
> Lee! Put that thing away.

LEE shrugs. Pockets roach. The sound of a hymn being sung – 'Lord of the Dance'.

> JAMIE
> This place is doin' my 'ead in.

MICK approaches.

> BACON
> Here we go.

> MICK
> Me and Jesus chose you to join our flock. Jesus 'ere reckons you was rude to him whilst I was 'aving a slash. Told him to piss off... Y'know I believe him cos he's the Lord.

> JAMIE
> Look Micky we're sorry we threw you ... and Jesus out the pub but you was scaring the punters... Anyway I don't remember telling... Er your mate to piss off.

BACON starts laughing. LEE looks very concerned.

MICKY glares at BACON.

> LEE
> Bacon, shut up.

> MICK
> You laugh at the Lord. You're laughing at me. I know your sort you shall never repent... eh ?

Listens to Jesus. Starts to look angry.

> MICK (CONT'D)
> Ah Bollocks to that no time for forgiveness now... it's too late. I gunna Baptise you in the showers in as many ways as there are holes. Yer gunner be dead before the end of – uurgh.

IRONBAR whacks him over the head with the side of his hand.

IRONBAR
Rest it.

He and BRUMMIE carry on walking over to the lads.

MICK
The Lord is punishing me...

BRUMMIE
Bollocks, these lads is working for me. That right, eh Lee?

LEE
Er yeah.

CUT TO:

TOOTHLESS nudges FRANKIE and turns away confidentially.

TOOTHLESS
Hear that? They're workin' for Brummie? Eh?

FRANKIE shakes his head.

FRANKIE
So what? What's that got to do with anythin'?

CUT TO:

BRUMMIE and IRONBAR stop in front of the lads.

LEE
I'm sortin' out yer cash. Pay yer next week.

BRUMMIE
Fuck the money. Get me some gear. Get yer birds to bring it
in for us. You'll get well looked after.

BACON
We don't need lookin' after.

IRONBAR
Micky ain't no bullshitter. But we'll 'andle 'im for yer.

BRUMMIE
Long as yer pay yer debts.

BRUMMIE has noticed something.

> BRUMMIE (CONT'D)
> Ironbar. Someone's sittin' on your bench.

IRONBAR wheels round.

> IRONBAR
> Eh? Shhhit.

Storms off towards a MAN sunning himself on a bench. His eyes closed, miles away.

BRUMMIE ambles behind. IRONBAR stares down at the MAN. Suddenly he swoops down.

CUT BACK TO:

LADS reactions as IRONBAR beats the guy up.

CUT BACK TO:

IRONBAR dropping the bloodied and semi-conscious interloper to the floor.

IRONBAR sits down on his bench.

The MAN crawls away, blood streaming from his face. MICK is creased up with laughter.

FOLEY comes running up.

> FOLEY
> You do this Ironbar?

> IRONBAR
> Me? Nah.

> FOLEY
> About your bench was it?

> IRONBAR
> It was old Santa. Suddenly went apeshit.

IRONBAR nods at an OLD CON with a white beard looking rather nervous.

> IRONBAR (CONT'D)
> Right lads?

The other CONS shrug and nod agreement.

FOLEY
Right Santa, you're off down to seg. Dose of the liquid cosh
might be in order...

SANTA'S face lights up. Everyone's happy, except the POOR BLOKE on his knees
bleeding, who's totally ignored.

LEE
This place is just mental.

BACON
Lee, concentrate. We gotter think of a way to...

CRAWLEY approaches. JAMIE catches his eye.

CRAWLEY
Alright, pretty boy?

JAMIE makes a move to deck him, but BACON holds him back.

BACON
Not now...

CRAWLEY
You always was soft.

CRAWLEY slouches off.

CUT TO:

INT. STAIRWAY OF PRISON -- DAY

The LADS pass Crawley again.

CRAWLEY
You ain't gunner 'ave protection for ever, twinkle.

JAMIE
Right, that's it.

Storms off after CRAWLEY.

BACON
Jamie! Lee? Ah bollocks to it.

BACON and LEE follow on. No great hurry.

CUT TO:

EXT./INT. HMP NICKHAM LANDINGS -- NIGHT

BACON and LEE react to the sounds coming from the cell. JAMIE comes out nursing his fist.

> BACON
> Really gettin' to yer, innit ?

> JAMIE
> Feel better after that.

They go.

CRAWLEY crawls out of his cell. TOOTHLESS watches from the next floor. They can see JAMIE nursing his fist.

> FRANKIE
> Didn't see no blade.

> TOOTHLESS
> Gave 'im a good shoein' though didn't they?

> FRANKIE
> Oh yeah. Wanna take 'em.

> TOOTHLESS
> You saw Brummie in the yard. He's protectin' 'em. Some
> reason.

> FRANKIE
> What we gunner do then? Go on the numbers?

> TOOTHLESS
> They ain't gunner let us in with the nonces. Not after we
> clattered that Tube groper.

> FRANKIE
> (Impatient)
> Just 'and the key over then.

> TOOTHLESS
> You mad? Tha's all we got to bargain with. No. What we
> gotter do is...

FOLEY interrupts them.

> FOLEY
> Cells!

427

                    TOOTHLESS
                    Hey Guv!

                    FOLEY
                    What?

                    TOOTHLESS
              Wanna put in for a transfer.

                    FRANKIE
                    An' me too.

                    FOLEY
                    (Hinting)
        Any particular reason I should... take into account?

                    TOOTHLESS
        Someone's got the finger on us, innit? Either we kill
                    or we die.

                    FOLEY
                    (Still hinting)
        Yeah, yeah. Gotta be convinced it's a pressing case.

                    TOOTHLESS
              Hundred quid. All we got.

                    FOLEY
              Bollocks. Yer robbed a bank!

                    TOOTHLESS
                    We got caught!

TOOTHLESS gives him the cash.

                    FOLEY
              I'll dig out the forms.

                                        CUT TO:

INT. HMP NICKHAM/VISITING ROOM -- DAY

CONS and their families. One YOUNG GIRL coughs something up and slips it over to a young con who then shoves it down between his ballbag and his arse. They carry on chatting casually as if nothing had happened.

SPECIAL BREW is getting a ticking off from a LITTLE WOMAN about half his size.

           LEE
Ugh, that's disgustin'.

He is looking at BRUMMIE who looks as if he's trying to hold his breath for the whole visit. Closer look reveals that he's getting a handjob from his female visitor.

MIAMI enters. Sits down. They wait for him to speak.

          MIAMI
You're makin' a meal outter this, lads. It's a very simple job.

          JAMIE
We'll be honest with yer, Mr Vice. We really don't wanna kill
'im.

          MIAMI
Then just get the key.

          BACON
We searched 'is cell.

          MIAMI
What for? He ain't gunner leave it there for yer. It ain't a
fucking treasure hunt.

          LEE
You reckon 'e keeps it on 'im all the time?

Pause.

          MIAMI
You what? You takin' the piss? Of course he keeps it on him,
it's up his arse you fucking half-wit. Where else is he going to
keep it? Ah, Jesus...

Suddenly there is a commotion. GUARDS steam onto BRUMMIE, pulling him away from his WOMAN.

          BRUMMIE
Ah, c'mon it's just a handjob, yer can't do me for that! Yer
bastards! What harm's a fuckin' handjob?

BRUMMIE is dragged out.

          BRUMMIE (CONT'D)
You fuckin' fascists. I'm goin' on 'unger strike –
it's not human!

CUT BACK TO:

MIAMI
Right. Listen, you lot. I went to a lot of time and trouble to
get you banged up and I expect results.

CUT TO:

INT. HMP NICKHAM/LEE AND BACON'S CELL -- NIGHT

BRUMMIE lying on his bed. FOLEY enters.

FOLEY
What's this crap I hear 'bout you being on 'ungerstrike?

BRUMMIE
I'm gonna take my case to Amnesty International. It's an
abuse of human rights.

FOLEY
BRUMMIE, just get off your arse an' get down the kitchens.

BRUMMIE
I ain't eatin' 'til I'm allowed conjugal rights.

FOLEY
You ain't married.

BRUMMIE
That's a fuckin' crime now is it, eh?

FOLEY
Don't be silly.

BRUMMIE
Silly, eh? You'll see.

FOLEY
You'll die if you don't eat.

BRUMMIE
I'll fuckin' die if I don't shag.

CUT BACK TO:

INT. HMP NICKHAM, JAMIE'S CELL -- NIGHT

BACON and JAMIE return from the shower room. Towels in hand.

LEE is puffing out the window.

                    JAMIE
            What you doin' in 'ere ?

                    LEE
        BRUMMIE's gettin' short-tempered. He's 'ungry.

                    BACON
                  (To JAMIE)
            Ain't paid 'im for his gear.

                    JAMIE
        Yer gunner 'ave to 'ave a shower sooner or later.

                    LEE
        Micky Farrel said I'd die in the shower.

                    BACON
        That stuff's makin' you paranoid.

                    LEE
    Paranoid ? Mick Farrel thinks God told him to drown me in
      the shower. I'm sharin' a cell with two hardmen who're
    gunner do me for debts I can't pay. An' I'm gunner be stuck
    'ere in this dungeon till I do over some geezer and pull a key
                    out his arse.

                    JAMIE
            We'll think of something.

                    LEE
                  I won't.

                                                    CUT TO:

INT. HMP NICKHAM, TOOTHLESS'S CELL -- NIGHT

Dark. Silent. TOOTHLESS wakes to hear stealthy movement. FRANKIE is slipping
out of bed – TOOTHLESS's whole body tenses. His lip curls with fury.

TOOTHLESS leaps up onto his bed and stands with his back to the wall.
Fists clench.

                    TOOTHLESS
    Fuck you! Judas! I'm ready! Thought you could slit my throat
                    in the –

                      431

FRANKIE is standing in his underwear with the SLOP BUCKET
up to his waist. Sighs wearily.

> FRANKIE
> Christ's sake Toothless, get a grip.

Sound of urine splashing into the bucket.

CUT TO:

INT. HMP NICKHAM, LEE AND BACON'S CELL -- DAY

Lock-up. IRONBAR reads the paper.

> BRUMMIE
> That's another day you ain't paid up. So you can double the
> smack.

> IRONBAR
> Typical innit? Be friendly to 'em, 'elp 'em out an' what d'yer
> get? Ripped off. Yer ripped Brummie off!

> BACON
> Just give us a couple days, alright?

> BRUMMIE
> Two days. Two. I'm countin' 'em.

> LEE
> Leave it with us. No worries.

BRUMMIE turns his attention back to IRONBAR who still reads the paper.
BRUMMIE pulls a Mars bar out of his pocket. Digs into it.

> BRUMMIE
> Ain't there nuffin' about my 'unger strike in there?

CUT TO:

INT. HMP NICKHAM, TOOTHLESS'S CELL -- DAY

FOLEY unlocks door and enters. TOOTHLESS sits up. FRANKIE raises his eyebrows.

> FOLEY
> You got yer transfer.

> TOOTHLESS
> Thank fuck. Not up North I 'ope?

                    FOLEY
                  No. Scrubs.

                  TOOTHLESS
               Scrubs? No... No!

                    FOLEY
     What you expect for a hundred quid? The Dorchester?

                   FRANKIE
             You can't send us there.

                    FOLEY
             You in danger there too?

                  TOOTHLESS
             Everyone's in danger there!

FOLEY slams the door.

                                                    CUT TO:

INT. HMP NICKHAM, KITCHEN -- DAY

It's lunchtime. SPECIAL BREW and TOOTHLESS are having an argument.

                 SPECIAL BREW
           It's mah turn to fry the fockin' chips.

                  TOOTHLESS
     Bollocks, it's your turn to chop the onions up an' you know it...

                 SPECIAL BREW
           Bloody onions make me cr-... eyes water.

A couple of chuckles from the CONS. SPECIAL BREW looks around.

                    MOON
             You could do 'alf each.

They both look at him as if he's a moron.

                 MOON (CONT'D)
              Look. Here y'are.

Hands a knife to SPECIAL BREW. KNIFE BLADE flops over. It's made of Baco-foil.

>   SPECIAL BREW
> Who's got the blade? C'mon! Fock's sake it's the only knife
>   that cuts.

No-one is owning up. SPECIAL BREW throws down the knife-handle.

>   SPECIAL BREW (CONT'D)
> If yae dinnae give me the blade, I'm goona kick the livin' shite
>   oota all o'yae.

SPECIAL BREW looks at each of them in turn. Stops on TOOTHLESS.

>   SPECIAL BREW (CONT'D)
>   It were fockin' yae, pal.

He steps towards TOOTHLESS.

>   TOOTHLESS
> Listen Brave'eart, I need a tool. I got hitmen on me arse. You
>   can have it back Wednesday cos I'm gettin transferred.

MOON's reaction – he mouths 'Fuck'.

>   SPECIAL BREW
> Well yae kin get choppin' the onions then can't yae?

>   CUT TO:

EXT. HMP NICKHAM, EXERCISE YARD -- DAY

MOON, walking out, whistles a tune. A line drops down. MOON hooks a piece
of paper on to it and walks away. The line is pulled up.

>   CUT TO:

INT. HMP NICKHAM, LEE AND BACON'S CELL -- DAY

JAMIE watches BACON's reaction as he reads the message.

>   BACON
>   Shit. Lee...

LEE is in a narcotic stupor.

>   BACON (CONT'D)
>   Lee?!

LEE raises his head and fixes BACON with a look of iron concentration.

LEE
What?

BACON shows LEE the note.

BACON
Toothless is out, he's gettin' a fuckin' transfer.

MICKY stands in the doorway twitching

MICK
It's Thursday tomorrow.

BACON and LEE look him up and down. Is he going to make a move?

MICK (CONT'D)
You know what's special about Thursday?
(He listens to Jesus)
That's right Jesus, it's the Day of Judgement!!
(Explosive)
When dirty shitty sinners go down and get their heads boiled
in the fucking cauldron!!

END OF ACT TWO

ACT THREE

INT. HMP NICKHAM, LANDING -- NIGHT

The LADS stride up to TOOTHLESS'S cell. Grim determination.

CUT TO:

INT. HMP NICKHAM, TOOTHLESS'S CELL -- NIGHT

TOOTHLESS smokes his rollie looking out the window as if someone might try
to sneak in through the bars.

Turns to see JAMIE, flanked by BACON and LEE. Quick as a flash he picks up a
chair as a shield and pulls the knife out of his trousers.

TOOTHLESS
Miami sent yer, didn't 'e?

JAMIE
He did as a matter of fact.

435

> TOOTHLESS
> I'm takin' you with me. Le's go, I've waited long en –

> BACON
> We ain't the hitmen.

> TOOTHLESS
> Bollocks. Who's first?

> JAMIE
> Look. We're the negotiators.

> TOOTHLESS
> The what?

The LADS edge closer to TOOTHLESS until he's surrounded.

> LEE
> Jus' hand the key over, eh?

> TOOTHLESS
> Well that's very good negotiatin'.

> BACON
> Y'know what 'appens if yer don't?

> TOOTHLESS
> I ain't afraid to take you lot on.

> JAMIE
> Ain't us you gotter worry about pal.

> BACON
> If we fail. Miami's got a back-up plan. Micky. Micky Farrel is
> Miami's hitman.

> TOOTHLESS
> Bollocks. I've heard him ravin' away. His pages are fallin' out!

> BACON
> It's just an act. Standard innit lads?

They nod.

> BACON (CONT'D)
> If he gets rumbled for doin' the job on you, he'll plead
> insanity. He's thinkin' ahead.

TOOTHLESS is taken aback. But still suspicious.

> TOOTHLESS
> How come he's screaming blue murder at you if yer all on the same team?

> LEE
> Think about it. We talk the key outter you an' 'e don't get to do the hit. He wants us to fail, so he can move in... an' get paid.

> TOOTHLESS
> Shit...

> JAMIE
> We don't like this. Hand the key over an' Mickey's our problem.

JAMIE holds out his hand for the key. TOOTHLESS believes them – we can see it in his face.

> TOOTHLESS
> Nah. Nah. I ain't givin' up without a fucking good fight.

LADS shake their heads, look disappointed.

> TOOTHLESS (CONT'D)
> Now get outta my cell.

The LADS give up on him. As a final thought:

> JAMIE
> Just don't come runnin' to us when Micky makes his move.

> TOOTHLESS
> I'll see 'im. No problem.

CUT TO:

INT. HMP NICKHAM, LANDING -- NIGHT

The LADS leaving TOOTHLESS'S cell.

> LEE
> Didn't buy it, did he?

> JAMIE
> What yer talkin' about? He took it 'ome in a carrier bag.

MICK makes his way to the toilets. Shouts to the LADS and beckons to them.

> MICK
> Come on lads! What's the matter? Scared to meet your maker?

Walks straight into the WALL... BANG... Raises his fist at the wall.

> MICK (CONT'D)
> (To the wall)
> I warned you... I fuckin' warned you... I gonna drive the Devil
> out of yer... After I been to the bog...

Walks into toilets.

CUT TO:

INT. HMP NICKHAM MICKY'S CELL -- NIGHT

MICKY is drowned in the toilet. MICK flails and squirms but FRANKIE and TOOTHLESS crush his head down. Squirming stops.

> TOOTHLESS
> Sweet. I'll do them lads too. That'll get us a bit of respect
> over at the Scrubs.

CUT TO:

INT. HMP NICKHAM/LANDINGS -- NIGHT

SPECIAL BREW and the LADS look down as SANTA is led away in handcuffs.

> JAMIE
> He was down the noddy shop learnin' to weave baskets. He
> can't have done it.

> SPECIAL BREW
> He didnae.

> LEE
> Well he don't look too bothered about takin' the blame.

> SPECIAL BREW
> He's gettin' a couple of ounces an' a bar of chocolate oot of
> it. One more life sentence is no bother to him. He's already
> got six.

> BACON
> Well that's one death threat out the way, innit?

They all think about this with relief.

                    BRUMMIE (O.S.)
              Oy, you lads. Come 'ere.

They look round. BRUMMIE arrives.

                    BRUMMIE (CONT'D)
        Right you fuckheads. Pay-up time. What is it now? Two
        ounces of hash and a couple of grams of smack, yeah?

                    LEE
              Right, the only thing –

                    BRUMMIE
        There ain't no problem. Visitin' day tomorrer. Get yer birds
                t'pick up the gear from this address.

Hands LEE a slip of paper.

                    BRUMMIE (CONT'D)
        Now, if the goods don't come through, I'll set Ironbar on yer.

They look over to IRONBAR.

                    LEE
        Yeah er... no worries I spoke to me bird she's up for it, she's
                gonna sort it out for yer.

                    BRUMMIE
              Yer good lads.

BRUMMIE turns away.

                    BACON
              You ain't got a bird.

                    LEE
        Worst comes to the worst I'll just get me old dear to pick up the stash.

                    BACON
              Your mum? You're fuckin' mad.

                    LEE
              She might do it.

                    JAMIE
        Lee. Get a grip on reality will yer.

Officer FOLEY approaching the BRUMMIE. LADS can just hear what's being said.

CUT TO:

FOLEY
You're lookin' remarkably well for a man on hunger strike.

BRUMMIE
Thanks.

FOLEY
Read your name in the paper the other day.

BRUMMIE
Yeah, what paper was it in?

FOLEY
Prison Gazette. Thing is they got yer name wrong. Said:
known to fellow prisoners as 'Gummie'.

FOLEY laughs, but BRUMMIE doesn't see the funny side.

BRUMMIE
Prison fuckin' Gazette. I need more fuckin' publicity than that. My
cause needs to be known. It needs to be a topic for debate.

FOLEY
I'll pin it on the noticeboard for you.

FOLEY strolls off. BRUMMIE pulls out a mars bar. Starts munching.

BACON has had a brainwave.

BACON
(To BRUMMIE)
Eh, Brummie!

BRUMMIE turns to look at BACON. LADS looking at BACON
wondering what the hell he is going to say.

BACON (CONT'D)
I hear you ain't getting much publicity for your cause...

BRUMMIE
What's it to you?

BACON
Well I think we can help you out.

> BRUMMIE
> Make it good, boy.

> BACON
> Hunger strikes never get much publicity unless you die... Nah the best way
> is a hostage situation... Yer threaten the lives of a few inmates and the whole
> of Fleet Street will be swarming round 'ere like flies round shit... Plus yer get
> the added bonus of exclusives from the rags... make a fuckin' fortune mate.

> BRUMMIE
> Wha's in it for you?

> BACON
> We wanna be the hostages.

BRUMMIE looks puzzled.

CUT TO:

INT. HMP NICKHAM, LEE AND BACON'S CELL -- NIGHT

Association. BACON, JAMIE and LEE stand plotting.

> JAMIE
> It's dodgy.

> BACON
> We'll be alright. Brummie ain't gunner bring Ironbar in on it.

> JAMIE
> Well, that's something.

> BACON
> Toothless just better be there.

> JAMIE
> Never misses Cookery.

> BACON
> Just remember. Make sure Brummie don't bottle out before
> Toothless has shat the key out.
> (To LEE)
> You gotter tell Tanya, right? Fucking fast-acting laxatives,
> nothing gentle.

> LEE
> I've seen this stuff work. It'll turn 'is insides out. Be like
> dredgin' a canal.

JAMIE
Sweet. Pass the key onto Moon an' we'll be out of 'ere for
the weekend.

LEE taps a PHONECARD against his hand.

LEE
I better call Moon as well, yeah?

BACON
You know what? Let's just surprise 'im.

CUT TO:

INT. HMP NICKHAM/LANDING -- NIGHT

LEE at the phone. Big queue behind him.

LEE
Allo Tanya. How are yer? Yeah we do actually.

CUT TO:

INT. VISITING ROOM -- DAY

LEE waits for TANYA. About to doze off. He is rudely awoken.

TANYA
Wake up will yer?

LEE jumps.

LEE
Ah, Tanya. Alright?

TANYA is having trouble speaking clearly:

TANYA
No. Dose bloody guar's shearch me more an' all de othersh.

LEE takes a look at the other prison wives and mums. Then looks back at TANYA.

LEE
I wonder why.

TANYA
Gig ush a kish den.

442

                              LEE
                        A kick? What for?

Annoyed, she points at her mouth.

                             TANYA
                        A kish. On da mouf.

                              LEE
                        Oh yeah, right, right.

They kiss. Long and lingering. TANYA shifts a package over to LEE with her
tongue. LEE almost chokes. Shifts the package around his mouth.

                          LEE (CONT'D)
                           Dice one.

                             TANYA
                       Just don't swallow 'em.

                                                          CUT TO:

INT. H.M.P NICKHAM, FOOD SERVING AREA -- DAY

Lunchtime. CONS queuing for food. The three LADS and BRUMMIE line up next
to each other.

                             JAMIE
                        Now's the time Brum.

Seeing CRAWLEY in front of him.

BRUMMIE's hyped up. Just needs a bit of a push.

                            BRUMMIE
                     Yeah? Y'reckon. Yeah, yeah...

                             BACON
                        Come on, let's go.

                              LEE
                  Yeah we can hole up in the kitchen.

                            BRUMMIE
                  Be handy. Now I'm back on the grub.

                             BACON
                      But no Ironbar OK?

BRUMMIE
Yeah, yeah... Let's do it.

JAMIE shoves CRAWLEY into the back of a LARGE CON who takes exception to his food flying onto the floor. He bears down on CRAWLEY.

CRAWLEY
It weren't me...

SMACK.

BRUMMIE looks round at two LARGE CONS. Him and the
LADS start to shove the big blokes. Fight breaks out. Alarm
bells ring.

BRUMMIE
Right. Let's go.

Fight spreads. Trays and cutlery fly. Mayhem.

JAMIE sees CRAWLEY cowering by the hotplate. Decides to give him another whack. BACON pulls him away again. The LADS and BRUMMIE jump over the hotplate. IRONBAR is behind them. GUARDS steam into the chaos.

BRUMMIE kicks the kitchen door open.

CUT TO:

INT. HMP NICKHAM, KITCHEN -- DAY

MOON, SPECIAL BREW and TOOTHLESS look up as BRUMMIE and the LADS storm in. IRONBAR follows.

BRUMMIE
Right, Special, you can go.

SPECIAL BREW
What yae want me oot for?

BACON
(Impatient)
I'm takin' 'ostages. You wanna be one?

SPECIAL BREW
I ain't leavin' a gallon o' mah best hooch for yae greedy
bastards to gulp doon.

BRUMMIE
Stay then. But we ain't lettin' yer out.

TOOTHLESS stares at the lads.

BACON
He stays.

TOOTHLESS
You fuckers ain't gunner do me.

Produces the KNIFE-BLADE from his trousers.

IRONBAR just walks across the room and breaks TOOTHLESS'S arm. The blade falls to the floor.

TOOTHLESS (CONT'D)
Aaaah...

TOOTHLESS drops to his knees in agony.

LEE
(To BRUMMIE)
We need one real hostage, innit?

BRUMMIE doesn't really understand why, but he's really getting into this.

BRUMMIE
Right, nice one. Ironbar? Barricade the doors.

LADS turn in horror to see: IRONBAR heaves the table up against the door. Piles all sorts of stuff on top of it.

LEE
(Quietly to BRUMMIE)
Thought you was... leavin' Ironbar outter this?

BRUMMIE opens a catering-size tin of spaghetti hoops.

BRUMMIE
Yeah, but look at him. Ain't a siege without old Ironbar.

MOON
(To lads)
What is goin' on?

JAMIE
Brummie's doin' a protest. He's taken us hostage.

445

(Winks)
Us an' TOOTHLESS.

MOON
Right. Weren't there nowhere else you could've done it?

BACON
(Sarcastic)
Sorry to drag you into our little difficulty, Moon.

MOON
I'm meant to be takin' Tanya to see that Abba musical...

LADS stare at him.

MOON (CONT'D)
What?

There is a banging on the door.

FOLEY (O.S.)
Right, open up. Playtime's over.

BRUMMIE
(Mouthful)
We ain't comin' out. An' we got 'ostages in 'ere.

JAMIE
Tha's good, right attitude.

FOLEY (O.S.)
That you Brummie?

BRUMMIE
Dead fuckin' right. Now get the Governor down 'ere, or I'll
start slicing someone up.

LEE, BACON and JAMIE nod encouragingly. MOON is slower to get into it.

FOLEY (O.S.)
Come on, Brummie. Open up now an' we'll pretend it
never 'appened.

BRUMMIE
I ain't speakin' to you. I'm speakin' to the Governor an' no
fucker else.

Footsteps.

BACON
Nice work mate.

BRUMMIE
Break out some hooch, then Special.

SPECIAL BREW
No chance.

BRUMMIE
C'mon. We'll sort you out good when we get out.

SPECIAL BREW
It's mah hooch, an' I ain't wastin' on the likes o' yae.

BRUMMIE shouts out the door.

BRUMMIE
Oy, you screws. We're givin' yer a hostage.

SPECIAL BREW
I'm stickin' wi' mah brew.

IRONBAR and BRUMMIE bear down on him with vegetable KNIVES. LADS glance at each other – how do they play this one?

SPECIAL BREW (CONT'D)
(Still defiant)
Fockin' rollin' pin's sharper than those knives.

IRONBAR
Just 'ave to use more force. I ain't got a problem with that.

Stand off. SPECIAL BREW thinks.

SPECIAL BREW
Yae kin have a couple of moothfuls each. And y'll owe me
for 'em.

Tension subsides a bit.

BRUMMIE
I'm a fair man.

SPECIAL BREW pulls out his hooch barrel. Dips mugs in and hands them out.

FOLEY (O.S.)
Where's this hostage then?

447

> ### BRUMMIE
> We changed our minds. You took too long. An' you're not the
> fuckin' Governor.

The LADS, BRUMMIE, IRONBAR and SPECIAL BREW chink glasses. TOOTHLESS
suffers in the corner.

> ### MOON
> (Muttered)
> What's yer plan?

> ### BACON
> We make Toothless shit the key out.

He shows MOON a PARCEL of pills.

> ### LEE
> Tanya smuggled them in.

IRONBAR takes TOOTHLESS a mug of hooch.

> ### IRONBAR
> No 'ard feelings.

> ### TOOTHLESS
> Look, I need medical attention. Let me go first, eh?

> ### BRUMMIE
> No. We'll cut yer up first if yer gunner be miserable.

BRUMMIE drinks from his cup.

> ### BRUMMIE (CONT'D)
> Not bad.

The LADS drink from their cups.

> ### BACON
> Tastes like stomach acid.

> ### BRUMMIE
> Yeah, sort of fruity.

CUT TO LATER:

Everyone is now sitting on the floor. BRUMMIE and IRONBAR have drunk rather
a lot.

GOVERNOR (O.S.)
BRUMMIE, lad? This is Governor Molby.

BRUMMIE stands self-importantly, but unsteadily.

GOVERNOR (O.S.) (CONT'D)
This is all very foolish. Nothing will come of this but trouble.
Now, if you think you've got a grievance, you open up and
we'll have a little chat. Just you and me. Man to man. See if
we can work something out.

BRUMMIE is in his element.

BRUMMIE
Bollocks.

LADS
Nice one... go on son [etc.]

GOVERNOR (O.S.)
Listen...

BRUMMIE
You listen. I want conjugal rights. For all cons.

He looks round at all the others. The LADS nod and egg him on.

IRONBAR
An' I want satellite TV an' a sofa in me cell.

BRUMMIE
Shut up, Ironbar, I'm tryin' to be serious.

IRONBAR
An' a microwave. Just me, nobody else.

BRUMMIE
(To Governor)
Forget about what Ironbar wants. Just listen to me.

The LADS look from BRUMMIE to IRONBAR. Tension is rising between them.
It does not auger well.

IRONBAR
Brummie, that ain't fair.

BRUMMIE
(To Governor)

449

An' I want this protest on the news. Else I'll start chopping
people up.

> GOVERNOR (O.S.)
> (Wearily)
> Look, I can get you onto the news. But conjugal rights... it's something
> that'll have to go through the Home Office. It takes months.

> BRUMMIE
> I ain't goin' anywhere.

> GOVERNOR (O.S.)
> Well. I'll give you twenty-four hours to think it over.

> BRUMMIE
> Got loads of food in 'ere. So you can fuck off, can't yer?

GOVERNOR'S footsteps retreat. LADS getting uneasy now. It's not really
under control.

> JAMIE
> 'E's rat-arsed.

> BACON
> Make some soup or somethin'. For old Toothless.

TOOTHLESS sees the LADS conspiring.

> TOOTHLESS
> Look... BRUMMIE. Them lads is gunner stitch you right up.
> They just wanna do me, an' pin it on you. Now, I'm gunner be
> flush when I get out... Forget all this bollocks about wife-
> shaggin', I'll make yer rich.

> BRUMMIE
> Rich?! I'm in 'ere for life, mate.

> TOOTHLESS
> They're fuckin' hitmen.

BRUMMIE looks over to the LADS. LEE shakes his head. JAMIE taps his head and
points to TOOTHLESS – Mad. BRUMMIE laughs.

> BRUMMIE
> Good for them.

> TOOTHLESS
> Yer gotter let me go. Whatever yer want it's yours.

IRONBAR
Why don't you shut up?

Smack. IRONBAR knocks TOOTHLESS out.

LADS look at each other – this doesn't make things any easier. The plan is
falling apart.

FADE TO BLACK

CUT TO LATER:

TOOTHLESS regains consciousness. MOON is holding a cup-a-soup in front of
him. Virtually pouring it down his throat. Stares up at the LADS. They stare
back at him.

SPECIAL BREW
How come I don't get one ?

MOON
That was the last one.

IRONBAR
(To BRUMMIE)
What about duvets ?

BRUMMIE
Leave it, will yer.

IRONBAR
Fuck you, Brummie.

BRUMMIE
An' stop drinking so much, yer turning into a joke.

IRONBAR
I ain't got no woman to come in an' give us a shag. I want
something outter this.

IRONBAR and BRUMMIE glare at each other.

SPECIAL BREW
Dinnae worry. Y'll get a gud beatin' an' a holiday doon on the
block.

TOOTHLESS puts the soup down. He's downed half of it.

> SPECIAL BREW (CONT'D)
> (To TOOTHLESS)
> Yer finished wi' that?

TOOTHLESS nods. SPECIAL BREW picks it up.

> SPECIAL BREW (CONT'D)
> Chicken.

> JAMIE
> I wouldn't, if...

Trails off.

> IRONBAR
> (To BRUMMIE)
> Is he right? We gunner get nuthin' outter this?

> BRUMMIE
> We'll get publicity.

> IRONBAR
> Publicity?!

> BRUMMIE
> For our demands.

> IRONBAR
> Your demands! I don't wanna spend a month in seg for a bit
> of publicity. I want some luxuries.

> BRUMMIE
> Alright, but think of something fuckin' sensible.

IRONBAR looks at BRUMMIE with psychotic distrust.

Meanwhile, TOOTHLESS is looking queasy. Distracts BRUMMIE.

> TOOTHLESS
> I'm gunner... dump me guts out.

> BRUMMIE
> Oh Jesus. Get in the cupboard and do it. Then chuck it out the window.

The LADS look at each other nervously.

> TOOTHLESS
> Ah, God.

BRUMMIE
Ah God, it's prob'ly typhoid, settin' in.

SPECIAL BREW
Ah, God.

SPECIAL BREW is now clutching his stomach.

LEE peers into the cup. All the soup is drunk.

TOOTHLESS grabs NEWSPAPER and crawls into the cupboard. BRUMMIE kicks the
door shut.

SPECIAL BREW (CONT'D)
Dinnae take too long there, pal.

IRONBAR
(Laughing)
It'll take 'im a while, with one good hand.

SPECIAL BREW
Yeah, well I cannae hold onto the Loch Ness Monster for long.

CUT TO:

INT. HMP NICKHAM, KITCHEN CUPBOARD -- DAY

TOOTHLESS' face is sweating profusely. Relief spreads across his face. He gets his
breath back – remembers:

TOOTHLESS
(Whispers)
Key... key...

WHAM. Door flung open by SPECIAL BREW. SPECIAL BREW grabs TOOTHLESS
and drags him out of the cupboard.

SPECIAL BREW
C'mon pal. I got a bomb waitin' to go off 'ere.

TOOTHLESS tries to pull up his trousers with his one good hand. NEWSPAPER
flying everywhere.

The LADS watch this scene unfold with consternation.

TOOTHLESS
'Old on, I ain't –

Door slams.

> TOOTHLESS (CONT'D)
> – finished.

LADS look at TOOTHLESS.

> JAMIE
> (Under his breath)
> Where's... the key ?

CUT TO:

EXT. HMP NICKHAM, ALLEY -- DAY

Moments later. Flying pasty thuds to the ground.

CUT BACK TO:

INT. HMP NICKHAM, KITCHEN -- DAY

BRUMMIE dusts his palms. Him and IRONBAR are now totally pissed.

TOOTHLESS is laid out on the floor, a broken man.

The LADS look at each other, aghast. They conspire in the corner.

> BACON
> Shit.

> MOON
> How does that fit into the old plan then, eh?

> JAMIE
> It's a setback.

> MOON
> Key's wrapped up in shitty paper out there and we're
> hostages to a couple of... psychos... who can hardly count up
> to their IQs...

SPECIAL BREW is still in the cupboard.

JAMIE takes BRUMMIE aside. IRONBAR is jealous.

> JAMIE
> Listen, Brummie. Why don't yer let the chef go? As a sign of
> good faith?

BRUMMIE
Eh?

JAMIE
Show 'em you ain't mental.

IRONBAR
Fuck that. I am mental.

BRUMMIE
Just makes us look weak, don't it?

IRONBAR
I'm not weak. You know what? I say it's time we showed 'em
we mean business.

BRUMMIE
Wait an' see if we're on the news.

IRONBAR
Chop someone's leg off an' we'll be on the fuckin' news.

BRUMMIE
We gotter be more cleverer. A siege is like a game of chess...

IRONBAR
Since when could you play chess?

BRUMMIE
Alright draughts. Same thing.

IRONBAR
They won't be expectin' us to chop no legs off. It'll catch 'em
on the 'op.

LEE
Wait a minute. Lads... we're in this together, innit?
Was our idea.

BRUMMIE
You said you'd be the 'ostages.

LEE
Yeah, but...

BRUMMIE
You wanna be 'ostages or not?

BACON
Easy boys...

IRONBAR and BRUMMIE are now not listening to the LADS at all.

IRONBAR
We could make 'em draw straws.

BRUMMIE
(To the lads)
Can't say fairer than that.

CUT TO LATER:

JAMIE is holding the short straw. Look of despair.

IRONBAR
I'll get the bread knife.

BRUMMIE
After the news.

IRONBAR
No. I'm bored.

JAMIE
Let's wait for the news, eh?
(To Lads)
Eh, lads?

LADS
Yeah... yeah...

IRONBAR
Where's the telly, Brummie?

BRUMMIE
Eh?

IRONBAR
What we gunner watch it on?

BRUMMIE
I was gunner get the Governor to send a telly down.

IRONBAR
Yer just make it up as you go along. I'm fuckin' cleverer 'n
you are.

BRUMMIE
We gotter play it cool, Ironbar. Cool, calm, c'lected –

IRONBAR
Bollocks. I'm bored. Them out there ain't takin' any notice
of us. An' I'm gunner cut that geezer's peg off. See
what 'appens.

BRUMMIE
Listen to me Ironbar.

IRONBAR
I ain't listenin' to you no more, yer full of shit.

IRONBAR pushes past BRUMMIE with the bread knife. BRUMMIE grabs
IRONBAR'S shoulder. IRONBAR spins round and slashes BRUMMIE'S throat.
BRUMMIE stumbles backwards, blood oozing from his throat. Slides down the
wall, staring vacantly at IRONBAR.

IRONBAR looks round at everyone, bleary-eyed.

IRONBAR (CONT'D)
Shut 'im up, didn't it?

SPECIAL BREW emerges from the cupboard as if it's a normal toilet. Chucks
newspaper out of the window.

Sees BRUMMIE. Stoops to have a look at him.

SPECIAL BREW
'E's nae gonna make it.

He looks up at IRONBAR. It's obvious that IRONBAR did it.

SPECIAL BREW (CONT'D)
Tha's yae focked. It's fockin' marder.

IRONBAR
Tha's right Taggart. You're next if you don't watch it.

SPECIAL BREW
Dinnae be threatenin' me, pal.

IRONBAR
This is my siuge now.

SPECIAL BREW
Ah used tae break skulls like yours for a pastime, mate.

                              IRONBAR
          Don't provoke me man, I'm ready to do the lotta yer. I'm like
          a cocked fuckin' shotgun, one wrong move an' you'll be...

CLONG. SPECIAL BREW whacks IRONBAR over the head with an oil drum.
IRONBAR drops like a sack of spuds. Knocked out, possibly dead.

                           SPECIAL BREW
                      What a pain in the arse.

JAMIE breathes a huge sigh of relief.

SPECIAL BREW walks over to the door, shouts through it.

                       SPECIAL BREW (CONT'D)
                        We're commin' oot.

Starts tossing aside the barricade. LADS look at each other. Look at MOON.

                              BACON
                  Pick it up on yer way 'ome, eh?

We finish on MOON'S reaction.

                                                             CUT TO:

EXT. HMP NICKHAM, ALLEY -- NIGHT

C.U. – MOON'S face as he bends down to the ground.

Sound of paper rustling, unwrapped. MOON grimaces then nods. He's found
what he's looking for.

MOON stands up with the flying pasty in his hand.

                           FOLEY (O.S.)
                      What you doin' there lad?

MOON spins round to see FOLEY.

                              MOON
                        Dropped me sarnies.

He holds up the ball of newspaper, wraps it up tight and stuffs it into his jacket
pocket, gulping and trying to smile.

                                                             CUT TO:

INT. MIAMI'S OFFICE -- DAY

MIAMI looks up as THREE FEET enters the office.

> THREE FEET
> Evenin', Guv.

> MIAMI
> Three Feet.

> THREE FEET
> We've, er...

Breaks off. Not sure how to play it.

> MIAMI
> What? What've you done?

> THREE FEET
> We found out... where that key's for. Place called
> 'Rocket Roger's'.

> MIAMI
> Restaurant?

THREE FEET shakes his head.

> MIAMI (CONT'D)
> Club?

> THREE FEET
> Yeah, sort of. A gym.

> MIAMI
> Oh. Train boxers do they?

> THREE FEET
> No. It's, er...

Leans closer to give MIAMI the terrible information...

CUT TO:

INT. ROCKET ROGER'S, LOCKER ROOM -- DAY

Steam. Row of lockers with pink numbers and pink keys. Young, ridiculously
well-conditioned, males walk past. Sound of skin being slapped. Hearty laughter.
A very happy place.

CUT BACK TO:

INT. MIAMI'S OFFICE -- DAY

MIAMI'S eyes widen in old-fashioned horror.

> MIAMI
> No...

THREE FEET nods, visibly distressed.

> MIAMI (CONT'D)
> Still. That's Jimmy Silver for yer. Tragic.

CUT TO:

INT. ROCKET ROGER'S, LOCKER ROOM -- DAY

MIAMI and THREE FEET storm into the locker room. Through the steam and the giggles.

> MIAMI
> Old Jimmy Silver, eh? Always takin' the piss.

> THREE FEET
> Had to have a laugh, didn't he?

They stop at locker 99.

> MIAMI
> It's the laugh last what counts, though. Eh, Three Feet?

> THREE FEET
> Yeah, well said.

THREE FEET pulls out the key, handles it with a white handkerchief.

MIAMI takes the key and opens the locker.

There is a wooden box. MIAMI takes the wooden box out. Exchanges a glance with THREE FEET. Opens the box. His smile fades.

> MIAMI
> You old...

C.U. - Photo of JIMMY'S smiling face, winking. A bomb, and a card with a message.

MIAMI (CONT'D)
... fucker.

The message reads: MIAMI! SEE YOU IN A SECOND. JIMMY

MIAMI'S jaw drops. Red light on bomb flashes.

CUT TO:

EXT. ROCKET ROGER'S -- DAY

Sound of explosion inside the health club.

CUT TO:

INT. H.M.P NICKHAM, VISITORS" ROOM -- DAY

MOON is visiting. Ashen-faced. There is a beautiful very sexy girl in the background.

MOON
He's still in a critical condition. They can't believe he made it through another night.

BACON
That's terrible.

LEE
That's a shame.

JAMIE
It is. Very bad news.

Pause. MOON bites his lip. Forces himself to speak.

MOON
That ain't the, er... really bad news.

JAMIE
You what?

BACON
What else 'as 'appened?

MOON
It's Barbie. She's took it all personal... She, er... she thinks you was in on the hit. On Miami.

461

>   JAMIE
>   Don't make no sense, we was workin' for 'im!

>   MOON
>   I know, I know. But 'er mind's made up. She ain't droppin'
>   the charges.

>   LEE
>   She's got to!

MOON shrugs. LADS are speechless.

>   MOON
>   I'll come and visit yer. When I get back from Tenerife.

MOON turns to the sexy girl. They leave together.

Close on the reaction of the LADS.

>   END

CAST AND CREW LIST

EPISODE 1

JAMIE	SCOTT MASLEN	Producer	Antony Wood
LEE	DEL SYNNOTT	Director	Sheree Folkson
BACON	SHAUN PARKES	Script Editor	Johnny Capps
MOON	DANIEL CALTAGIRONE	Casting Director	Julia Duff
MIAMI VICE	RALPH BROWN	Director of Photography	Katie Swain
THREE FEET	CHRIS ADAMSON	Production Designer	Iain Andrews
NEFARIUS	GEORGE YIASOUMI	Costume Designer	Jayne Gregory
KOUROS	MARIO KALLI	Film Editor	Nick Arthurs
BARBIE	LORRAINE CHASE		
TANYA	LISA ROGERS		
LAURA	NIKKI GROSSE		
JOHANN	CHRIS ROWE		
JORDI	NIKOLAJ COSTER WALDAU		
FIREBUG	CLINT DYER		
HAPPY JACK	NICHOLAS BEVENEY		
ROY	DEL ANDERSON		
UNCLE DEREK	NICK BRIMBLE		
UNCLE BRIAN	IAN BRIMBLE		
ANARCHIST	MARTIN RUTHERFORD		
MICHAEL	JACK WARREN		
AMBER	VICTORIA BLACKHOLLY		

EPISODE 2

JAMIE	SCOTT MASLEN	Producer	Antony Wood
LEE	DEL SYNNOTT	Director	Rudolf Mestdagh
BACON	SHAUN PARKES	Script Editor	Johnny Capps
MOON	DANIEL CALTAGIRONE	Casting Director	Julia Duff
MIAMI VICE	RALPH BROWN	Production Designer	Anna Higginson
THREE FEET	CHRISTOPHER ADAMSON	Director of Photography	Tim Plamer
NEFARIUS	GEORGE YIASOUMI	Costume Designer	Jayne Gregory
KOUROS	MARIO KALLI	Film Editor	Nick Arthurs
ROBBIE ROSSI	ANTHONY BARCLAY		
TREVOR TRUSCOTT	ANDY LINDEN		
KERRY DOWD	NICK BARTLETT		

EPISODE 3

JAMIE	SCOTT MASLEN	Producer	Antony Wood
LEE	DEL SYNNOTT	Director	Nick Jones
BACON	SHAUN PARKES	Script Editor	Johnny Capps
MOON	DANIEL CALTAGIRONE	Casting Director	Julia Duff
BARBIE	LORRAINE CHASE	Production Designer	Anna Higginson
TANYA	LISA ROGERS	Director of Photography	Katie Swain
JOHANN	CHRIS ROWE	Costume Designer	Jayne Gregory
JORDI	NIKOLAJ COSTER WALDAU	Film Editor	Sue Wyatt
MR BONE	TIM PERRIN		
LARRY HARMLESS	BRADLEY WALSH		

EPISODE 4

JAMIE	SCOTT MASLEN	Producer	Antony Wood
LEE	DEL SYNNOTT	Director	Rudolf Mestdagh
BACON	SHAUN PARKES	Script Editor	Johnny Capps
MOON	DANIEL CALTAGIRONE	Casting Editor	Julia Duff
MIAMI VICE	RALPH BROWN	Production Designer	Anna Higginson
THREE FEET	CHRISTOPER ADAMSON	Director of Photography	Tim Palmer
BARBIE	LORRAINE CHASE	Costume Designer	Jayne Gregory
TANYA	LISA ROGERS	Film Editor	Nick Arthurs
LAURA	NIKKI GROSSE		
JOHANN	CHRISTOPHER ROWE		
JAAP	MARTIN FREEMAN		
SPAGHETTI EDDY	ANDY LUCAS		
TONY 'PEACEMAKER' GIBBS	PAUL McNEILLY		
CANDICE	TARA ELLIS		
HEINRICH	ANDREAS WISNIEWSKI		
DEBBIE	JELENA BUDIMIR		

EPISODE 5

JAMIE	SCOTT MASLEN	Producer	Antony Wood
LEE	DEL SYNNOTT	Director	Nick Jones
BACON	SHAUN PARKES	Script Editor	Johnny Capps
MOON	DANIEL CALTAGIRONE	Casting Editor	Julia Duff
MIAMI VICE	RALPH BROWN	Production Designer	Anna Higginson
THREE FEET	CHRISTOPER ADAMSON	Director of Photography	Katie Swain
TANYA	LISA ROGERS	Costume Designer	Jayne Gregory
MOIRA	ELIZABETH COUNSELL	Film Editor	Sue Wyatt
HAGGIS MOSS	RONNIE LETHAM		
GREASY JOHN	DAVID SCHAAL		
RAINHAM RAY	GARY POWELL		
TWO SIPS	DAVID SCHOFIELD		
CAPTAIN	DONALD PELMEAR		
NO HOPE HARRY	HARRY MILLER		
TERRY GARDNER	MICHAEL McKELL		

EPISODE 6

JAMIE	SCOTT MASLEN	Producer	Antony Wood
LEE	DEL SYNNOTT	Director	David Thacker
BACON	SHAUN PARKES	Script Editor	Johnny Capps
MOON	DANIEL CALTAGIRONE	Casting Director	Julia Duff
MIAMI VICE	RALPH BROWN	Production Designer	Anna Higginson
THREE FEET	CHRISTOPER ADAMSON	Director of Photography	Tim Palmer
NEFARIUS	GEORGE YIASOUMI	Costume Designer	Jayne Gregory
BARBIE	LORRAINE CHASE	Film Editor	St John O'Rorke
UNCLE DEREK	NICK BRIMBLE		
UNCLE BRIAN	IAN BRIMBLE		
MICHAEL	JACK WARREN		
ATTILA	MATTHEW MARSH		
MACCA	SCOTT WILLIAMS		
TERRY JIFFER	JOHN LABANOWSKI		
YURI	SERGE SORIC		

EPISODE 7

JAMIE	SCOTT MASLEN	Producer	Antony Wood
LEE	DEL SYNNOTT	Director	David Thacker
BACON	SHAUN PARKES	Script Editor	Johnny Capps
MOON	DANIEL CALTAGIRONE	Casting Director	Julia Duff
MIAMI VICE	RALPH BROWN	Production Designer	Anna Higginson
THREE FEET	CHRISTOPHER ADAMSON	Director of Photography	Tim Palmer
BARBIE	LORRAINE CHASE	Costume Designer	Jayne Gregory
TANYA	LISA ROGERS	Film Editor	St John O'Rorke